The
ENGLISH
TABLE

OUR FOOD
THROUGH THE AGES

Jill Norman

REAKTION BOOKS

For my grandchildren, Saskia, Olivia, Alex, Eva and Chloe

Published by
REAKTION BOOKS LTD
Unit 32, Waterside
44–48 Wharf Road
London N1 7UX, UK
www.reaktionbooks.co.uk

First published 2024
Copyright © Jill Norman 2024

Printed and bound in India by Replika Press Pvt. Ltd

A catalogue record for this book is available from the British Library

ISBN 978 1 78914 933 3

CONTENTS

Preface

In this book I have tried to describe the food of England over its long history. My aim has been to explore food and drink and how they were prepared from the time hunter-gatherers first settled in what is today known as England through the Neolithic, Bronze and Iron Ages to the present. The early inhabitants probably ate quite well: wild foods were available, although their food preparation was basic.

The Romans introduced new foods, their cooking techniques were sophisticated and their meals were more refined and more elegantly presented and served. The only record of Roman cookery is the ninth-century manuscript attributed to Apicius, which has been translated into English as *The Roman Cookery Book*. When the Romans left to defend their European mainland empire, many imported foods also disappeared.

The Anglo-Saxons and Vikings who arrived after the Romans were closer culturally to the people whose land they moved into; their foods were simple and basic, although they cultivated more crops, and knew how to salt and dry foods to preserve them. The Norman conquerors who followed and ruled the whole country were great hunters and loved eating and feasting; they introduced more spices to season their food. They also brought with them elements of French cooking that became interwoven with the food they found in England.

The earliest English collection of medieval recipes is *The Forme of Cury*, compiled in the fourteenth century. A surviving scroll in the British Library ascribes it to the master cooks of Richard II (1377–9). It is likely that the king's cooks dictated their recipes to a scribe. Thereafter, cookery manuscripts and books gradually became more common. The earliest were written by cooks to royalty and the nobility; they were the only ones whose head of the household and possibly the master cook were literate.

Many ingredients eaten in medieval times are still eaten today, but not necessarily prepared in the same way. The prominent use of spices and sugar (which was valued as a new spice) were not to hide the taste of bad meat, as is often said, but to demonstrate wealth. Ingredients tell us a lot about developments in agriculture and in trade; spices and other goods came from the East. European merchant bought spices and other valuable goods from merchants in Alexandria and later from the Venetians who traded widely with Asia. From 1600, when Elizabeth I granted a charter to the East India Company, spices and other goods from Asia – silks, china, carpets – became more readily available.

Nevertheless, only the very rich could afford these expensive imports. The king and the nobles hunted for much of their meat; fruit and vegetables came from their estates; beer was brewed, wines imported. Wealthy Elizabethans ate well, as had their predecessors; influences from France, Spain and Italy are evident in many dishes of these times. With three fish days a week (although poultry was considered as fish at times) – Mondays, Wednesday and Fridays – and fish permitted all through Lent, recipes for fish were essential.

Meals changed when foods came from the Americas in the sixteenth century. Roasted birds were always popular and by 1591 recipes for roasted turkey appeared, at the same time as recipes for larks and peacocks disappeared. As empire expanded, so did the variety of foods available.

Later books were written by scientists, doctors and herbalists who were also good cooks. By Elizabethan times it was quite common for fairly wealthy households to keep notebooks where family recipes were recorded, both for food and for medicine; some were handed down and also have additions made at later dates. A few books dealt specifically with food for banquets when they were at their height in popularity; others had a section devoted to banqueting. Cookery books reveal information about the times in which they were written: what ingredients were available, fashionable or new, and the typical cooking methods at the time. They might also explain how to present the finished dish, and some have drawings showing how the dishes should be presented on the table.

By the seventeenth century books for a wider audience became available, although many recipes were still drawn from an earlier time. Robert May's *The Accomplisht Cook*, originally published in 1660, is addressed to master cooks and their apprentices, and looks back, somewhat regretfully, to the gastronomic triumphs of the period before the civil war. His book is nevertheless also clearly focused on his own time. In the early eighteenth century books such as Lamb's *Royal Cookery* (1716) contain no antiquated dishes; they are focused on recipes for other contemporary professional chefs.

At about this time, the ladies of the household, who were responsible for the stillroom, for preserving fruit and flowers and for making creams, jellies, syllabubs, mead, sack and cordials produced recipes for these popular foods and drinks that were consumed for health reasons as well as for pleasure. There were more vegetable dishes – salads and pottages, and meat dishes with recurring flavours of verjuice and herbs, or beef stewed with anchovy and onion. Hannah Woolley's book of 1670 includes a number of recipes for bread. More middle-class mistresses of large households turned to writing for women. More than a century later, Mrs McIver's *Cookery and Pastry* (1784) is certainly more upper middle than upper class. Hannah Glasse was the most influential woman writer of the period, her recipes are clear and well explained, though not yet with all quantities or cooking times given.

By the eighteenth century, women began to publish cookery books, sometimes in protest against those by chefs – many of the latter included French recipes that were considered extravagant. They also wanted to encourage girls to learn to cook and to extend their knowledge of preserving and potting. The nineteenth century brought more books by women authors as well as those by chefs. Confectionery became more important as new shops opened and extended their range of sweets.

None of these cookery books tell us anything of the food of the poor, who comprised the largest part of the population. Their food was often unpalatable, minimal and comprised very few ingredients. Many poor people were very near starvation level for much of their lives. It was not until the nineteenth century that writers turned their attention to the food of the poor and wrote recipe books with simple dishes that could be cooked with the minimum of equipment. It was also in the late nineteenth and early twentieth centuries that studies were undertaken to examine the diet of the poor and its deficiencies, and steps taken to improve it.

In the first half of the twentieth century cookery books and food journalism flourished. Marcel Boulestin, a French chef who settled in London in the 1930s, wrote several books in English and a column for the *Evening Standard*. Ruth Lewinsky and Hilda Leyel published charming, small books, often introducing Middle Eastern and Asian dishes to their readers. Florence White produced her authoritative collections of English recipes. Before the Second World War upper- and middle-class cooking drew heavily on French cuisine, but when the number of domestic cooks dwindled after 1945 more women had to take over their own kitchens and fewer complicated French dishes were made.

During the Second World War many small books and pamphlets published by the government helped people make the best of the rations they had and taught them to be enterprising in foraging and growing their own or keeping pigs or chickens. In 1946 Constance Spry, originally a flower arrangement specialist, opened the Cordon Bleu Cookery School with Rosemary Hume, and a decade later published the *Constance Spry Cookery Book*. They – or probably Rosemary Hume – invented the coronation chicken for Elizabeth II's coronation. Elizabeth David started to publish her books on European food aimed at single-cook households at this time; Robert Carrier took a similar approach, but with an American perspective; Jane Grigson devoted books to both English and French cooking. Claudia Roden introduced us more comprehensively to the cuisines of the Middle East than earlier writers had done. They all wrote for newspapers and magazines as well.

In the later twentieth century, TV food programmes became popular, and Derek Cooper started the BBC Radio 4 Food Programme for the British audience to listen to while cooking their Sunday lunch. The post-war period saw a significant increase in immigration to all parts of the UK, meaning more foods were imported from Asia, Africa, the Middle East and the Caribbean, and more shops and restaurants opened specializing in the foods of these regions. Writers like Yan-kit So, Ken Hom and Madhur Jaffrey taught the domestic cook how to produce dishes that they had learned as children growing up in other countries. Our palates adjusted and our food became much more varied.

Since the post-war period, England has changed significantly; it has become more cosmopolitan and our food has changed significantly, much for the better but some for the worse. Now we live in a world of celebrity chefs, a plethora of food programmes on television, recipes in magazines or posted online, and new cookery books published every week. We can buy foods from every corner of the planet online, and if we don't want to cook, we can buy ready meals, get takeaways or have meals delivered to our door.

Mosaic panel showing two hunters returning home with a deer slung on a pole, Roman villa, East Coker, Somerset, c. 350–400 CE.

1

First Settlements to the Earliest English Society

It is possible that the first inhabitants of Britain arrived here some 900,000 years ago when it was a peninsula of Europe and glaciers covered most of the planet. The ice retreated about 10,000 BCE and the climate became milder. Britain became an island around 6000 BCE when the last ice sheets receded. This was the time when continuous human occupation began. The land slowly changed from tundra to forests of pine, birch, hazel, oak, elm and lime, with a variety of soils: chalk, clay, peat and sand. The earliest inhabitants were hunter-gatherers; they hunted with spears, bows and arrows the deer, beaver, wild boar and oxen that roamed the forests; those who lived near the sea caught fish and shellfish; freshwater fish were abundant in lakes and rivers. They fished with lines or basketwork traps and may have worked from coracles in inshore waters. The large quantities of shells of limpets, mussels, whelks and oysters found at archaeological sites around the coast and in river estuaries indicate the importance of these foods. At a few sites fishbones have also been found.

Wild ducks, gannets, cormorants, herons, cranes and other large birds were trapped in snares or clubbed. Edible wild plants such as wild carrots, fat hen, ramsons, nettles, sorrel, mustard and dandelions, and wild fruits such as crab apples, bilberries, blackberries, strawberries, raspberries, sloes and nuts were eaten in season; nuts were probably stored for winter. Wild bees' nests were raided for honey. Women were usually the gatherers; their role was as important as that of the hunters because if the men returned without meat, the group depended on the gathered foods.

Fire existed in the wild: dry plants burned in hot weather. Perhaps the most important step in human development was the ability to start a fire – for warmth, light and cooking. In his study of Brazilian tribes, Claude Levi-Strauss suggested that cooking symbolized humanity's control over nature.[1] Until people learned how to make a fire, and to tame it, all food was eaten raw. Cooked food was usually more digestible; cooking reduced waste and spoilage, and increased the amount of energy obtained from food. While the men continued to hunt, it is likely that the women had the responsibility of cooking. In *Catching Fire: How Cooking Made Us Human*, Richard Wrangham notes, 'The extra energy gave the first cooks biological advantages. They survived and reproduced better than before. Their genes spread. Their bodies responded by biologically adapting to cooked food, shaped by natural selection to take maximum advantage of the new diet.'[2] Wrangham also noted that the French gastronomist Brillat-Savarin wrote in 1825, 'It is by fire that man has tamed Nature itself.'[3] Meat was valued even more when people learned to make a fire and cook it.

Around 4000 BCE people started to settle on the land, domesticating animals and planting crops. More settlers arrived by boat from the northern areas of the Continent, bringing seed corn and domestic animals. The first farmers grew emmer wheat and barley; early cultivation was slash and burn – parts of the forests were cut down and burned, and the corn planted in the soil and ash of the clearings. When the soil was exhausted they moved on to another area. Wild foods continued to be an important contribution to the diet.

Throughout the Neolithic, Bronze and Iron Ages new settlers arrived, bringing peas and beans, and later oats and barley. They developed simple tools and started to make pottery and jewellery.

In time, more sophisticated stone tools were produced and the inhabitants mined for tin, copper and silver. By the middle of the Bronze Age, around 1000 BCE, the land became more settled, and small groups of simple houses were established alongside field systems, which meant the permanent destruction of forests, transforming the landscape to a patchwork of dwellings and fields but still with extensive forest areas.

A problem for these early inhabitants was how to preserve meat, birds and fish. It is likely that they dried them in the wind or smoked them by hanging them close to a fire. Domestic animals, kept for meat and milk, were slaughtered in autumn because there was no fodder for the winter. The exceptions to the slaughter were breeding animals.

Early cooking was done over an open fire; meat was roasted on spits and fish broiled on hot stones. People knew how to clean and stuff the gut of an animal with its liver, brains, innards and fat to make a 'sausage' that was cooked slowly in the embers. No part of the animal was wasted. Cereals and pulses were cooked in water in earthenware vessels at the edge of the fire, and the addition of wild vegetables and herbs, or wild fruits and honey, improved the flavour of these pottages. On the coast seaweed may have been used. Tougher pieces of meat were also stewed, breaking down the tissues and making the meat more tender.

Wild foods continued to provide an important part of their diet. Pastures were valued for raising domestic cattle, goats, sheep and pigs. Our ancestors made butter and cheese; in some parts of the country butter packed into baskets or leather containers was buried in peat bogs to preserve it, a practice that continued into the fifth century (Anglo-Saxon times). Caches have been found even in relatively recent years. It is possible that Neolithic adults were lactose intolerant, and making butter and cheese was one way to remove the lactose from the curds, which could then be eaten as they were or processed further into butter or cheese.

The production of salt from seawater started in the Bronze Age, about 1100 BCE, along the coast of Lincolnshire, East Anglia and Essex. Water was left to evaporate in salterns – usually a series of ponds – along the coast. Sometimes the concentrated brine was then transferred to small briquetage vessels to reduce further. These were thick-walled pans of coarse ceramic material which were heated from below until the water evaporated and only salt remained. At that point, the vessel was broken to remove it. The remains of broken briquetage vessels from the Bronze Age have been found at sites along the east coast. Later they were made of iron. Salt was a valuable trading commodity. It added flavour, particularly to cereals and pottages, and by drying the flesh of meat and fish through osmosis speeded up the process of preserving these foods. Some cheeses were probably brined too.

Cereals continued to be consumed daily and better techniques were developed for processing them. Saddle querns – flat stones over which a rubbing stone, rather like a heavy rolling pin, was pushed back and forth – were widely used. By the Iron Age (about 800 BCE until Roman times) these were replaced by rotary querns made with two heavy, flat, round stones. The upper one had a hole in the middle to pour in the grain and smaller holes on opposite sides into which fitted the wooden handles used to turn it. The weight of the stone crushed the grain. The coarsely ground grain could then be baked into basic unleavened bread on a hearthstone.

Grain was stored in underground pits to provide a supply until the next year's harvest. Barley was processed for malt used to make ale. Ale barm began to be used as a leaven for bread, probably originally by accident. The stomach contents of Lindow Man, the body of a man who lived in the first century CE and was found in a peat bog at Wilmslow in Cheshire in 1984, show that his last meal was unleavened wheat and barley bread and a small amount of mistletoe pollen, which may have been in ale.

In addition to ale, people drank milk and a type of mead made from honey fermented in water, along with wine imported from southern Europe. Unclean water was drunk too, but the parasites it contained infected the drinker; this persisted until the water only became safe to imbibe when it was boiled before drinking.

During the Iron Age, skills developed in crafts ranging from weaving to pottery, wood and metalwork. People learned to work with copper, bronze and later iron, making more tools to improve their farming and to provide knives, spoons and cauldrons for cooking. Meat, grains and vegetables were cooked in large cauldrons suspended over a fire, and long-handled flesh hooks were devised for removing food from the pot. Later, firedogs were made which could hold spits for roasting or grilling. Tin, copper and silver together with grain, cattle and wool were traded for goods from Europe; tin and minerals were traded with the Phoenicians in exchange for Mediterranean goods.

Roman Britain

In Rome, Caesar's invasion of Britain in 55 BCE was considered daring and enterprising; very little was known about the strange northern land except that it was an island beyond Gaul (present-day France) with valuable mineral resources. Tribes in the southeast of the country accepted Roman protection following the arrival of the Roman forces. Some forces were left behind when Caesar returned to Rome, and trading relations were established.

Almost a century elapsed before Claudius arrived with four legions in 43 CE to take possession of the island. In the intervening time Roman traders who had settled in Britain had extended the market beyond the southeastern tribes to those to the north and west, and knowledge of these areas was available to the armies. Nevertheless, it took almost another hundred years before all the tribes were subjugated. The most difficult to defeat were those who resided in Wales and on the Scottish border. Most of the Welsh tribes were eventually subdued, and the emperor Hadrian largely resolved the latter problem by ordering the construction of the barrier that became Hadrian's Wall, which was completed in 128 CE. The area south of Hadrian's Wall, and including a large part of Wales, became Roman Britain, a province of the Roman Empire until 410 CE. Britain was strategically necessary to the empire at this time, and was also a source of raw materials and taxes. It was worth the expense of occupation and so a permanent garrison was installed to protect Rome's island asset.

Writing at about the same time as Claudius' arrival, Strabo described Britain:

> Most of the island is flat and overgrown with forests, although many of its districts are hilly. It bears grain, cattle, gold, silver, and iron. These things, accordingly, are exported from the island, as also hides, and slaves, and dogs that are by nature suited to the purposes of the chase.[4]

Imports were numerous too: wine, silver tableware, fine pottery from Italy and Gaul, Roman furniture, glass and jewellery.

The population of Britain at this time was about 3 million, and most of the populace were settled in the central regions and the south. Trade with Rome had grown in the years since Caesar's conquest, with increased exports of wheat, minerals and slaves. The tribal chiefs and their families of the southeast and the southern coastal region appreciated imported luxuries, including food and wine, and coinage had been adopted to facilitate trade. Further inland, the warring and warrior tribes were less disposed to trade, and further still were the tribes living in the forests and mountains.

The Romans set about conferring peace and order, establishing civic organizations that would lead to a rise in the population and to prosperity. The cost of the army in Britain was offset by the revenues from the conquered land. They made treaties with most of the tribal leaders and absorbed their lands into the imperial territories as the army advanced through the country. The Roman influence was enormous in all spheres of life, leaving marked leaps in progress on the landscape and the people, transforming much of the conquered island. Civic organization was just as important as military power to the Romans as they extended their control. They built cities, roads, fortifications, aqueducts and public baths, sanitation and wastewater systems; they drained marshes and cultivated them. Farms had enclosures, and villas had orchards and dovecotes to encourage wood pigeons to breed. Many Roman villas had mosaic floors, walls painted with frescoes, hypocaust heating systems and a bath house. In all aspects of life, the Romans were more cultivated, and they encouraged the local elites to adopt Roman behaviour and manners and to educate their sons in Latin. The tribal lords regularly purchased Roman goods and learned to live and dine in the Roman manner.

Roman tastes in food were far more sophisticated than those of their subjects, and substantial supplies of foods they enjoyed were imported. They enclosed land to rear deer and smaller enclosures at their houses to rear rabbits, hares and pheasants. Roman feasts have been described by many classical writers; they were occasions for ostentation and gastronomic excess, which led cooks to extend their culinary skills to the utmost and offer extravagant presentations. They loved to disguise food in both its appearance and its taste.

One ingredient essential to almost any dish was liquamen or garum. Fish entrails and small fish were put in an earthenware bowl and salted, and the bowl was left to ferment in the sun. When it was judged to be ready, the liquid was strained off. The best was made from the entrails of tuna and its juice, gills, blood and sufficient salt. This was left for up to two months before the side of the vessel was pierced to allow the liquamen to flow out.[5]

Many new foods were introduced into England, such as pheasants, peacocks, guinea fowl, grapes, cherries, figs, mulberries, walnuts and chestnuts. The Romans cultivated a wide range of herbs and vegetables: parsley, sage, rosemary, mint, marjoram, thyme, garlic, onions, leeks, cucumbers, radishes, cabbage, chicory, celery, beets and turnips. They planted vineyards in the south and different varieties of apple and sweet cherry trees. They imported wine, olive oil, pine nuts, almonds, figs, raisins, the essential garum and spices, especially pepper, ginger and cinnamon. They also introduced new cooking equipment and techniques, including the pestle and mortar.

Oysters, mussels, cockles and other shellfish were popular Roman fare; their shells have been found in large quantities on the sites of Roman towns. Sea fish – notably cod, bream, haddock and grey mullet – were also enjoyed, as were wild fowl such as swan, duck, goose, woodcock and plover. Dormice were fattened on acorns, snails on milk, wheat and must. Beef and veal were served with rich sauces, often sweet and sour with raisins, honey, vinegar, spices and herbs. Pigs were plentiful: pork and suckling pig were roasted and served with spicy sauces, while ham and bacon were salted (salt was obtained by boiling down brine). Apicius has a recipe for cooking a ham with dried figs.[6] Birds were roasted or boiled and often stuffed before cooking. One stuffing consisted of pepper, lovage, ginger, chopped meat, boiled spelt grits, pounded brain, eggs, liquamen, a little oil, whole peppercorns and plenty of pine kernels.[7] Lard was used for cooking when olive oil was unavailable.

Emmer and einkorn wheats continued to be grown, and the Romans introduced kilns for drying hulled wheat to make threshing easier and more efficient. They built granaries at farms and forts, and used querns driven by donkeys to grind large amounts of grain; rotary hand querns were still used in domestic kitchens. Bread was the staple food of the army, so the grain stores and domed bread ovens built at army camps were essential.

To prepare even an ordinary Roman meal required more equipment for cooking than the simple cauldron suspended over a fire. Most Roman kitchens had a raised brick hearth that held a charcoal fire, over which cooking pots were placed on gridirons or tripods. Meats were grilled on gridirons and large animals roasted on spits. Domed earthenware ovens were used for baking and roasting; they were heated by making a fire inside and once the right level of heat was reached, the ashes were raked out, the food put in and the opening closed. Cooking pots and pans were increasingly made of iron and bronze, while pottery bowls of all sizes were used for mixing. Wine and oil were stored in amphorae.

The Romans expected their food to be served elegantly, so tableware was important too. Diners ate much of the food with their fingers, but also had access to knives and spoons, napkins, silver plates and bowls made of pewter or Samian ware (decorated red tableware) imported from Gaul. Napkins were essential. Wine was served in silver, glass or pottery cups or goblets, and there were elaborate strainers and ladles for serving it. They also had bronze, silver and pewter jugs.

The huge Roman army had to be housed, clothed and fed, which led to the further development of a monetary economy. London became an important port for imports from Europe and for the export of grain to feed the Roman armies in Gaul. A network of towns grew up across the country, each with paved streets, a forum, a basilica (meeting house), shops, a good water supply, public baths and private houses. Industries such as ironworking, potteries and glass manufacturing were established in some towns; there were also market towns for agricultural produce and fruit and vegetables from market gardens and orchards. The well-maintained road network made travel relatively easy.

The country prospered under the Romans until the fifth century, when the Roman armies could no longer defend the furthest limits of their empire. The Roman forces left England and returned to the Continent to defend against Germanic invasions at the heart of the empire. On the emperor Honorius' orders in 410, the local peoples in Britain were left to defend themselves.

Anglo-Saxon farmers and settlers

In the second half of the fifth century Angles and Saxons arrived from northern Germany and southern Scandinavia, gradually taking over most of the country that the Romans had colonized. They saw it as good land to settle in and farm. In his *Ecclesiastical History of the English People*, written in the late eighth century, Bede described it as an 'island rich in crops and trees of various kinds'.[8] The newcomers lived in small tribal communities and for a century or more there were wars between the tribes as each one sought to have the upper hand. It was not until the seventh century that they agreed to divide the land into seven small kingdoms.

The Anglo-Saxons were surprised by the richness and refinements of urban culture they found. They lacked the sophistication of the Romans; their food culture was basic and they knew nothing of Roman tastes in cooking or dining. Birds that required care in rearing, such as the guinea fowl, died out. Nor did they know how to build in stone or repair stone buildings; they lived in lath and plaster dwellings in small farming communities. In his history, Bede described what remained of the Roman temples and cities in his day. But many of the Roman cities and towns were already neglected and less populated before the invasions. As the centralized administration was abandoned, the political function of the governance centres and outposts ceased to be relevant and they fell into disrepair. The road network that crossed the country to connect the cities and towns was not maintained.

At first there was little trade between the early Anglo-Saxon communities, and they were largely self-sufficient except for salt to preserve their meat and fish and metals to make tools. Slowly trade increased, particularly in foodstuffs: fish was traded from most coastal areas; dairy produce, particularly cheese, from low-land pasture areas and sheeps' wool and cheese from uplands. By the sixth century a thriving export trade with Europe existed for clothing, wool and pigs and also for enslaved people. English slaves continued to fetch a high price in the market in Rome.

Larger settlements became towns, often built on earlier Roman sites with arable land and pastures that were shared by the inhabitants, but they could seldom produce enough food to be self-sufficient. They grew into commercial centres where skilled artisans and tradesmen, merchants and other professionals settled.

The most significant development in Anglo-Saxon times was the arrival of Christian missionaries from Rome under the leader-ship of Augustine in the late sixth century, who in little more than a century converted most of the population in the British Isles to Christianity. Churches and monasteries were built, usually near to the lord's manor in the centre of the community, to affirm links between Church and state. They received some landed endow-ment, but their main income came from dues paid to them. Like the nobles, the monasteries and minsters leased the best land and organized farming. They set the local population to work on the land and took substantial amounts of food from the peasants and farmers as rent. One ninth-century monastic rent was a cask of beer, a vessel full of honey or its equivalent in mead, one plough beast, one hundred loaves, one sheep and one pig.[9]

The nobles, or thanes, lived on their estates; those who owned more than one estate travelled between them. Their houses, built of wood in the early days and later of stone, consisted of a great hall used for daily business, meals and entertainment, and as sleeping quarters for the retainers. Smaller buildings provided bedrooms for the family and their guests, and the whole was fortified, surrounded by a stockade. They had many officials and retainers, as did the ecclesiastical lords. A thane's responsibilities were, first, military duties to the king, then to keep order in his own household, attend assemblies and assist in suppressing lawlessness. Thanes also had obligations to the Church and the more senior nobles had duties at court. At home, they enjoyed hunting and hawking, feasting and drinking, entertainment and music. Minstrels and singers travelled from hall to hall, but not all musicians were professionals; sometimes the lord played or sang. In the old English epic poem *Beowulf*, at the court of the king of the Danes, Hrothgar, the harp is played, and the king's thanes themselves provide the entertainment on another occasion.

Some thanes were literate, and their sons were encouraged to learn Latin and study theology. The monks who came to England from the Continent were scholars and introduced their tradition of learning. The monasteries were centres of learning with well-stocked libraries; many books in Latin and Greek were imported and copied in the scriptoria. The renowned Lindisfarne Gospels were produced at the monastery in the eighth century and about two hundred years later translated into Old English. Translations of other texts followed, and knowledge of Latin began to decline. In the ninth century King Alfred of Wessex introduced educational reforms to spread the ability to read in the vernacular and establish a literary tradition. Poems and songs that had been recited or sung became the earliest vernacular literature. By the end of the century most thanes were literate, and it is possible that their wives were too. In Anglo-Saxon society an upper-class woman had considerable freedom: she could be an independent land holder and act in legal transactions, and she held the power to free her slaves.

A freeman was called a churl; he paid dues to the Church, attended assemblies and did the military duty required of him. He was not bound to the land and could travel. A churl owned one hide of land – the area of land considered necessary to support a modest family – or more. Lesser freemen – villeins, who had been given part of a hide, animals and tools by their lord – had to work for two or three days a week for the lord and pay rent in kind. All other men and women were slaves, who were the main workforce on the land. Slaves were granted a daily corn allowance, with more allotted to men than women. In winter one or two animal carcasses were added in order to keep them fit enough to work. Slaves could earn free time for themselves and were given additional foods at Christmas and Easter. The spread of Christianity and the influence of churchmen helped to mitigate their lot.

The only records that survive about land ownership and its use are those for the Church and the wealthy. Within the village community the open field cultivation ensured a fair share of good and less good land to each individual and each had a voice in the agricultural policy. But overarching this system were the feudal power and legal rights of the thane.

Hides were usually divided into three, with one part left fallow in each season and cereals and pulses grown on the other two. They were farmed in long, narrow strips, each a furrow long: hence 'furlong'. In the eighth century oxen were used to draw harrows, though by the tenth century horses had been introduced as they were faster and more efficient. Farming was the most important activity throughout the country and cereals – wheat, barley, millet, oats and rye – the most important crops. Barley provided malt for brewing as well as played an important role in bread making.

To avoid famine, it was essential to dry, thresh and store the grain. Several techniques developed for grinding it. The saddle querns that had been used since earliest times were replaced by more efficient mills with staves to drive the grinding stone. Nevertheless, it was still arduous work, usually done by the women in the household. By the eighth century, large communal mills driven by oxen were used, and water mills were introduced where a suitable water source was available. Communal mills were the property of the lord, and peasants who used them had to give

Medieval watermill with undershot wheel, from the Bodley bestiary, 1201–50.

part of their grain as the fee, so many continued to grind their grain at home. According to the Domesday Book commissioned by William I after the Norman Conquest, published in 1086, there were some 6,000 water mills for grinding grain in settlements across England.

Animal husbandry remained important. Beef had been the preferred meat of the Roman legions, and it was widely enjoyed by the Anglo-Saxon gentry. Pigs provided the meat of the poor, but their ham and bacon were appreciated at all levels of society; goats and sheep were kept, the latter valued not only for their meat and milk but for their wool. Deer and wild boar were hunted by the aristocracy. Shepherds and cowherds had milk from their animals, but they drank skimmed milk, whey or buttermilk; full milk was a luxury. The women of the household made butter and cheese; a small amount of fresh cheese was consumed locally but butter and most cheeses were salted to preserve them. Dairy families may have had a little butter and cheese to barter, but all the full milk, butter and cheese were the property of the lord of the manor. Large estates sold their surplus cheese and butter.

The monasteries were in close touch with their sister houses in Europe, not only about sacred texts but about daily life. Monks in England were familiar with Holy Roman Emperor Charlemagne's capitulary of the ninety aromatic and vegetable plants to be grown on his estates, written around 800 CE. Those suited to a northern European climate were planted in monastery gardens, including red, purple and black carrots, beets, parsnips, turnips, black radish, celery, garlic, sage, parsley, mint, dill, lovage, rosemary and caraway. Apple, pear, plum, cherry and mulberry trees grew in the orchards. Many of these vegetables and fruits were also introduced into local

The Town Mill, Lyme Regis, thought to be one of 5,000 pre-Domesday mills. The present site dates back to at least 1340.

thanes' estates. Wild foods continued to be an important part of the diet too – fungi, wild greens, herbs and fruits were gathered in season. The poor relied on these essential additions to their diet.

In the eighth and ninth centuries the wealth of the country and the settled Anglo-Saxon society drew invasions from Viking, mostly Danish, warriors, who plundered the north and east of the country, particularly the wealthy monasteries. The Danes encountered a rich and civilized society with a system of local government and taxation and a growing literary culture. The Anglo-Saxons established the kingdom of England and aspects of their government survive, for example, in the shire counties. The country was divided into shires, and each shire had courts with officials appointed by the king to maintain the law and collect taxes. They also established the spoken (and later written) language now called Old English.

The Vikings plundered and destroyed, but were halted by Alfred of Wessex in 871, and eventually they were assimilated, mainly in northern and eastern areas. The Vikings had a strong belief in the individual, and in time introduced some social and political changes in the northern and eastern shires. They also introduced a number of culinary skills, including different methods of salting, drying and smoking fish as well as pressed and smoke-dried beef.

Leechdoms – texts concerned with remedies and healing – included instructions on gathering, drying and consuming foods. Preserving food was extremely important for the whole population. Some foods were dried in the sun, in an oven or by a fire; the staple cereals and pulses were the most important crops to dry, and herbs and fungi were dried for use in winter. Salting was the most important method of preserving, used for meat, fish, butter, cheese and some vegetables. The salt was obtained from pans around the coast and from the salt mines of Cheshire and Worcestershire. Brining was the cheapest and most common method for fish and meat; curing – dry salting – required more salt, and so was more expensive. Ham and bacon were the most popular cured meats. A traditional curing mixture in Yorkshire and Westmoreland was common salt, bay salt, saltpetre, black pepper and honey. The hams were turned and rubbed with the mixture twice a week for a month, then soaked for 24 hours and hung up to dry.[10] These were green hams, dried without smoking. Many cured meats were smoked after drying.

After the Romans left, very little olive oil reached Britain, and butter or lard were the only cooking fats available. Most foods were cooked slowly in a liquid with limited use of fats. Salt fish and meat and dried vegetables had a thorough soaking in water before cooking in clean water or milk, or on rare occasions in butter. Dried beans and cereals were commonly used in stews and pottages simmered in a cauldron over an open fire. If the pot containing the food could not be put over the fire, heated stones were put into it. Beef was marinaded in herbs and vinegar, and fruits in wine and honey. Unplucked seabirds were baked in the embers, their feathers encased with clay.[11] Pits were dug outdoors and filled with heated stones before meat wrapped in straw was put into them and covered with more stones and turf. It was a good way to cook a large meat joint for a rich household.

More commonly, earthenware ovens were heated with a pile of brushwood, as in Roman times. After the bread was baked, the oven could be used for food that required slow cooking. In the ninth century monasteries and manors established bakehouses at some distance from the main building (lest they caught fire). A century or so later, cooking for large numbers led to the construction of kitchens near to the bakehouses, and the first mentions occur of men employed as cooks. Bakers and cooks also set up bakeries and cookshops in towns to feed travellers, pilgrims or local people with few or no cooking facilities. In small houses a part of the main room was used for cooking; if a fire was kept going, a

Sage and coriander, miniatures from a pharmacopeial compilation,
c. 1150–75.

cauldron containing cured meat and vegetables could be left simmering while people were at work. The fuel was primarily wood or preferably charcoal, which burned at a more predictable heat and did not produce a lot of smoke. Coal from outcrops was also used, as was peat.

Kitchen equipment was fairly basic; a poor household would have an earthenware cooking pot and a few utensils, while a modest household enjoyed a brass, copper or bronze cauldron that could be suspended or placed over a fire, a frying pan or griddle, a spit, earthenware basins and bowls, hair sieves, an axe for chopping bones, knives, ladles, sieves, a pestle and mortar, and bellows for the fire. A grander household had more of the same equipment, probably made in better materials. Meat and bones were cut up for stews, food could be chopped into small enough pieces to be stuffed into animal membranes to make sausages, and soft foods were puréed with a pestle and mortar.

Bread was the staple food on the table at all meals, including those of high-ranking families. The poor baked their bread on a hearthstone; unleavened bread was flat and hard, while yeasted bread had a lighter texture. Some devised a simple oven by inverting a pot or cauldron over the dough and covering it with embers. The Celts had learned to add beer barm to their bread to lighten it; the other method was to leave a mixture of flour and water to ferment. A lump of the fermented dough could be kept and used to start a subsequent baking. Oven-baked yeasted bread was a great improvement on unleavened bread.

The poorest had barley bread or maslin made from a mixture of wheat and rye. Wheaten bread was for the well-to-do and white for the Eucharist. Leechdoms describe the qualities of ground meal, from coarse to very fine; several recipes call for 'fine wheaten flour' or 'very fine flour' for the bread of the rich, whereas there are fewer references to barley or rye meal.[12] Bread was eaten plain or spread with butter, lard or fresh cheese, and perhaps accompanied by a handful of herbs. The rich could extend and vary their meals with meat or vegetables or fish.

Little is known of the food of the poorest. Their daily diet was monotonous and essentially consisted of carbohydrate – bread and/or pottage made with peas or beans. In the depths of winter, when there were no vegetable crops to procure fresh food from, their diet was even more restricted (except for dried supplies). Harvests frequently failed due to bad weather, leading to regular famines which would disproportionately impact the poor, as too did outbreaks of plague.

Athelstan, the early tenth-century king of the West Saxons, decreed that one destitute man on each of the royal estates was to receive monthly provisions of meal and bacon or mutton. As noted earlier, serfs and villeins received a daily allowance of corn; they might receive meat at festival times, and some may have had a piece of land on which to grow vegetables.

When the Vikings settled in Britain, they were already skilled in brewing with wheat and barley. They were great ale drinkers and made a number of special brews, sometimes using herbs. Ale, whey, skimmed milk and boiled water were the everyday drinks of most of the population. Mead was the drink of both the Celtic and Anglo-Saxon upper classes and liberally consumed at feasts. It was also drunk to celebrate religious festivals in the richer monasteries. Wine was served at feasts both secular and religious.

There are few records of meals in Anglo-Saxon times. The usual pattern seems to have been to eat two meals a day, one in the early morning and one in the evening, leaving time to be spent in work or other activities. Surviving fragments of texts indicate that Anglo-Saxon monks ate well, though less well than the nobility. They kept several saints' days throughout the year as feast days, following the many biblical references to eating. On these days the monks had two meals instead of just one that was usually at midday. Some monastic orders followed a more ascetic line and consumed no flesh except fish or fowl. A meal in a monastery usually consisted of two cooked courses and one of fruit or vegetables; a poor household would have only one, and the upper classes four or five. Spices were one of the few luxuries allowed to monks. Bede recorded sharing his spices among his fellow monks at the end of his life.

The Church sought to impose frugality and curb gluttony among the rich and worldly. Fast days were observed on Friday, Saturday and for six weeks throughout Lent, when one meal, without meat, was the rule. Fasting was seen as a Christian duty and the entire population (except children and the sick) was expected to observe Lent and some other fast days.

Anglo-Saxon
maslin bread.

Feasts are the most commonly recorded events, both religious and secular. Landowners held feasts associated with events in the agricultural year – ploughing, mowing and harvest – to which all their workers, including slaves, were invited. The poor also enjoyed the great feasts of the Christian year. Funeral feasts to appease the gods were important in pagan times and were soon incorporated into the Christian calendar. A receipt for a funeral feast at Bury St Edmunds included 5 ore (a Swedish currency) for malt and fuel, 42 pence for bread, 17 pence for a pig, 2 ores for a bullock, 1 ore for 3 bucks, 8 pence for a cheese, 3 pence for fish and 4 pence for milk.[13]

Royal and noble feasts, occasions for ostentation and display, were held in the great hall, sometimes known as the mead hall. The Church's calendar of fasts and feasts was followed, while the function of the secular feast was to display the king's or lord's power. Feasts were a demonstration of the prestige and generosity of the host, who provided a lavish array of rare and choice foods – the best cuts of roast meat, the finest fish and fowl were served with rich sauces made with fruit or vinegar, honey and herbs. Religious feasts on Fridays would have offered only fish, probably the highly esteemed salmon. The cooks demonstrated their skills in producing delicacies for these occasions. Sweets were not neglected: dishes of curds or sweet omelettes with flowers or fruits, summer puddings of blackberries, raspberries or whortleberries contained in bread, and cereal-based flummery. The rich enjoyed imported oil and spices; the latter were highly regarded but used more sparingly than later on. Drink was as important as the food: ale, mead, wine and fruit-based drinks. Ritual, music and spectacle were as essential as the food and drink. Feasts were designed to keep the lord's followers loyal; considerable status was attached to feasting and this became even more important later in the Middle Ages. They also kept the men well fed, which was essential if they were to be fit enough to fight for their lord.

Anglo-Saxon recipes

Green soup

Michaël Fant, *Vikingars gästabud* [The Viking Feast]
(Copenhagen, 1998)

150 g (5 oz) fresh spinach or about 250 g (8 oz) frozen
10 cm (4 in.) white part of a leek
1.2 litres (2 pints) good vegetable stock
salt
dash of pepper
dash of ground ginger
2–3 egg yolks
120 ml (4 fl. oz) cream
grated nutmeg

Wash the fresh spinach and parboil it or thaw the frozen. Rinse the leek and slice thinly. Bring the stock to the boil; add the spinach and leek and let it boil for 7–8 minutes. Season with salt, pepper and ginger. Whisk the egg yolks with the cream. Remove the pan from the heat and pour this mixture slowly into the soup, stirring briskly. Grate a little nutmeg over the top and serve with bread. *Serves 4*

Hare, rabbit, veal or chicken stew with herbs and barley

Michelle Berriedale-Johnson, *The British Museum Cookbook*
(London, 1987)

50 g (1½ oz) butter
1–1.5 kg (2½–3½ lb) (depending on the amount of bone) of either hare, rabbit joints, stewing veal or chicken joints

450 g (1 lb) trimmed leeks, washed and thickly sliced
4 cloves garlic, chopped finely
175 g (6 oz) pot barley
900 ml (1½ pints) water
3 tbsp red or white wine vinegar
2 bay leaves
salt and pepper
15 roughly chopped fresh sage leaves
or 1 tbsp dried

Melt the butter in a heavy pan and fry the meat with the leeks and garlic until the vegetables are slightly softened and the meat lightly browned. Add the barley, water, vinegar, bay leaves and seasonings. Bring the pot to the boil, cover it and simmer gently for 1–1½ hours until the meat is really tender and falling from the bone. Adjust the seasoning to taste and serve in bowls. The barley will serve as a vegetable.
Serves 6

Lozenges or curd cheese pastries

Robert I. Curtis, *Ancient Food Technology* (Leiden, 2001)

225 g (½ lb) wholemeal shortcrust pastry
225 g (½ lb) curd cheese
25 g (1 oz) very finely chopped stem or crystallized ginger
or plump raisins
15 g (½ oz) roasted and chopped pine nuts
sugar to taste
lemon juice to taste

Roll the pastry out very thin and cut it into small rectangles, approximately 15 × 8 cm. You should have at least 24. Bake them in a moderately hot oven (190°c/380°f) for 10 minutes or until they are crisp and brown. Remove them and cool on a rack.

Meanwhile mix the curd cheese with the ginger or raisins, pine nuts and sugar, and lemon juice to taste. Set aside. When you are ready to serve, sandwich together two pieces of pastry with the cheese mixture. They can be used as a dessert or as a snack.

Serves 6

Honey oatcakes

Robert I. Curtis, *Ancient Food Technology* (Leiden, 2001)

350 g (13 oz) rolled oats
225 g (½ lb) butter
225 g (½ lb) honey
pinch of salt

Melt the butter in a pan and add the remaining ingredients and stir until well mixed. Spoon the mixture on to a greased baking tray and press it down well. Bake at 170°c (340°f) for 30 minutes until golden brown. Mark into squares while still warm and serve cold.

Serves 10–12

2

From 1066 to Chaucer

B y 1066 England was a country of long-established regional traditions and local government, and all inhabitants were subjects of the king. There may have been little overall political unity, but the country already had a well-developed legal system, its own currency – the silver penny – and a system of national taxation. The king had an army, a ready rank of soldiers, and could summon men to defend the country, but the men were not warriors.

The Vikings, who had settled in northern France and established a duchy there, remained a culture of fighters specialized in the art of warfare; the English were no match for Duke William's men in the Battle of Hastings. The Norman invasion was the conquest of a warrior who came to rule, unlike those of the Angles and Saxons, who came to settle. The Bayeux Tapestry, commissioned in the eleventh century to celebrate the Conquest, shows castles surrounded by moats, men in armour with their weapons, and others catching the animals to be cooked for the feast to mark the duke's safe arrival. Some food is simmering in a cauldron suspended over a fire; meat and birds are roasted on spits and passed to the men who serve the meal. There is fish on the table. The duke and his senior commanders sit at the table with bowls of food and cups of wine.

William lost no time in dispossessing the old nobility and distributing their lands to his followers, who built fortified castles up and down the country. By the time the Domesday Book was compiled in 1086, almost all of the king's noble tenants were of Norman origin. By the beginning of the next century, the Normans and the English had almost become integrated as a unified nation.

The king and his army moved around the country, partly to ensure there were no revolts and partly to enjoy hunting in the royal forests. Hunting was the sport and recreation of the medieval nobility, and only they could afford it. Good horses, hounds, skilled servants – huntsmen and falconers – spears, daggers, crossbows and shooting gloves were essential; and the horses, hounds and staff had to be housed and fed. A trained falcon or hawk could cost as much as £10 and a fine horse up to £28. Hunts were well-planned events, where each participant had a specific role to ensure that no one was put in danger or lost. The ritual was as important as the animal killed. Young boys often joined the hunt to learn how to handle a horse, use a weapon and travel through forests with others.

The deer was the most valued animal hunted, specifically the hart: the adult male red deer. The noblest form of hunting was considered to be *par force de chiens*, to let the dogs chase the deer to exhaustion before one of the hunters would kill it with a sword or spear. There were eight stages in this style of hunt, each to be observed in sequence. Boar were hunted and killed in the same way. Falconry became a favourite sport and a means of hunting wild fowl: herons, cranes, mallards, swans, gulls and curlews were on the table as well as chickens and geese.

The nobles moved between the manors on their land for similar reasons to the king. It was a way of quelling any discontent among those subject to them and offered opportunities to hunt for pleasure. It was therefore done as a matter of necessity. Their huge households had to be provided with two meals a day from the hunt and the produce of the estate. When one manor's supplies were depleted, they moved on.

Manor houses were usually fortified, often with a moat and drawbridge and an enclosed courtyard. The domestic offices were to one side of the yard and the living quarters to the other. They were large, if primitive, with a great hall where public life was conducted and where meals were taken – on a high table for the lord and his guests and on lower tables for less important people. The hall and the kitchens had to be large enough to feed visiting nobles and even occasionally the king and his retainers.

A lord's household had to provide for fifty or more servants in addition to family members, and a series of visitors, usually accompanied by their own retinue, throughout the year. Provisioning was a key concern for such a household, particularly as transport was slow and uncertain due to the state of the roads. Supplies were laid in during autumn to prepare for winter. In 1260 the Earl of Leicester's household consumed between 400 and 1,000 salt herrings costing 10*d* per hundred during Lent; 3,700 eggs costing 3½–4½*d* per hundred were used in one week. Sturgeon cost 31*s* per

Scenes of cooking and feasting, Bayeux Tapestry, 1066–82.

barrel, pears cost 10*d* per three hundred (being bought by the hundred) and earthenware dishes were purchased by the thousand (6*s*
8*d*). Milk, butter and cheese; vegetables (peas, beans, onions, garlic,
leeks, cabbages and herbs); and fruit (apples, medlars, quinces,
pears and cherries) were provided on the estate.

Two hundred years later, Sir John Howard's accounts recorded
the purchase in September of twenty great oxen (£17), twenty cows
(£10 10*s*), ten bullocks (£6) and eight hundred dried salt fish (£9
12*s*), as well as salt, wine and spices. Spices were always the most
expensive item: pepper (10*d*–2*s* per lb), ginger (10*d*–2*s* 6*d* per lb),
zedoary (2*s* per ½ lb), saffron (10–14*s* per lb). Other expensive
imported foods were sold alongside spices, including sugar (1–2*s*
per lb) and almonds (1*s* for 5 lb).

The price of ale depended on the price of barley: it could range
from ½*d* to ¾*d* per gallon. Beer was not yet known because hops
were only introduced in the fifteenth century. Wine was a major

import and prices varied depending on quality, but averaged about £2 per tun (252 gallons). The Leicester household consumed about ¾ tun per week.[1]

The working day was long, from 5 a.m. to 9 p.m.; dinner was served at 9 a.m. and supper at 5 p.m. They were substantial meals. If any breakfast was taken, it was light and eaten in the private chambers.

Manors continued to be organized on the basis of subsistence farming. The peasant had a contract with the landowner which determined his right to land and the labour that he was obliged to provide for the lord. The existing structure of great open fields was maintained, usually with the lord's demesne within the fields. For most people life went on as it always had done, following the rhythm of the agricultural year. It was gruelling, hard work, day after day. The peasants farmed their own strips of land, which were often in different parts of the field. Some fields were arable, others were meadows for hay and one in three usually lay fallow in each season. The regulation of the fields was organized by the village as a whole to ensure each man had his fair share of good and poor land, and a voice within the community.

The feudal authority of the lord of the manor lay over this sharing, democratic structure. The peasants were serfs of the lord; they had no legal right to leave their land. They were bound to the soil, and to work on the lord's land for a prescribed number of days a year under the supervision of the bailiff. They were paid in kind for their work; this was not a monetary economy. They grew much of their own food, reared animals, and built their own cottages and furniture; the women baked, brewed, cooked, spun and wove cloth.

The feudal law of the manor held throughout the country. Village society was made up of the lord and his staff on the one hand and the serfs on the other. There were very few freemen, certainly fewer than in Anglo-Saxon times. In 1215 the first English parliament was convened to establish the rights of the barons to act as consultants to the king on matters of government. Its members, who were all lords, drew up Magna Carta in 1215, which granted rights to the peasants and to freemen. It put into writing the principle that the king and his government were not above the law. No man could be imprisoned or stripped of his possessions or his rights except by the judgement of his equals or by the law of the land. In 1265 a more representative parliament was convened with lords and freemen, and in 1295 Edward 1 decreed that a greater balance between lords and freemen was required, following the Roman legal doctrine that 'what touches all shall be approved by all.' The House of Lords, where the barons sat, and the Commons, composed of knights and burgesses, were established. Edward called his parliament once or twice a year, usually to raise taxes to pay for his wars.

Many aspects of medieval life were regulated by the Church and the monasteries, including food and drink. The Bible has many references to feasting and enjoying food, but also occasions when restraint is required. In some stories indulgence in eating and drinking is encouraged, while in others austerity and self-denial are called for. People lived with these contradictions. Hospitality and generosity were expected, especially sharing with the poor. Medieval people observed the rules of hospitality scrupulously, particularly in wealthy households and monasteries. All food left on the table was given to the almoner (distributor of alms) to gift to the poor instead of being sent back to the kitchen. Fasts and feasts followed each other through the year; the main fasting period was Lent, followed by Easter celebrations; in winter the Advent fast was followed by Christmas.

For the nobility the culinary traditions followed those of pre-Conquest times. Feasts were the most recorded meals, but the occasion was recorded rather than the food served. The documents that survive are from noble and royal houses or from monasteries and only describe the food of the rich. There was an emphasis on

Work during a year on an estate such as Sir Geoffrey Luttrell's, including scenes of servants preparing food, marginalia from the Luttrell Psalter, 1325–40 (*counter clockwise*): a wattle pen full of sheep; tethered hen with her chicks; servants roasting meat; stewing, chopping green vegetables and pounding with a pestle and mortar; carving the meat and serving the feast; feasting scene at a table.

adiutor eorum + protector eorum est.
qui timent dominum sperauerunt

formality and courtesy, good table manners, and the careful and elegant presentation of the food, although bones were dropped for the dogs that accompanied their masters in the hall.

The rich and powerful throughout Europe ate similar foods, but they were unavailable to most of the population. Access to fresh meat and game in winter was a mark of their status, as was consumption of river fish, the largest and finest sea fish, and plentiful poultry, particularly capons, and wild fowl.

One of the earliest menus for a feast is from the thirteenth century 'Treatise of Walter of Bibbesworth', which tells us that bread, ale and wine are essential. The first course consisted of boar's head, venison and a variety of cranes, peacocks, swans, kid, pigs and hens. Then came rabbits in gravy covered with sugar, roast birds – pheasants, woodcock, partridges, larks, blackbirds and song thrushes – and fritters with sugar mixed with rose water. The feast finished with sweet spice powder, mace, cubebs and wafers.[2]

From accounts such as this, it seems that gargantuan amounts of food were consumed, but some feasts lasted for more than one day, and we do not know how many people were present. At the feast for the enthronement of the Archbishop of York in 1466, some 3,000 people were present, and at court there were thousands of guests and retainers to be fed daily. Feasts were a demonstration of political or ecclesiastical power and wealth, a display of conspicuous consumption. They were occasions to show the ties of power and dependence: the size of the feast and the choice of the principal guests confirmed the host's importance. Other guests were seated lower down the hall from the host's table.

The food at feasts had to be expensive and copious, and flavoured with rare spices. Display and visual effects were as important as the food itself – the diners first appreciated the offerings with their eyes. Bright colours, particularly yellow and red sauces, and the use of gold leaf were highly regarded, whereas plain roast or grilled meats were often spurned because they were not artful enough unless 'endored' with a glaze of saffron or egg yolk. Peacocks and swans cooked and reassembled in their plumage, or a vivid, gilded boar's head, were borne into the chamber to impress.

Artifice was another essential skill. Cooks prided themselves on disguising foods and presenting them in an unexpected form. The preparation often involved a great deal of pounding to transform the food, and its flavour was likely to be changed by adding spices. The first course for the feast to celebrate the enthronement of the Bishop of Salisbury in 1414 included a dish of *pomes en gele*, in which the apples were meatballs coloured green, mawmeny (minced chicken, rice flour, sugar and spices mixed with almond milk), boiled capons and swans. The second was roast meats – venison, suckling pig, heron, partridges and crane – and the third course was rabbit, pigeons, larks, quail, fritters and pastries.

Expensive spices fulfilled multiple roles: their aromas aroused the appetite and their use showed the status and sophistication of the host, as well as adding complexity to the food. Then came tasting the expensive ingredients: fine cuts of meat, fish such as lampreys, sturgeon or turbot, and exotic birds.[3]

In addition to these, the sotelties or entremets – small fanciful dishes presented between courses – were designed to exhibit the skills and artistry of the cook. These luxurious, decorative delicacies such as glazed and stuffed chickens, tarts, fish or meat jellies, wafers, marzipan hedgehogs with almond quills, and other spiced sweetmeats were eagerly looked forward to.

Feasts were leisurely occasions and sometimes there were entertainments between courses from travelling players, jugglers, acrobats or musicians. Strict social hierarchy was followed in the seating of guests, and it is likely that some of the grander, more expensive dishes were admired by, but not served at the tables of the lower orders.

Whether for a feast or for daily dining, dinner usually consisted of three courses, each with several highly spiced and coloured dishes. The number of dishes in each course varied according to the occasion. Supper was usually a smaller meal. Whether at the end of a feast or on a quieter occasion, a meal often ended with a glass of hippocras or other spiced wine, fruits and wafers, with caraway and other spice comfits to aid digestion.

The hall of the manor house or palace had many functions other than dining and had to be cleared after meals. The furniture for dining was simple and could easily be set up and removed. Long boards were laid across trestles and most diners sat on benches called bankers, though the royal family and high nobles had chairs. The table was covered with a fine white cloth, and white napkins were provided for the guests, who often provided their own knife and spoon. The salt cellar was placed in the centre of the table: the

Richard II feasting with the Dukes of Gloucester, York and Ireland in 1386, miniature from a manuscript dated c. 1480.

Trencher, British, late 16th–early 17th century, painted wood.

grander the salt cellar, the more splendid the occasion. Trenchers (plates) of thick slices of maslin bread were laid for each person, and a cup for wine, which was often mixed with water. Sticks of bread – never the fingers – were used to mop up sauces. Trenchers were replaced by clean ones for the delicacies at the end of the meal. Hands were washed before and during the meal. Good table manners were expected at all levels of society, as was careful and courteous handling of the dishes put on the table. Usually a few dishes were placed for a group of diners to share easily. The carver underwent lengthy training to prepare for his role, and his skills in cutting all kinds of meat and fish were observed and appreciated.

Wynken de Worde's *Boke of Keruynge*, published in 1513, was a manual to teach upper-class boys how to behave at court. Among other things, it explained how to arrange a feast, the correct way to lay the table, how to prepare and carve meat and fish, and which sauces should be served with them. For many years, kings, princes, dukes and archbishops no longer ate in the hall except for the great annual religious feasts or state occasions. The private chambers where they had their meals were often large enough for favoured guests, but tables still had to be erected and removed between meals. In royal palaces these chambers usually had their own kitchen and bakehouse.

Cooks and their kitchens were not much written about or illustrated. In many kitchens there were dogs sniffing around for food; a fifteenth-century edition of *Aesop's Fables* shows two plump rats enjoying the foods in a larder. The master cook was a trained craftsman who knew how to prepare a wide range of dishes. His team of apprentice cooks did the basic work, and other kitchen staff did the heavy work of getting water and wood for the fires. The cook would account to the steward for expenses incurred for the food and kitchen materials. Grand medieval households had well-equipped kitchens situated not far from the hall, usually still in the courtyard, close to the fuel store, the well, the larder, the cellar, the bakehouse and the pantry. The twelfth-century scientist and theologian Alexander Neckam describes such an establishment:

> In the vivarium let fish be kept, in which they can be caught by net, fork spear or light hook, or with a basket. Small fish for cooking should be put in a pickling mixture, that is water with salt.
>
> In the kitchen there should be a small table on which cabbage may be minced, and also lentils, peas, shelled beans … and other vegetables of the kind that can be cut up.
>
> There should also be pots, tripods, a mortar, a pestle, a hatchet, a stirring stick, a hook, a cauldron … and a large spoon for removing foam and scumming.[4]

Kitchens had separate areas for cleaning meat and poultry, and for fish. In addition to the utensils Neckam listed, there were knives and cleavers, ladles, an array of metal and ceramic pots and pans, bowls, platters, spoons, a griddle, a hand mill and a meat axe. There was also a cupboard in which spices and other expensive ingredients were secured.

One of the most important household books of the time was *Le Ménagier de Paris*, written between 1392 and 1394 by a wealthy (but not noble) Parisian householder for his young wife. It deals with all aspects of housekeeping, but the largest part is devoted to food and cooking. This section starts with specimen menus for dinners and suppers, for winter or summer, fast days or feast days; then follows a series of recipes for meat and meatless pottages, freshwater and sea fish, highly spiced meats and sausages, pungent sauces based on wine, verjuice and vinegar, and dishes are flavoured with galangal, pepper, ginger, cinnamon and cloves. The final part has recipes for preserves, wafers, pastries and spice mixtures. The *Ménagier*'s dishes are very similar to those eaten in England, as the foods of northern Europe were common throughout the region.

Reconstruction of a medieval kitchen, 14th century: Abbot's Kitchen, Glastonbury Abbey.

Cereal foods, particularly bread, provided the substantial part of most meals. Over time, the variety of breads increased. On big estates, bread, whether fine white bread, brown breads or maslin, was baked in bakehouses with domed brick or stone bread ovens. Maslin was the most common, made with a mixture of rye and wheat flour. Cheaper breads included husk and at times beans and peas. In the north and west of the country barley bread and oatcakes predominated. Thick slices of stale maslin provided trenchers for the table; the rich would have several at each meal, but the poor just one.

As early as 1202 laws were applied to commercial bakers to regulate the price of bread and the baker's profit; in 1266 these simple laws grew into the Assize of Bread, which governed the weights and prices of bread until the end of the sixteenth century. The Assize set out to regulate the weight of a penny loaf according to the prevailing price of grain and the grade of flour used. This meant that at any given time the penny loaf would have three different weights, depending on the quality of the flour used. The white loaf (manchet or payndemayn) was made from flour bolted (sifted of coarse bran) as finely as possible; next was the wheaten loaf (brown or yeoman's bread) made from more coarsely bolted meal, which was half as heavy again as the white loaf. The third loaf, the biggest and heaviest, was made from unbolted meal. In 1329 the price of wheat was about 6s a quarter (232 kilograms or 512 lb) and the white loaf weight was 1.7 kilograms (3 lb 13 oz), the wheaten loaf 2.6 kilograms (5 lb 12 oz) and the third 3.5 kilograms (7 lb 11 oz).[5]

The other staple food common to all people was pottage. It was eaten most days and sometimes served at feasts. A pottage was anything cooked in one pot. It was something like a soup-stew and varied greatly in the ingredients used – vegetables, cereals, fruit, dairy products, meat and fish, though vegetable pottages based on peas and beans were the most common. Pottages were thickened with old bread, flour paste, cereals and, for the rich on special occasions, ground almonds. The cooks knew that ingredients should be added at different stages of the cooking process to preserve their texture, flavour or colour.

Fish was important because of the Church's insistence on the observance of fast days, and during Lent dairy produce was also prohibited. For the rich, fasting days didn't mean that less food was provided, but rather that the food was that prescribed for fast days. For the poor, the food was the same as usual, although there would be no bacon scraps in the pot. People living near the coast could easily get fresh fish as well as oysters, whelks, crabs and lobsters. The rich could buy more expensive river fish and some had stocks of carp, eels and tench in their stews (fishponds). Some fresh fish was shipped to nearby towns inland, but much of the common fish such as cod, mackerel and herring was salted or pickled when it reached port. Salted fish had to be soaked in water for several hours and was then simmered in a pot of water suspended over a fire. Stockfish, wind-dried cod, was so tough that it had to be softened with a wooden hammer before it was considered ready for soaking and cooking. Mustard sauce or melted butter were served to help make it palatable.

Cattle, goats, pigs and sheep were kept as in earlier times, but sheep's wool to trade to the Continent was becoming more important than mutton. Pigs were the poor man's animal; a pig could forage and did not need to be fed, the meat could be salted or pickled and made into sausages, and the lard could be spread on bread or used in cooking. Most animals continued to be slaughtered in autumn because there was no food for them through winter; the best meat was salted and the offal, blood and marrow were eaten fresh. Farm animals provided most of the meat; wild boar and venison were highly prized, but hunting was only affordable for the very rich. The finer cuts of meat and whole small animals and birds were roasted, but in order to stop the flesh cooking too quickly it had to be turned on a spit in front of the fire. Spit turning was an unenviable job done by boys. The juices and dripping collected in a tray set beneath the spit and were scooped up to baste the meat. Some dishes were simmered or braised in a lidded pot over a fire. Most were highly spiced and flavoured with herbs; meats were often simmered in wine, and some were sweetened; fish was cooked in verjuice or vinegar, and almond milk used with poultry.

Cows and ewes were milked to supply milk, cream, butter and cheese for the manor house. Some young fresh cheese would have been kept for the lord's table, but the butter and most of the cheese were salted to preserve them. Curds and cream were popular with the wealthy, as were milk custards and warm possets. Butter and lard were still the most important cooking fats. Almond milk was used more widely in the kitchens of the rich as it would keep for much longer than fresh milk.

Monasteries had established vegetable gardens in the seventh century, and over the years manor houses developed kitchen gardens where they grew many of the same plants: leeks, onions, root vegetables, cabbage, lettuce, radishes, spinach and a variety of savoury herbs – rosemary, mint, fennel, sage, parsley, marjoram, mostly used as pot-herbs for stews. By the late fourteenth century herbs considered necessary for a garden numbered about a hundred, some for pottage, some for sauces, some to flavour drinks. In *Food and Drink in Britain*, C. Anne Wilson gives an early salad recipe, recorded about 1393:

> Salad. Take parsley, sage, garlic, chibols, onions, leek, borage, mints, porray, fennel, and garden cresses, rue, rosemary, purslain; lave and wash them clean; pick them, pluck them small with thine hand, and mingle them well with raw oil. Lay on vinegar and salt and serve it forth.[6]

They also grew fruit trees in their orchards – apples, wardens (a type of pear), plums and cherries – and big estates had pigeon lofts.

There was no shortage of food for the most part, and choice was limited only by the season and by wealth – or lack of it. Food was a clear indicator of social class: the rich could afford the finest fresh ingredients and the most expensive flavourings, while the poor had what was left and suffered from inadequate nutrition and, when crop yields were low, from hunger.

Arab and Asian flavours contributed greatly to the taste of food in Europe. By the ninth century Spain and Sicily were governed by Muslim rulers. They enjoyed a subtle yet complex and refined cuisine, and as European travellers discovered these flavours, the influence spread northwards and new techniques and flavours were introduced. More spices were imported, and with them sugar and probably a greater use of almond milk. Exotic foodstuffs such as pomegranates, dates, figs and pistachios were enthusiastically adopted in English and French kitchens.

Change in the kitchen was only a small part of the contribution Asian and Muslim cultures made to Europe. Other luxury imports from Asia included silks, porcelain and carpets. By the twelfth century a combination of Christian and Muslim influences led to the establishment of new universities, medical schools and the spread of knightly chivalry and courtly love, as in the Arthurian legend and *Le Roman de la rose*. The Middle Ages were a time of construction: Gothic cathedrals, abbeys, guildhalls, castles and fortifications were built, thanks to the increasing number of architects, master masons and skilled craftsmen. The forests that still covered much of the land provided the timber essential for building houses and ships, for the iron furnaces and for fuel.

Spices had been imported since Roman times and were now used in larger quantities and in greater variety thanks to Asian and Arabic influence. The Normans loved spices, perhaps learned from their cousins who now ruled Sicily with its sophisticated Arabic cuisine. Their selection was wider than that used in many Roman dishes. Nevertheless, the style of many medieval dishes is similar to those found in *The Art of Cooking* by Apicius because they combine spices and herbs with sweet and sharp flavours. Cloves, cinnamon, cardamom, nutmeg, mace, galangal, grains of paradise, turmeric, mastic, cassia and cubebs were in demand, as were local mustard and the saffron grown in East Anglia. Piquant flavours were widely enjoyed, as were 'egerdouce', sweet-sour dishes flavoured with vinegar or verjuice, honey or sugar and currants. Two 'powders' were frequently used: *poudre douce* made with ginger, cinnamon, cloves, grains of paradise and sugar, and *poudre forte*, a combination of ginger, cinnamon, cloves and black pepper. Combinations of spices were added to dishes served at different stages of the meal, and ambergris, musk and rose water added their scents. The wide range of herbs in kitchen gardens – fennel, coriander, parsley, rosemary, borage, pennyroyal, mint, lavender, sage, tansy, hyssop – all had a place in the kitchen alongside dried fruits, honey and sugar, vinegar, verjuice and wine.

It is clear from the range of ingredients and the ways they were combined that the upper classes enjoyed sophisticated and complex cooking daily, not only for feasts. While the combinations of ingredients may sound strange or excessive to modern readers, surviving collections of recipes and kitchen documents from many parts of Europe indicate that this highly flavoured, elegantly presented food was enjoyed throughout the region.

Cane sugar, discovered by the Crusaders on the plains of Tripoli on their way to Jerusalem at the end of the eleventh century, arrived with the spices. It came in different forms: powdered, loaf, candied or flavoured. Initially, it was mainly used as a medicine and spice, kept in the locked kitchen cupboard with the spices. In 1176 the royal kitchen of Henry II bought 15 kilograms (34 lb) of sugar at 9*d* per pound.[7] A century or so later a conical loaf of sugar cost 1–2*s* per pound. In 1180 Henry established the Guild of Pepperers to control imports of these luxury foods and confiscate any that were adulterated.[8] All the guilds had the power to fine members for dishonesty; regulations were strictly enforced, whether about the quality of a loaf of bread, selling bad meat or adulterating food. There was also legislation about how to dispose of food waste. Spices and sugar remained expensive; Edward I (r. 1272–1307) spent £1,600 on spices in one year. In 1287 the royal kitchens used 307 kilograms (677 lb) of plain sugar, 136 kilograms (300 lb) of violet sugar and 862 kilograms (1,900 lb) of rose sugar. The head cook continued to control their use.

The poor made do with mustard, garlic and onions for their flavourings and used honey as a sweetener. Strong seasonings added flavour to the salted meats that were so common, and it is sometimes said they helped to mask tainted meat, as did washing it with vinegar. However, the upper classes had fresh meat from the manor farm, supplemented by game in winter, but this too was heavily spiced as their palates were accustomed to strong aromatic flavours. Fruits and vegetables did not escape liberal spicing either. In one recipe strawberries, washed in red wine, were simmered in almond milk with raisins, saffron, pepper, sugar, ginger, cinnamon and galangal, sharpened with vinegar, a little white fat added, and then the dish was coloured red with alkanet and decorated with pomegranate seeds.[9] It is difficult to imagine that any of the original strawberry flavour survived, but no doubt it looked handsome. Colour was as important as flavour: saffron was in demand as a rub for chickens and to make egg dishes more yellow; red colouring came from the plant alkanet or the tree sanders imported from India, while green was pressed from parsley, purple from heliotrope, and white from rice, milk or ground almonds. Dishes were garnished with a sprinkling of ground spices or studded with almonds or cloves.

The peasants' diet varied from year to year depending on the harvest. In general they ate what they could provide themselves. A bad harvest meant little food, disease and famine; in good years a dinner of pottage, maslin bread and ale might be enriched by eggs, milk, cheese (called white meats), vegetables or a bit of bacon. Meat was a luxury they could not afford to buy, and only rarely might a small piece of salt beef or pork be added to the pot. The diet was monotonous, with most meals a simple mixture of grains and vegetables cooked in a cauldron. They picked wild foods – nettles, sorrel, wild garlic, mushrooms, fruits and nuts – to supplement the vegetables they could grow. Poaching for rabbits, hares and birds was common.

The diet changed with the season; most animals were slaughtered in late autumn, and during winter the only meat available was salted or game. During Lent fasting was observed, and by spring, as the weather improved, fresh foods became available again.

In the Great Famine of 1315–17 many peasants died of starvation. The Black Death of 1348–9 decimated all classes of the population. When life returned to normal, there was vacant land to be farmed and more animals to be shared; meat eating increased as a result. There were still famines and shortages, but in general a wider choice of food was available to the poor after 1349. The meagre diet that was their lot for most of the year was similar to that of the poor widow in Chaucer's 'Nun's Priest's Tale':

> There was no *sauce piquante* to spice her veal
> No dainty morsel ever passed her throat
> She drank no wine, nor white nor red had got.
> Her board was mostly served with white and black,
> Milk and brown bread, in which she found no lack;
> Broiled bacon or an egg or two were common.[10]

By the end of the fourteenth century manor houses were changing from fortified castles to more comfortable, and often elegantly ornamented, houses. The buildings were still within a courtyard, with the kitchen, bakehouse, brewhouse and other offices to one side and living quarters to the other. Chapels were often given more prominence, but the focal point was still the hall. Manors continued to be largely self-sufficient because much of the land between them was marsh or forest. The Normans developed the few small Anglo-Saxon towns and created new ones. These were centres for markets where corn, meat and wool could be sold, and salt, spices, wine and some household or farm implements bought. In time they grew larger with more merchants, craftsmen and shopkeepers. Food markets and cookshops became essential in all towns. They mostly served the lower classes of town dwellers, many of whom had no cooking facilities, or could only occasionally afford fuel to cook for themselves. Small landowners who could not grow enough to feed themselves were regular customers too. As markets expanded, they came to be used by servants from the well-to-do for foods they didn't grow themselves and for other less common ingredients. Markets and cookshops were tightly controlled by the victual laws, which regulated quality, measure and price, prohibited adulteration and unsanitary conditions, and enforced punishments. A baker who sold an adulterated or underweight loaf could be tied to a sled with the loaf round his neck and driven through the streets. The other common punishment was a spell in the stocks.

In the thirteenth century the manorial system had changed from subsistence farming to working for profit. Manors developed as independent 'businesses' with officials – bailiff, smith, steward, shepherd, ploughman – who supervised and organized the work. The old contracts between the peasants and the landowner were being terminated. Bailiffs and stewards now kept the accounts in a professional manner. The peasants became leaseholders of their land and received payment for their labour. Those who leased good land could be almost self-sufficient families with crops, cattle, pigs, sheep and hens. These changes continued through the early years of the fourteenth century, until in 1348–9 the Black Death decimated the population and led to unrest and a shortage of labour.

The surviving labourers were in a strong bargaining position and demanded higher wages. Some peasants acquired more strips of land left derelict and became themselves employers of labour and members of a new yeoman class. Landowners gradually increased the acreage of land leased and paid the higher wages demanded by landless peasants. Many manors were broken up into freeholdings and the lord became an absentee landlord. Although the legal obligation to work for the lord was gone, most peasants continued to lead a life very similar to that of their forebears, although in good years they probably ate better. Trade and industry were increasing, but the main occupation was still agriculture, and the country was largely self-supporting in food. However, there were conflicts between peasants who wanted land to grow crops and the demand for enclosures to keep sheep. Changes continued in agriculture, but open fields and enclosures continued to exist side by side in parts of the country until the nineteenth century.

Prosperous peasants and yeomen began to combine farming with artisan work or a trade; the money they made was used to extend their farms. Some now kept sheep for their wool, joining the nobles and abbots who had flocks of thousands. A weaving industry grew up in peasant homes, giving these families greater independence and wealth. A middle class began to emerge of yeomen farmers, merchants and manufacturers.

The wool trade was the most important and most lucrative trade of the Middle Ages. Wool merchants were members of the Company of Merchants of the Staple in Calais, which guaranteed the quality of the wool offered for sale to the weavers of Flanders. Its members were wealthy and respected, the leading figures in many towns and ports in the country, and eventually the company became bankers to the king. By the twelfth century sheep had become more valued for their wool than their meat, and large flocks were kept in southern and eastern counties. This trade was the basis of England's wealth and persisted until the Merchant

Adventurers, drawing on the increasing manufacture of cloth at home, started to export woollen cloth in the fifteenth century. Both domestic and capitalist production continued to develop well into Tudor times.

The new middle class was open to fresh ideas and people started to move away from the constraints of the Church with its emphasis on tradition. Anti-papal movements increased as monasteries became lax in the observance of their rule and corrupt senior clerics focused on wealth and power. Social unrest at the entrenched, privileged position of the Church and its role in the state grew. This new class turned to industry and trade and became increasingly self-reliant. It began to understand its importance within the state and grew in confidence.

Chaucer's franklin could have belonged to the upper level of this class. Franklins were free-born landowners but not members of the gentry. Chaucer's franklin was a justice who enjoyed the good life in a country town:

> He made his household free to all the county,
> His bread, his ale were the finest of the fine
> And no one had a better stock of wine.
> His house was never short of bake-meat pies,
> Of fish and flesh, and these in such supplies
> It positively snowed with meat and drink
> And all the dainties that a man could think.[11]

In the fourteenth century the transition from the medieval to the modern began, the evolution apparent in life and in language. Many more schools were endowed by wealthy landowners to educate local boys to be merchants, lawyers and estate managers or assume civic roles. The endowment of schools continued to increase in the fifteenth century, offering education to the sons of the yeomen and burghers as well as the local gentry. Boys were taught in Latin, with some translation into English, and some schools taught French. Latin was essential for any career in the Church, law, medicine, diplomacy or as town clerk because many documents were in Latin. Many boys went on to university at Oxford or Cambridge in their mid-teens.

While French remained the language of the court for some time yet, the provincial dialects of Old English and some French and Saxon words blended into a common English language, although spelling was far from standardized. This was essentially the English of Chaucer. In 1477 William Caxton set up a printing press in Westminster and published books in the English spoken in London, helping to standardize this dialect. By Tudor times, as books and education spread, this vernacular had become the language of the country. Caxton translated several books into English and printed Chaucer and the poet John Gower as well as his translations of Cicero and Virgil. Education slowly spread this English throughout the land.

There was a substantial well-educated middle class by the end of the fifteenth century. Most upper-class and many middle-class men and women could read and write. Books helped to form opinion in middle-class circles and gradually their homes became a focus of social life in towns, replacing the Church. The comfort of home life had not been important until now; it was not suited either to a peasant shack or to travelling noble households. Middle-class values developed as people's interest in industry, the material world and scientific experiment grew, displacing the old order of the Church. Personal initiative and awareness of the individual came to the fore.

The social fabric of the country was disturbed in the mid-fifteenth century by sporadic fighting during the Wars of the Roses. For thirty years branches of the House of Plantagenet – the House of York, symbolized by the white rose, and the House of Lancaster, symbolized by the red rose – fought for the crown. In

August 1485 Henry Tudor, Earl of Richmond, and the Lancastrians defeated Richard III at the Battle of Bosworth Field. Richard was killed, bringing to an end the Plantagenet dynasty, and Henry became the first Tudor king. The new king restored order throughout the country, but otherwise little changed in the rhythm of life; that did not come until his son Henry viii replaced him.

The Catholic Church was increasingly unpopular, but the bishops remained state counsellors, and Cardinal Wolsey, the pope's representative, embodied the power of the medieval Church. He considered himself superior to the nobles and gentry, drawing widely on the revenues of bishoprics and abbeys and other sources to become one of the wealthiest men in the land. However, though greedy and a lover of luxury, he used some of his great wealth to found schools and colleges and remained chancellor, serving Henry vii and Henry viii for many years.

London remained relatively peaceful during the wars; the city was governed by members of the merchant companies – the Goldsmiths, Grocers, Drapers and Mercers. They kept out of struggles for the crown and focused on enriching themselves, their guilds and the city. Much of their wealth came from exporting wool, cloth and grain; a large proportion of it was poured back into extending and improving their country estates. London, which had a population of about 18,000 when the Domesday Book was written in the eleventh century, grew rapidly as overseas trade expanded. It was a market town with a busy port. By the fourteenth century it had about 45,000 inhabitants, but other towns grew more slowly; many were little more than extended villages with around 3,000 inhabitants and they remained partly rural with gardens and orchards. Town dwellers had a strip of the town field to grow their crops and could graze their animals on common town land; the urban and rural were still intertwined.

As towns developed, a more fluid society evolved based on the flow of money. A professional class – lawyers, merchants, doctors, not stondyng and messe it forth.

Vyaunde Ryal. xx. iiij. xix.

Take wyne greke. oþer rynysshe wyne and hony clarified þerwiþ. take flo(ur) of rys powdo(ur) of gyng(ur) oþ(er) of pep(er) & canel. oþ(er) flo(ur) of canel. powdo(ur) of clowes. safroun. sug(ur) cypre. mylberyes. oþer sandr(es) & medle alle þise togid(er). boile it and salt it. and loke þat it be stondyng.

Compost. C.

Take rote of p(er)sel. pasternak of rasens. scrape hem and waisthe hem clene. take rap(es) & caboch(es) ypared and icorue. take an erthen panne wiþ clene water & set it on the fire. cast alle þise þ(er)inne. whan þey buth boiled cast þ(er)to peer(es) & p(ar)boile hem wel. take alle þise thyng(es) up & lat it kele on a fair cloth. do þ(er)to salt whan it is colde in a vessel take vyneg(er) & powdo(ur) & safroun & do þ(er)to. & lat alle þise thyng(es) lye þ(er)in al nyȝt oþ(er) al day. take wyne greke & hony clarified togid(er). take lumbarde mustard & raisons corance al hoole. & grynde powdo(ur) of canel powdo(ur) douce & aneys hole. & fenell seed. take alle þise thyng(es) & cast togyd(er) in a pot of erthe. & take þ(er)of whan þ(ou) wilt & serue forth.

Gele of fyssh. C. i.

Take tench(es). pyk(es). eelys. turbut and plays. kerue hem to pecys. scalde hem & waisshe hem clene. drye hem wiþ a cloth do hem in a panne do þ(er)to half vyneg(er) & half wyne. & seeþ it wel. & take the fysshe & pike it clene. cole þe broth thurgh a cloth in to an erthen panne. do þ(er)to powdo(ur) of pep(er) and safroun ynowh. lat it seeþ & skym it wel. whan it is ysode. dof þe grees clene. cowche fisshe on chargeo(ur)s & cole the sewe thorow a cloth onoward & s(er)ue it forth.

Gele of flessh. C. ii.

Take swyn(es) feet & snowt(es) and the eerys. capouns. conynges. calues fete. & waisshe hem clene. & do hem to seeþ in the thriddel of wyne & vyneg(er) and wat(er). and make forth as bifore.

Chysanne. C. iii.

Take roches. hole tench(es) and plays & smyte hem to gobett(es). fry hem in oyle blaunche almaund(es). fry hem & cast þ(er)to raisouns corance. make lyo(ur) of crust of brede. of rede wyne & of vyneg(er). þe thridde part þ(er)of fyg(es) drawen. & do þ(er)to powdo(ur) fort and salt. boile it. lay the fisshe in an erthen panne & cast the sewe þ(er)to. seeþ oynouns ymynced & cast þ(er)inne. kepe hit and ete it colde.

Congur in sawse. C. iiii.

Take the cong(ur) and scald hy(m). and smyte hy(m) in pecys & seeþ hym. take p(er)sel. mynt. pelet(er). rosmarye. & a litul sawge. brede and salt. powdo(ur) fort and a litel garlec. clow(es) a lite. take and grynd it wel. drawe it up wiþ vyneg(er) thurgh a cloth. cast the fyssh in a vessel and do þ(er)on þe sewe onoward & s(er)ue it forth.

Rygh in sawse. C. v.

Take rygh(es) and make hem clene and do h(em) to seeþ. pyke h(em) clene and frye hem in oile. take almaund(es) and grynde h(em) in wat(er) or wyne. do þ(er)to almaund(es) blaunched hole fryed in oile. & raisouns corance. seeþ the lyo(ur) grynde it smale & do þ(er)to garlec ygronde & a litel salt & v(er)ious powdo(ur) fort & safroun & boile it yfere. lay the fysshe in a vessell and cast the sewe þ(er)to. and messe it forth colde.

Makerel in sawse. C. vi.

Take makerels and smyte hem on pecys. cast hem on wat(er) and v(er)ious. seeþ hem wiþ mynt and wiþ oþ(er) erbes. colo(ur) it grene or ȝelow & messe it forth.

Pykes in brasey. C. vii.

Take pykes and undo hem on þe wombe(s) and waisshe hem clene. and lay hem on a roost irne. þenne take gode wyne and powdo(ur) gyng(ur) & sug(ur) good wone & salt. and boile it in an erthen panne & messe forth þe pyke & lay the sewe onoward.

Porpeys in broth. C. viii.

Make as þou madest noumbles of flessh with oynouns.

Balloc broth. C. ix.

Take eelys and hilde hem and kerue hem to pecys and do hem to seeþ in wat(er) and wyne so þat it be a litel ou(er)stepid. do þ(er)to sawge and oþ(er) erbis wiþ fewe oynouns ymynced. whan the eelis buth soden ynowh do hem in a vessel. take a pyke and kerue it to gobett(es) and seeþ hym in the same broth. do þ(er)to powdo(ur) gyng(ur) galyngale. canel and pep(er). salt it and cast the eelys þ(er)to & messe it forth.

Eles in brewet. C. x.

Take crust(es) of brede and wyne and make a lyo(ur). do þ(er)to oynouns ymynced. powdo(ur) gyng(ur) & canel. & a litel wat(er) and wyne. loke þat it be stepid. do þ(er)to salt. kerue þin eelis & seeþ hem wel and s(er)ue hem forth.

Cawdel of samoun. C. xi.

Take the gutt(es) of samoun and make hem clene. p(ar)boile hem a lytell. take hem up and dyce hem. slyt the white of lekes and kerue hem smale. cole the broth and do the lek(es) þ(er)inne wiþ oile and lat it boile togyd(er) yfere. do the samoun ycorue þ(er)in. make a lyo(ur) of almaund(es) mylke & of brede & cast þ(er)to spices. safroun and salt. seeþ it wel. and loke þat it be not stondyng.

Plays in cyuee. C. xii.

Take plays and smyte hem to pecys and fry hem in oyle. drawe a lyo(ur) of brede & gode broth & vyneg(er) and do þ(er)to powd(our) gyng(ur). canel. pep(er) and salt. and colo(ur) it with saundr(es) grene. & loke þat it be not to stondyng.

For to make flaumpeyns. C. xiii.

Take clene pork and boile it tendre. þenne hewe it small and bray it smal in a morter. take fyg(es) and boile hem tendre in smale ale. & bray hem & tendre chese þ(er)wiþ. þenne waisshe hem in wat(er) & þenne lye hem alle togid(er) wiþ ayren. þenne take powdo(ur) of pep(er). or els powdo(ur) marchant & ayren and a porcioun of safroun and salt. þenne take blank sug(ur). eyren & flo(ur) & make a past wiþ a roller. þenne make þ(er)of smale pelett(es) & fry hem broun in clene grece & set hem asyde. þenne make of þat oþ(er) deel of þat past long coffyns & do þat comade þ(er)inne. and close hem faire with a countoo(ur) & pynche hem smale aboute. þanne kyt above foure oþer sex wayes. þenne take eu(er)y of þat kuttyng up & þenne colo(ur) it wiþ ȝolkes of ayren. & plant hem thick in to þe flaumpeyns above þat þou kuttest hem. & set hem in an ovene and lat hem bake eselich. and þanne s(er)ue hem forth.

For to make noumbl(es) in lent. C. xiiii.

Take the blode of pykes oþ(er) of cong(ur). and nyme the paunch(es) of pykes. of cong(ur) and of grete code lyng. & boile hem tendre & mynce hem smale & do hem in þat blode. take crust(es) of white brede & strayne it thurgh a cloth. þenne take oynouns iboiled and mynced. take pep(er) and safroun. wyne. vyneg(er) aysell oþ(er) alegar & do þ(er)to & s(er)ue forth.

For to make chawdoun for lent. C. xv.

Take blode of gurnard(es) and cong(ur) & þe paunch(es) of gurnard(es) and boile hem tendre & mynce hem smale. and make a lyre of white crust(es) and oynouns ymynced. bray it in a morter & þanne boile it togyd(er) til it be stondyng. þenne take vyneg(er) oþ(er) aysell & safroun & putte it þ(er)to. and s(er)ue it forth.

Furmente with porpeys. C. xvi.

Take clene whete and bete it small in a morter and fanne out clene the doust. þenne waisshe it surgeons, master craftsmen – was becoming increasingly prominent. They became administrators, formed the guilds and town councils, and played a dominant role in the commercial and political life of the town. Chaucer, for example, was clerk of the works at Westminster Palace, the Tower and other royal manors. This bourgeoisie began to challenge the nobility and the Church in demanding a share of control of the country.

There is little doubt that artisans, traders, servants and apprentices who lived in towns generally had a more varied diet and a better standard of living than the peasant farmers. But many of the poorest in the towns had no cooking facilities of their own; bread, pickled herring, cheese and ale would have been a large part of their diet. For cooked food they had to rely on cookshops and victuallers, who were increasingly tightly controlled for the safety of their food and also for prices. There were street cookshops or food pedlars in the larger towns throughout the country: pie and pasty bakers, cheesemongers, cooked meat and sausage vendors shouted their wares in the streets. In the twelfth century, in his *Description of London*, William FitzStephen described a London cookshop:

> Moreover there is in London upon the river's bank, amid the wine that is sold from ships and wine-cellars, a public cookshop. There daily, according to the season, you may find viands, dishes roast, fried and boiled, fish great and small, the coarser flesh for the poor, the more delicate for the rich, such as venison and birds both big and little . . . Those who desire to fare delicately need not search to find sturgeon or 'Guinea-fowl' or 'Ionian francolin', since all the dainties that are found there are set forth before their eyes. Now this is a public cook-shop, appropriate to a city and pertaining to the art of civic life.[12]

Section from the oldest complete copy of the *Forme of Cury*, 1420s, scroll.

Two centuries later, in 1378, London prices for various cooked dishes were laid down by ordinance of the Cooks and Piemakers: 'The best roast pig for 8*d*. Best roast goose 7*d*. Best roast capon 6*d*, Best roast rabbit 4*d* . . . Best roast wodecock 2½*d* . . . Best roast pheasant 13*d* . . . Three roast thrushes 3*d* . . . The best hen baked in pastry 5*d*. The best lamb roasted 7*d*.'[13] The better-off, who had their own meat, could send a joint to the cookshop to be cooked. Chaucer's cook had all the techniques of medieval cookery at his fingertips:

> They had a Cook with them who stood alone
> For boiling chickens with a marrow-bone,
> Sharp flavouring-powder and a spice for savour.
> He could distinguish London ale by flavour,
> And he could roast and seethe and broil and fry,
> Make good thick soup and bake a tasty pie.[14]

The first practical cookery text in English, *The Forme of Cury*, was compiled by the master cooks of Richard II in the fourteenth century. It was probably dictated to a scribe by the cooks, who may have been illiterate. However, these men did not need written recipes; they were master craftsmen who had memorized techniques, flavours and quantities during their years of apprenticeship. Early cookery texts were for the householder and his steward.

Many of the recipes are similar to those in *Le Ménagier de Paris* and *Le Viandier* of Taillevent, which indicates that the wealthy, whether in Europe or in England, enjoyed the same dishes. At the beginning of *The Forme of Cury*, Richard is described as 'the best and royallest viander of all Christian kings'. A huge brigade of cooks worked in the royal kitchens to feed the thousands of people daily at court. There are recipes for hens, capons, pigeons, partridges, ducks, geese, cranes and herons. Oxen, mutton, beef, kid, pork and rabbit were the main meats; fish included cod, haddock, hake, turbot, mackerel, trout, carp, pike, crab, mussels and oysters. Although vegetables were not considered grand enough for court feasts, many were eaten on other occasions, as the recipes for skirrets (described in Gerard's *Herball* of 1597 as a root 'sweet, white, good to be eaten'), parsnips, turnips, garlic, onions, leeks, peas and beans indicate.

One list of foods required for the royal kitchens in 1387 includes fourteen salted oxen, fourteen boars, fifty swans, fifty capons, three hundred marrowbones and 11,000 dozen eggs. Eggs were cooked in a wide range of ways, but presumably many of this huge number were used for glazes, garnishes and gilding.

Meals at court always included roast meats and made dishes, both savoury and sweet. Dishes were highly coloured and well spiced. Roast meats were served by the skilled carver and eaten with the hands and a knife. The accompanying dishes had a soft consistency and could be eaten with a spoon. The food was copious and elaborate, designed to indicate the king's status, as did his palaces, his armies and his wealth.

Medieval recipes

Caboches in potage

The Forme of Cury (fourteenth-century collection of recipes)

Take a cabbage, quarter it and stew the pieces in a good stock with chopped onions and the white of leeks, sliced thinly. Add saffron and salt, and season with 'powdour douce' (a sweet spice mixture, which probably included cinnamon, ginger, grains of paradise, galangal, nutmeg and sugar).

D　It is reported, ſaith *Dioſcorides*, that Deare are preſerued from bitings of Serpents, by eateing of the herbe *Elaphoboſcum*, or wilde Parſnep, whereupon the ſeed is giuen with wine againſt the bitings and ſtingings of Serpents.

† Both the figures that formerly were in this chapter were of the Garden Parſneps ; the firſt being that of *Lobel*, and the ſecond that of *Tabernæmont*. that which ſhould haue beene in the ſecond place, was formerly put for *Sphondylium*.

Chap. 406. *Of Skirrets*.

Siſarum. Skirrets.

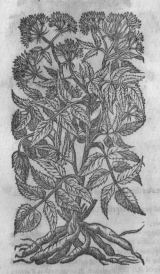

¶ *The Deſcription.*

THe leaues of the Skirret do likewiſe conſiſt of many ſmall leaues faſtened to one rib, euery particular one whereof is ſomething nicked in the edges, but they are leſſer, greener, & ſmoother than thoſe af the Parſnep. The ſtalkes be ſhort, and ſeldome a cubit high; the floures in the ſpokie tufts are white, the roots bee many in number, growing out of one head an hand breadth long, moſt commonly nor a finger thick, they are ſweet, white, good to be eaten, and moſt pleaſant in taſte.

¶ *The Place and Time.*

This skirret is planted in Gardens, and eſpecially by the root, for the greater and thicker ones being taken away, the leſſer are put into the earth againe: which thing is beſt to be done in March or Aprill, before the ſtalkes come vp, and at this time the roots which bee gathered are eaten raw, or boyled.

¶ *The Names.*

This herb is called in Latine, *Siſarum*, and alſo in Greeke, σίσαρον; the Latines do likewiſe call it *Siſer*; and diuers of the later Herbariſts *Seruillum* or *Cheruillum*, or *Seruilla*. the Germans name it, **Sterlin**; *Tragus*, **Zam garten Rapunkelen**: in the Low-countries, **Suycker wortelen**, that is to ſay, Sugar roots, and oftentimes, **Serillen**: in Spaniſh, *Cheruia*: in Italian, *Siſaro*: in French, *Cheruy*: in Engliſh, Skirret and Skirwort. And this is that *Siſer* or Skirret which *Tiberius* the Emperour commanded to bee conueied vnto him from Gelduba, a caſtle about the riuer of Rhene, as *Pliny* reporteth in *lib.16.cap.5*. The Skirret is a medicinable herbe, and is the ſame that the foreſaid Emperour did ſo much commend, inſomuch that he deſired the ſame to be brought vnto him euery yeare out of Germany. It is not, as diuers ſuppoſe, *Serapio* his *Secacul*, of which he hath written in his 89. chapter: for *Secacul* is deſcribed by the leafe of *Iulben*, that is to ſay, of the peaſe, as *Matthiolus Syluaticus* expoundeth it: and it bringeth forth a blacke fruit of the bigneſſe of a Cichpeaſe, full of moiſture, and of a ſweet taſte, which is called *Granum Culcul*: But the Skirret hath not the leafe of the peaſe, neither doth it bring forth fruit like to the Ciche-peaſe; whereupon it is manifeſt, that the Skirret doth very much differ from *Serapio* his *Secacul*: ſo farre is it from beeing the ſame.

¶ *The Temperature and Vertues.*

A　The roots of the Skirret be moderately hot and moiſt ; they be eaſily concocted; they nouriſh meanly, and yeeld a reaſonable good juyce : but they are ſomething windie, by reaſon whereof they alſo prouoke luſt.

B　They be eaten boiled, with vineger, ſalt, and a little oyle, after the manner of a ſallad, and oftentimes they be fried in oile and butter, and alſo dreſſed after other faſhions, according to the skill of the cooke, and the taſte of the eater.

The

Skirrets in John Gerard's *The Herball; or, Generall Historie of Plantes*
(1597; this edn 1636).

Salmon rostyd in sauce

Harleian MS 4016

Take 4 salmon steaks and brush with oil or melted butter and grill. Stir a little cinnamon into about 200 ml (7 fl. oz) wine. Chop an onion finely and put it into a pan with the wine and cinnamon and simmer gently. Then dissolve a little ginger in 2–3 tbsp verjuice or mild vinegar and stir into the wine. When the salmon is lightly browned on both sides, put the steaks on a serving dish and pour over the sauce.

NOTE: verjuice is the acidic juice of crab apples or unripe grapes. If you don't have verjuice or a mild vinegar, lemon juice would be a better choice than a strong vinegar.

Chike endored

Harleian MS 4016

Rub oil over the chicken and roast on a spit. When it is almost ready, brush it with egg yolks mixed with a little flour, salt, ginger, pepper and saffron to gild it. Don't let it brown. If you roast the chicken in a pan, make sure to turn it when coated with the egg yolk mixture so that it is evenly coloured.

Lamb, kid and other meats were also endored, but recipes for chicken are the most common.

Frumenty

Jill Norman, ed., *Elizabeth David's Christmas* (London, 2011)

250 g (9 oz) cracked wheat
600 ml (1 pint) creamy milk
60 g (2 oz) seedless raisins
150 ml (¼ pint) double cream
ground cinnamon

Put the wheat into a stainless steel pan and cover it with milk. Add the raisins and cover the pan. If you cook on gas or electricity, put the pan on a metal trivet over the source of the heat. This is important: the milk and wheat mixture catches and sticks easily. Let the wheat and milk cook over very low heat for 15–20 minutes until the whole mixture is creamy but not too solid. Stir in a little of the cream and leave until the next day. By this time the wheat will have swelled again. Stir in the rest of the cream. To serve the frumenty, spoon it into bowls. It can be eaten hot or cold – I prefer it cold – with the cinnamon sprinkled on at the last moment.

3

Excess and Hardship in Tudor and Stuart Times

Henry VII, the first Tudor king of England, brought much-needed stability to the country after the thirty years of disruption caused by the Wars of the Roses. However, daily life in 1485 continued much as before for most of the population. People remained in their small communities. Travel was not easy: the rough tracks through scrub, forest and marsh were more suited to walking or travelling on horseback than journey by carriage. Rivers were increasingly used for heavy transport and pack horses only for short distances. Villages continued to be self-supporting with a hierarchy of earls, barons, knights, squires, yeomen and labourers. The rich were extremely rich and the poor remained very poor.

The manor was still the focal point of the community; the lord was the king's tenant, and the former sublet parcels of land to the peasants. Increasing changes in agriculture meant that tenant farming had almost completely replaced the earlier feudal system. Towns expanded slowly as craftsmen made harnesses, implements, clothing, shoes and boots, and the professional classes grew. Both towns and villages were generally ordered societies in which people knew and accepted their place. A monetary economy was coming into use and this helped to create a more fluid society, where villeins became freemen and tenants became yeomen. However, prices rose steadily early in the sixteenth century and caused hardship, particularly for day labourers. Early Tudor England was largely self-sufficient for housing, fuel, food and clothing, although life for the poorest peasants and labourers remained precarious.

After restoring order in the country Henry recalled parliament, but the extension of its functions did not come about until the reign of Henry VIII. Civic liberties and the courts of justice were established, and medieval English common law became the basis of modern English law. The long-simmering hostility to the papacy and what was seen as a corrupt ecclesiastical bureaucracy continued, but Cardinal Wolsey thrived, probably by serving the king more assiduously than he did the Church. The works of Erasmus and Thomas More, and William Tyndale's translation of the Bible into English, were published with the hope that they could reform and liberalize the Church.

The monasteries were great landowners, and many thought the land could be better managed, most notably those families who were their tenants. A huge change occurred throughout English society in the 1530s when Henry VIII ordered the dissolution of the monasteries. Henry acquired the monasteries' assets and their income, and sold most of the estates to the nobles and gentry to replenish the treasury and to finance his wars. The rule of the country was still hierarchical, but this led to some blurring of social class, to changes in ownership and wealth at all social levels. Broadly speaking, most people moved up the landowning scale. The nobles and gentry enlarged their estates; yeomen farmers also acquired more land, while some moved into business. Cottagers and labourers often gained another strip of land for their own use, and the remaining villeins who had belonged to the monasteries won their freedom.

Clerical privilege and power were abolished and slowly secularism and Protestant ideas were adopted. Parliament passed the Act of Supremacy in 1534, which made Henry supreme head of the Church of England. This was not simply a religious change, but a social and political change. The bishops were nominated by the king and were also civil servants; priests often acted as business agents for the local gentry and these roles continued. Some abbots were executed, but most monks, friars and nuns were given a sum of money and sent out into the world.

Inequalities of class and sex did not change. Women, whatever their class, were considered inferior. Before marriage a woman was the subject of her parents; after marriage her husband took the place of her father. Marriages were usually arranged, often between children. Only as a widow did a woman have any freedom to organize her own life and dispose of her property. Women were not permitted to hold public office or have a profession. Women's education began to be taken seriously during the Renaissance, a time when England had two queens, but nevertheless capable women were not allowed to participate in public life. However, all women were expected to organize their household. Upper-class women had privileges but no rights, though their accomplishments were important: they were expected to be skilled in languages, music, dancing and needlework. The lady of the house supervised domestic activities and often made preserves and other sugar confections with her daughters and maids, except within the highest noble families, who usually employed a steward to run the household. Yeomen and their wives and daughters lived much more modestly, but by the end of the sixteenth century, as they became richer and better educated, this had changed significantly. The women in poorer households continued to do manual work, often in the fields, in addition to their household work.

Households at all levels of society kept livestock, though cottagers had only hens or a pig. Most animals continued to be slaughtered in autumn because there was insufficient food in the winter, with the meat salted or pickled to last the households through the coming season. The rich hunted, while the poor trapped rabbits and birds with snares. The fishponds of the rich continued to provide carp and pike for the table; others, if they could afford fish for fast days, had salt ling or stockfish. Inland, fresh fish came only from streams and rivers. Sea fish were available near the coast, and as before all fish to be transported inland continued to be smoked or salted before being dispatched. In his *Compendyous Regyment or a Dyetary of Helth* of 1562, Andrew Boorde claimed: 'Of all nacyons and countres, England is best served of Fysshe, not onely of al manner of see-fysshe, but also of fresshe-water fysshe.'[1]

According to the means of the family, food was grown and processed, beer brewed, butter and cheese made, preserves and herbal remedies produced in the stillroom. Soap and candles were made, while flax, wool and hides were used for clothing. The nobles and gentry had staff to do this work – ladies' maids, seamstresses, launderesses, dairy maids, outdoor maids and labourers – and in grand households there were often a hundred or more employed in these roles.

England was also part of a wider European economy, which meant transactions were common for large export orders, but imports were still restricted to luxuries for the rich. Metals had long been exported and the important wool trade of the Middle Ages was gradually replaced by the export of woollen cloth, which created work for weavers, dyers and other craftsmen. Some merchants ventured to the Mediterranean, but most shipping was to and from the Netherlands and northern France. The dominance of the Hanseatic League fleet in the North Sea led John Cabot to sail from Bristol in 1497 to find a northern route to the Spice Islands. Instead, he found the cod-rich waters of North America. Henry VII gave Cabot a pension and named the new territory Newfoundland, but not until many years later was a well-organized business in fishing Newfoundland cod established.

Henry VII had built up a royal navy and his son used some of the monastic funds to increase it and build naval bases and dockyards. In Elizabeth I's reign (1558–1603), Francis Drake, Walter

Raleigh and other adventurers sailed the seas, discovering new lands and new merchandise. Some joined in the slave trade from Africa to central America and the Caribbean islands. There was further exploration across the Atlantic to the American coast and unsuccessful attempts to navigate the Northwest Passage, but England remained behind Spain, Portugal and the Netherlands in naval exploration.

The Tudor years were a period of creativity, intellectual pursuits and political and religious change. The culture of Renaissance Italy had a considerable influence on the Tudor court, culminating in the reign of Elizabeth. The Italian influence was seen in architecture as the Gothic style was replaced by buildings, designs and ornaments in Renaissance style. Palaces were built or rebuilt, and the Tudor love of display was as evident here as in their magnificent costumes and jewels, and in the style of their ceremonies and entertainments.

This period has been described as a brief golden age: of Shakespeare, Jonson and Marlowe, of drama and lyric poetry, of Byrd, Campion and Dowland, and of madrigals, masques and compositions for the Chapel Royal. According to historian G. M. Trevelyan, 'Shakespeare's England had a charm and a lightness of heart, a free aspiring of mind and spirit not to be found elsewhere in the harsh Jesuit-Calvinist Europe of the day ... a people freed from medieval and not yet oppressed by puritan complexes and fears.'[2] Shakespeare and his colleagues were followed by the Jacobean poets, dramatists and prose writers – Milton, Donne, Marvell, Dryden, Congreve and others.

In early Tudor times, food continued to be served in the medieval manner. The royal palaces had extensive catering establishments to feed the hundreds of people always present at court. In addition to the kitchens there were bakehouses and cellars, larders and pantries, and a huge staff under the lord steward to turn out sumptuous banquets for as many as a thousand diners. The grand country houses of the nobles had similar facilities and staff, albeit on a more modest scale, to cater for their own needs and to accommodate visits from the king and court.

The largest surviving Tudor kitchens are at Hampton Court Palace. Henry VIII extended them in 1529 to comprise 52 rooms covering some 280 square metres (3,014 sq. ft), and they were staffed by at least two hundred people. The entry was through a gatehouse occupied by the Cofferer (kitchen accountant) and his staff, the Clerks of the Green Cloth, who monitored the arrival of staff and goods to the kitchens.

The Office of Spicery held all imported spices, as well as local mustard and herbs from the palace garden. It was also responsible for all the fruit grown in the palace gardens and orchards. There were six huge fireplaces with spit-racks in the great kitchen (one is still in use). A smaller kitchen housed charcoal stoves for making small preparations such as sauces, pancakes, preserves and confectionery. These needed the constant attention of a cook and careful control of the heat. The boiling house had great cauldrons for boiling meat and making stock. The pastry house had four ovens for baking savoury and sweet pies and pastries. The confectionery produced sweet dishes for the most important members of the court, and for banquets. All had shelves of ceramic bowls, pots and jugs, large pans and cauldrons, tables for preparing food, and hand tools – knives, spoons and ladles, pestles and mortars, bundles of twigs or rushes that served as whisks. Forks were used for cooking, carving and serving, but they were not much used at table until the seventeenth century. The king's food was prepared in a separate kitchen by his own team of cooks.

There were three larders: a flesh larder for meat, a wet larder for fish and a dry larder for pulses, grains, nuts and vegetables. In addition, the palace had three cellars – the wine cellar for casks of wine for the courtiers, the privy cellar for wine and ale for the king, and the great cellar where ale was stored. It is estimated that about

Tudor kitchens, Hampton Court Palace, 16th century.

2.75 million litres (600,000 gal.) of ale and about 340,000 litres (75,000 gal.) of wine were drunk at court each year.

When Elizabeth I lived at Hampton Court, the kitchens remained the same, and a wider selection of foods was available following the exploration of the New World. A kitchen list from the time of her reign shows the continuing importance of meat;

in one year 1,240 oxen, 8,200 sheep, 2,330 deer, 760 calves, 1,870 pigs and 53 wild boar were cooked in the kitchens. No part of the animal was wasted; the lung, spleen and udder were preserved in vinegar or brine, and black pudding was stuffed into intestines. Roast swan and peacock dressed in their feathers or boar's head were still served for special occasions.

Dinner was served at 10 a.m. and supper at 4 p.m. At court the king presided over meals in the great hall on the most important festive occasions, but otherwise Henry dined privately with a small number of his courtiers. A German visitor to Greenwich Palace later noted that Elizabeth ate alone, 'with very few Attendants'.[3] By now, this manner of dining had spread to noble households; the lord and his family took their daily meals in a private dining parlour instead of the great hall, apart from on festive or state occasions. On farms and small estates, the family and household continued to eat together.

On 6 January 1508 the Duke of Buckingham celebrated the Feast of the Epiphany with two meals for 459 guests and household. Much of the food was grown or produced on his estate, but it was also included in the daily accounts. Over forty foods are listed, including 678 loaves (18s 11¼d), 33 pottles of Gascony wines (66s), 259 flagons of ale (21s 7d), 36 rounds of beef (21s), 12 carcasses of mutton (14s), 22 rabbits (4s 7½d), 2 peacocks (2s), 3 dozen larks (9d), 6 large fresh eels (3s 4d) and 24 dishes of butter (2s).[4]

The nobility continued to use gold and silver tableware, but silver goblets were replaced by fashionable Venetian glasses. Knives and spoons were part of the place setting. Although forks were now being introduced from Italy, they were widely spurned: clean hands were considered sufficient. Only at the end of the sixteenth century and into the seventeenth were forks used regularly because dishes such as hashes and fricassees were easier to eat with a fork. Trenchers of wholemeal bread were replaced by pewter or wooden boards, often with a small indentation in one corner for salt. Salt was taken from the grand elaborate salt cellar in the centre of the table and put on individual boards. Earthenware cups started to replace the earlier wooden ones. Napkins were slung over the left shoulder and servants carried round ewers of water to rinse hands between courses.

Meat, and particularly beef, remained the most popular food. English meats were quite fatty and well flavoured because the animals fed on good pasture. Spit-roasted meats were preferred. The spits were now turned by dogs trained to walk within a wheel. In *The English Huswife* (1615) Gervase Markham gave detailed instructions as to the temperature of the fire for roasting different kinds of meat, the best bastings (butter, oil or dripping), how to dredge the surface of the meat with breadcrumbs or oatmeal to prevent it drying, what forcemeat to use and how to know when the meat is ready. He also describes how to carbonado meat: 'Carbonadoes, which is meat broiled upon coals ... are of divers kinds ... for there is no meat either boiled or roasted whatsoever, but may afterwards be broiled.' He recommends joints of mutton and venison basted with melted butter, and insists that it must be done on a broiling iron, which is made of plate iron with hooks on which to hang the meat. On a gridiron the juices dropping from the meat would make the fire smoke and the meat stink. The broiling iron is set close to the fire so that the meat cooks on both sides from the heat of the fire and from the heat of the plate. Markham serves the carbonado with vinegar, butter and minced onion. Presumably in a grand household the accompaniments would have been more complex and of grander ingredients.

Cooked meat, chopped finely and often spiced, was potted under a layer of butter, and cooked fowl and fish were often preserved in the same way. In *Delights for Ladies* (1605) Sir Hugh Plat included a recipe for cooked beef pickled in vinegar. Sausages continued to be popular. Usually they were made with pork, breadcrumbs, herbs and spices, but there are recipes using veal, beef or

capon. Cooks started to pot well-seasoned sausages, taking out the meat to fry when needed, coated in flour to prevent them sticking. Potted sausages saved time cleaning and filling intestines.

Intestines were also used to make black and white puddings; the meat was lightened with breadcrumbs or oatmeal, eggs yolks and cream, and flavoured with spices and dried fruits. Some white puddings were made without meat. Puddings were stuffed into guts and boiled, then often browned in front of a fire before serving. But as intestines were being dispensed with for sausages, so also for puddings. They were put into a bag or a cloth that was tied at the top and then suspended in boiling water. Sir Kenelm Digby, in his *The Closet of Sir Kenelm Digby Opened* (1669) offers several pudding recipes from the seventeenth century, some cooked in intestines, others in cloths and some that are baked between pieces of puff pastry.

Fast days were strictly observed in Tudor times, when only one meal a day was eaten instead of two. The state joined the Church in ordering that only fish could be eaten on Saturdays in addition to Fridays, possibly because of a scarcity of cattle and the high price of meat. In 1583 Elizabeth I added Wednesdays too. Penalties for breaking the fast on a secular fish day were severe – three months' imprisonment if the fine could not be paid.

For those who could afford it, fish was plentiful and of high quality. When in 1561 Elizabeth I dined at Ingatestone Hall in Essex on a Saturday, the household accounts show '2 firkins of sturgeon at 23/4 the piece, 46/8, carriage from London 5d'. Flounder, plaice, sole, gurnard and other fish cost £4 3s.[5] If a royal banquet had to be served on a fish day, sole or salmon would have been on the menu as well as sturgeon.

Robert May was cook to noble families over several decades, and his book, *The Accomplisht Cook*, includes several recipes for all

Great Hall, Guildhall, London, the setting for the annual
Lord Mayor's Banquet since 1502.

three, stewed, roasted, fried, jellied or baked. Sturgeon pies were popular, and he provides several versions, some to be served cold, others hot. Versions for winter and summer are included too. In one to be eaten hot, the sturgeon is cut into pieces the size of a walnut, flavoured with pepper, nutmeg and salt, and put into a pie shell on top of a layer of butter. On top of the fish,

> put to it a good big onion or two whole, some large mace, whole cloves, slic't ginger, some large oysters, slic't lemon, gooseberries, grapes or barberries and butter, close it up, and bake it, being bak'd, fill it up with beaten butter, beaten with white-wine or claret, and juyce or slices of lemon or orange. To this pye in Winter, you may use prunes, raisins, or currans, and liquor it with butter, verjuice, and sugar, and in Summer, pease boil'd and put in the pye, being baked, and leave out the fruit.

Pies such as these must have been very rich Lenten fare. May's pie recipes are accompanied by illustrations of the appropriate shapes the pies should take: 'Make your sturgeon pyes or pasties according to these forms.' He also includes recipes for turbot, lamprey, eel, plaice, halibut, crab, prawn, lobster and oyster.

Markham's recipes for the gentlewoman-housewife are more modest; they include baked eel and carp, stewed trout, and boiled gurnet or rochet. His simple instructions for small fish – roach, dace, gudgeon or flounder – are to

> boil white wine and water together with a bunch of choice herbs and a little whole mace, put in your fish, and scum it well: then put in the sole of a manchet, a good quantity of sweet butter, and season it with pepper and verjuice, and so serve it upon sippets, and adorn the sides of the dish with sugar.

Small fish were usually served on sippets or sops (small pieces of bread), often with melted butter.

Salt fish was at least somewhat better than stockfish; it was also eaten with mustard and butter, and was used in great quantities along with salt meat to provision ships' crews.

The aromatic flavours of earlier years were still enjoyed, and the use of spices continued to demonstrate wealth. The Portuguese reached India in 1488 via the Cape of Good Hope and established trading posts. For the next hundred years they kept the price of spices high, higher sometimes than they had been when the Venetians controlled the trade. Spices were still essential to many sauces and made dishes; cinnamon, mace, nutmeg, cloves, ginger and pepper were the most widely used while cubebs, galangal and grains of paradise started to fall out of favour. Rose water and petals were also popular Tudor flavourings.

Saffron growing in East Anglia reached its peak early in the sixteenth century, and in 1514 Henry VIII granted the town of Walden a charter and its official name became Saffron Walden. There was high demand for the saffron from rich Europeans in spite of its high price.

An entry dated 1 April 1549 in the household accounts of Ingatestone Hall, the home of Sir William Petre, Secretary of State to Edward VI, lists the cost of spices and other imported foods:

½ pound mace	6s 8d
½ pound cloves	2s 6d
1 ounce saffron	20d
20 pounds currants	8s 4d
4 pounds dates	2s
1 pound ginger	3s 4d
½ pound cinnamon	2s 10d
6 pounds pepper	14s

1 pound caraways   14*d*

6 pounds almonds   2*s*[6]

The only inexpensive spice was locally grown mustard, which was prepared at home and served with most fish and meat, whether fresh or salted. Medieval *poudre blanche* was replaced by cinnamon or clove-scented sugar. 'Kitchen pepper' (a variety of spices such as nutmeg, cloves and cinnamon mixed with pepper) and other blends of ground spices continued to be used, and whole spices flavoured some dishes. Dyeing food with cochineal and sanders became less common.

Sugar, which had hitherto been a luxury and treated as a medicine and spice, was imported in larger quantities and at different grades. Some included molasses, while others were more refined. The best sugar was sold in domed loaves of 1.4–1.8 kilograms (3–4 lb) glistening like snow. Supplies now came from new Spanish plantations in the West Indies and Portuguese plantations in Brazil, and in the 1540s a refinery was established in London. By the 1640s sugar was being imported from English-owned estates on Barbados. This new colonial trade had a widespread economic and social effect on the country. Imports increased dramatically and more refineries were built in and around London. Coal, equipment for the plantations as well as other goods needed by the plantation owners were shipped to Barbados. A few voices were raised about the conditions of the African slave labour in the plantations, but they were not heeded. In earlier times many dishes had been both sweet and savoury; complex, highly spiced sauces and condiments almost always included sugar. Sugar continued to be used with vinegar or verjuice in sweet-sour sauces, but a distinction was now being made between sweet and savoury dishes. For the nobility sugar took the place of honey as a sweetener, and it was used liberally to prepare crystallized fruits, sweetmeats and preserves. Tooth decay (among the rich) became a serious problem.

The rich enjoyed a wide variety of wines; large quantities were imported from Germany, France, Italy, Spain and Portugal. Sack (sherry) from Spain was fashionable and thought to last longest. In *The English Huswife*, Markham tells the reader to 'observe that your claret wines be fair coloured, and bright as a ruby'. Claret referred to the light red colour, not the origin of the wine. 'For your white wines, see they be sweet and pleasant at the nose, very short, clear and bright and quick in the taste.'

The poor drank ale and beer. Ale houses and taverns were popular places, as we know from Shakespeare's Falstaff. Ale and beer were also brewed at home until a royal edict stopped this practice in 1637. From this time, beer had to be bought from a registered brewer in order to make it easier to levy a tax on brewing. Cider was popular; hippocras (spiced, sweetened wine) was still enjoyed, and distilled waters were being made.

Sir Digby's *The Closet Opened*, published posthumously, gives many recipes for making meath (mead) and metheglin. Meath was made with hops, sweet herbs and honey. Metheglin was based on herbs (rosemary, marjoram, hyssop, borage and thyme) boiled in water. The liquor was strained and heated again with honey and spices (cinnamon, mace, cloves, nutmeg and ginger). This was strained and cooled, ale yeast added, the container covered and the metheglin left to ferment. After two weeks it was ready to drink, and it would keep for six months.

The main meals, dinner and supper, continued to be taken in the late morning and early evening, and a substantial breakfast might be eaten before hunting. The rich lived well on a high-protein diet of meat, fowl and fish, usually highly spiced, accompanied by wine and ale. Beef, veal, pork, mutton, venison and all manner of birds, sometimes including swans and peacocks, freshwater fish such as pike and carp and fine white manchet bread were served. Also popular were fricassees, hashes, bisks (bisque), carbonadoes and other dishes introduced from France and elsewhere in Europe.

Table laid for a traditional Tudor Christmas dinner at
Shakespeare's Birthplace, Stratford-upon-Avon.

Made dishes, including some pies and tarts, tended to be extravagant, and were often described as being in the French or Italian fashion. The court of James I (r. 1603–25) was known for its lavish entertaining, rather in the manner of Henry VIII; £100,000 a year was the total amount for household expenditure, twice as much as Elizabeth I had spent for all her love of good food, wine and entertainment.

The word 'banquet' had two meanings in Tudor and Stuart times; one was a grand feast, such as those given at court; the other was an elaborate dessert. A court banquet would last for several hours and consisted of several courses, each with a wide variety of dishes. In the early days of the Tudor monarchs, a formal banquet consisted of three meat courses followed by three of fish. Each course would have up to ten or twelve different dishes and finish with an elaborately executed sweetmeat or jelly. The dishes for each course were put out on the table, and the diner ate from those nearest to him. For a large party, the dishes would be repeated along the table.

The household accounts of Ingatestone Hall also include the foods served at a feast for about a hundred people to celebrate Twelfth Night in 1562: nine pieces of boiled beef (about 9 kilograms/20 lb per piece), six pieces of roast beef (about 14 kilograms/30 lb per piece), a haunch and leg of pork, two legs of veal, a whole young pig, a loin and breast of veal, two rabbits, and finally ten beef pasties, two mutton pasties and four venison pasties, all of which were very large. There were also geese, capons, woodcock, partridges, teals and larks. Most dishes would have had dressings, sauces and stuffing.[7]

It is impossible to know whether animals were kept and slaughtered for this occasion, or whether they were slaughtered in autumn, as was customary for all but breeding stock, and the meats

Selection of 16th- and 17th-century food including marchpane (marzipan) cake (heart-shaped decorations) and mince pyes, Little Moreton Hall, Cheshire.

salted or cured. Venison, rabbits and birds would have been the only fresh meats readily available in winter. In the country many families kept hens, sometimes geese and ducks. Manor houses had dovecotes; the rich bought capons, peacocks and pheasants. Birds were usually roasted, and small ones were served on sops of bread to absorb the butter and juices. Throughout the winter months birds were regularly on the menu to provide variety at table; only the very rich could afford venison. By the late sixteenth century some animals could be fed through the winter and a little fresh meat was available. The demand for the less interesting small birds and seabirds dropped during this period too, and falconry gave way to guns for killing birds.

The banquets of sweetmeats, fruits and sweet wines, sometimes accompanied by entertainment, were held in a separate banqueting chamber in winter, and in summer special banqueting houses in the park allowed guests to enjoy their surroundings. There were many recipes for 'banquetting stuffe'; sugar was still expensive, so a banquet of sweet confections was an indication of wealth and status. Banquets were also occasions for display, with elaborate table decorations sculpted in sugar. Often the lady of the house, rather than the male cook, organized the sugar work with her daughters and maids in the stillroom. They also made distilled waters, with, according to Sir Hugh Plat's *Delightes for Ladies* (1609), 'borrage flowers and cynamon for melancholie', clove water for stomach problems, sage water for colic, and 'the best waters for the smoothing of the skin, and keeping the face delicate and amiable'.

The title page of *Delightes for Ladies* continues: 'to adorne their persons, tables, closets and distillatories with beauties, banquets, perfumes and waters'. His recipes range from rose syrup and candied flowers to jellies and sugar paste animals in moulds. There are instructions for distilling waters from herbs, flowers and spices, practical information on 'bags sweet to lie among linens', a 'ball to take out staines', and a chapter on 'cookerie and huswiferie' that includes butter and cheese-making and keeping 'lobsters, crafishes, &c sweet and good for some fewe daies'.

A Queen's Delight; or, The Art of Preserving. Conserving and Candying, first published in 1655, was compiled by 'WM', who was in the service of Henrietta Maria, wife of Charles I (r. 1625–49). One of the most popular books of its time (it was reprinted frequently), it contains recipes for preserving and candying all kinds of fruit for 'marmalets' and 'biskets', and for making 'marchpane' (marzipan), candying and gilding it. At royal banquets the dishes and trenchers were sometimes made of sugar, often lavishly decorated with gilding.

Markham's *The English Huswife* gives several recipes for banquet dishes and tells the housewife how to present a banquet:

> You shall first send forth a dish made for show only, as beast, bird, fish, or fowl, according to invention: then your marchpane [marzipan], then preserved fruit, then a paste, then a wet sucket [fruit in syrup], then a dry sucket [candied fruit], marmalade, comfits, apples, pears, wardens [a type of pear], oranges and lemons sliced; and then wafers, and another dish of preserved fruits, and so consequently all the rest before: no two dishes of one kind going or standing together, and this will not only appear delicate to the eye, but invite the appetite with so much variety thereof.

The attributes of a good housewife, according to Markham, also included knowledge of gardening – when to plant and harvest herbs, fruits and vegetables – as well as cooking. His recipes are for people accustomed to eating well but not grandly. Most are for fricassees, broths, roast and baked meats, pies and tarts; the 'banquetting stuffe' is only for special occasions.

The recipes in *Elinor Fettiplace's Receipt Book* (1604) are also for less complicated dishes. This Elizabethan manuscript was handed down through generations of the family of Hilary Spurling's husband and published in 1986. It is clear that simpler daily meals were becoming more popular among the gentry, who did not have to reckon with court entertaining. The standards of cooking remained high, and the food was imaginative and elegantly presented, but it was not excessive or extravagant. Many ingredients came from the orchard or garden. Lady Fettiplace has recipes for apple pie, gooseberry wine, pickling samphire, buttered crayfish and buttered sweet potatoes (with rose water, sugar, orange zest and juice). There are several recipes for preserved fruits, quince paste, marchpane and crystallized fruits, as would be expected from the lady of the house.

Eggs and butter were widely used in cooking. Olive oil was still rare and kept for dressing salad, so butter or lard were used for frying. Melted butter sauces were poured over dishes when they were served, particularly vegetables and puddings. Omelettes were introduced from France, replacing the earlier English tansy. (A tansy was an egg dish flavoured with the herb tansy and made only in spring, when tansy is not poisonous.) The tansy, with added breadcrumbs, spices, sugar and cream, was eventually transformed into a sweet pudding boiled in a cloth. Recipes for spiced and plain pancake batters appeared. Fritters of egg batter and fruits, herbs or vegetables were well liked, particularly those with apples or skirrets. The popularity of fried eggs with collops (roasted rashers of bacon) continued. Otherwise, eggs were fried, poached in broth or water, or roasted in the embers. Eggs boiled in their shells became common in the sixteenth century. Many egg dishes were served on fasting days, especially buttered (scrambled) eggs. Fresh 'green' cheeses and soft and hard cheeses were part of the diet. Soft cheeses, often flavoured with herbs, were made everywhere in summer and served as part of a banquet course. By the sixteenth century most cheeses in England were made of cow's milk; ewes and goats were still milked in upland regions, but the milk was usually drunk.

Cereal pottages continued to be staples for most people for breakfast, and for the poorest, pottage remained the staple for most meals. Buttered cereals became popular: the cereal was boiled until very soft, then served with butter, a little spice and sugar, and eaten with a spoon. Frumenty, a kind of porridge made with cracked wheat enriched with eggs and milk, and sometimes coloured with saffron, was still popular on feast days. Towards the end of the seventeenth century sago arrived from Malaya and vermicelli from Italy. Both were used in the new, clear pottages or soups. By this time also bread, salted fish, meat and beer were added to the breakfast menu. Toast – long popular – spread with scrambled or poached eggs, chopped veal kidneys, ham or melted cheese was on the breakfast table.

Small households baked their own bread in a metal bowl on the hearth. The grand houses had bread ovens attached to their kitchens, but when kitchens were incorporated into the house, the bakehouse often remained outside. The oven was heated by burning wood within it and then removing it to slide in the dough on a peel. The door was put in place, sealed round the sides with mud, and the bread left to bake. In towns professional bakers sold a variety of breads and would also bake customers' dough. According to Dr Thomas Moffett in 1655, 'Bread is the best nourishment of all other, being well made.'[8] He maintained that bread made with medium coarse meal containing a proportion of bran was easier to digest and more nutritious than the white manchet made from finely bolted white flour. This was in contrast to the food of the rich at this time, who ate more manchet than 'household brede'. Bread made with barley or oats was still baked in poorer households.

Richer breads started to be produced with spices, egg yolks and butter added to the dough, some made into buns, others into large cakes. Gingerbread changed from its uncooked medieval form of breadcrumbs flavoured with ginger and other spices. It was now made with flour, spices, treacle and preserved fruits, and baked.

As towns and cities expanded, cookshops were set up to sell cooked meats, pies, puddings and other dishes to cater to travellers and to the many poor households who still had very limited cooking facilities. The increase in wealth of the merchants and landowners did not reach down to the poor. Poor townspeople lived on pottage, bread and pickled herring. The wages of farm labourers increased, but not enough to make a significant difference to their diet. Their meals still consisted of broth prepared with vegetables, maybe a little salt meat or bacon, bread and cheese.

By the early years of the seventeenth century, the population of England had grown to about 4 million, but most people lived in the southeast or along the coasts. The population of London, the biggest port, which employed thousands of people, rose to about 400,000. There was also severe poverty and disease among the slum dwellers, many of whom were dependent on charity.

The woollen and weaving industries remained cottage industries: middlemen commissioned goods, supplied the materials and sold the finished items. The work was still largely done in family units, and apprentices lived with their masters. Demand extended the industry to Yorkshire, East Anglia and the West Country. The rural economy was increasingly dominated by the demand from London for food and goods. The Dutch brought their talents for market gardening to England and the range of fresh produce widened. Markets sprang up around St Paul's Cathedral in London. The stalls spread into the churchyard and in 1673 the Lord Mayor restricted them to certain streets. London was spreading westwards. Covent Garden, where there had been a garden and orchard supplying food to a convent and hospital, came into the ownership of the Earl of Bedford. The fourth earl commissioned the most important architect of the day, Inigo Jones, to design a public square in 1630. Some years later it became London's foremost market for fresh fruit and vegetables.

Permanent food shops started to open in competition with the market, and charters were granted for retail markets in Leadenhall, Newgate and Billingsgate. Foods were subject to inspection, and the weights of cheese and butter were controlled. The Assize of Bread set up in 1266 to control the weight of a penny loaf had become unworkable and was dropped. Prices – now higher than a penny – still varied depending on size of the loaf and the grade of flour used.

London was now an important international mercantile centre. Elizabeth I had granted a royal charter to the East India Company in 1600. Even though the company came late to the international race for the spice trade, fortunes were made in this and other ventures. A new wealthy class of urban professionals – lawyers, merchants and industrialists – developed alongside master crafts-men, artisans, traders and servants. They formed livery companies and had a dominant role in commercial and political life. They also bought up or built large country estates, and this educated class of landowners and farmers was keen to learn and experiment.

Many of this new middle class were members of the House of Commons; under Elizabeth the Commons met more frequently, set taxes and made laws, but she refused to let them interfere in foreign policy or matters of religion. They were becoming increas-ingly frustrated at their lack of political power and the inability of parliament to force through change. James I lacked Elizabeth's firmness and did not deal with the situation so resolutely. This led to parliament making demands that the king should modify some of his traditional rights, most of which he resisted.

Religious undercurrents were woven into this society; Elizabeth had been made supreme governor, not head, of the Church in which Protestant and Catholic elements co-existed, and she ensured this balance was maintained. However, several sects developed within the Protestant movement, with the Puritans coming to the fore at the end of the sixteenth century. James I managed to maintain a balance in his dealings with parliament on religion and matters of government, but his son, Charles I, lacked his skills. He opposed the Puritans and married the Catholic Henrietta Maria, sister of Louis XIII of France. Charles dissolved parliament in 1629 and ruled directly for eleven years, recalled parliament briefly to try to raise funds to fight the Scots, and when parliament convened again in 1642, it 'met in a black mood, determined not on reform, but on revolution'.[9] Civil war broke out and continued until 1649, when Charles I was beheaded; this was a war in which the parties were divided on religious and political grounds, not social or economic. Oliver Cromwell became lord protector of the puritanical Commonwealth for a decade. The Commonwealth conferred prestige and power on the propertied class, strengthening the bourgeoisie, but the poorest remained untouched.

The Restoration of 1660 brought in a constitutional monarchy, returning the nobles and gentry to their former roles and the bishops to the Church. Some of the king's supporters went into exile but many kept their places in parliament. Charles II reopened the theatres closed by the Puritans and his interest in science led to the foundation of the Royal Society under his patronage. The 'natural philosophers' John Evelyn, Kenelm Digby, Isaac Newton and Christopher Wren were among its first members.

Once again, the royal household and court led the way in setting the fashions of the day, including in the kitchen. Many Catholic families who had fled to France returned with their French cooks and a taste for European dishes. Employing a French chef conferred prestige. Books by renowned French chefs were translated into English; La Varenne's *Cuisinier françois* was published as *The French Cook* in 1653, and François Massialot's *Cuisinier royal et bourgeois* as *The Court and Country Cook* in 1702. They were widely used by both French and English cooks in noble households.

Robert May was the most interesting English professional cook of the time. Born in the reign of Elizabeth i, he worked until the reign of Charles ii. A Catholic, he cooked for several aristocratic Catholic families and left for France when his employers did during the Commonwealth. His book, *The Accomplisht Cook*, was published in the mid-1600s on his return to England. It shows some nostalgia for the grand meals and set pieces of the past, but it consists largely of everyday dishes. They are grander than Markham's, because May was writing for other professional chefs to the nobility, not for gentlewomen and housewives. His years in France exposed him to many French, Italian and Spanish dishes.

His monthly bills of fare for dinner for two courses, each with six dishes, are more modest than those of the past. For feasts the two courses run to twenty dishes each, and for those on fasting days and in Lent the courses each have sixteen dishes. In addition to introducing European dishes, he also brings in new ingredients like the turkey and the potato. Turkey is suggested in the first recipe, which is for a grand version of a Spanish peasant stew, *olla podrida*, which became olio podrida in English. Many versions were published, most of them far more luxurious than the original. Into 13.5 litres (3 gal.) of water in a large pot over a charcoal fire go a rump of beef, Bolonia sausages, neats' (ox) tongues, followed after two hours by mutton, venison, pork and bacon, 'all in gubbins (pieces) as big as a duck's egg', then carrots, turnips, onions, cabbage, all cut 'in good big pieces, as big as your meat', a faggot of sweet herbs – whole spinach, sorrel, borage, endive, marigolds and 'other good pot-herbs'. Cloves, mace and saffron are added towards the end. Meanwhile, birds are cooked separately in salted water: a goose or turkey, two capons, two ducks, two pheasants, two widgeons, two partridges, four doves, four teals, eight snipe, 24 quails and 48 larks. Next, bread, bone marrow, artichoke bottoms, yolks of hard-boiled eggs, whole mace, boiled and blanched chestnuts, two cauliflowers and saffron are cooked together in 'good sweet butter, a little white wine and strong broth'. The olio was served as a magnificent pyramid with the beef or pork at the bottom, then the venison, mutton, tongue, sausage and root vegetables. Above these were the largest fowl, followed by the smaller ones, and at the top the fine vegetables and eggs. Some of the strained broth was poured over the olio and the rest served separately. A dish like this was intended to impress a large party for a special occasion. It could only be made in a well-staffed and well-equipped large kitchen.

Around this time there was renewed interest in cultivating vegetables and fruit. The gentry began to pay more attention to their gardens and started to grow a wide range of produce for the kitchen. Radishes, skirrets, turnips, parsnips and cucumbers were cultivated alongside cabbages, onions and many different herbs. Large numbers of Huguenot refugees, fleeing religious persecution in Europe, settled in southeast England, bringing their knowledge of horticulture and many new varieties of plants, including asparagus, spinach and artichokes, and also their skills in weaving silk. Several cookery books of the period have recipes for sallets; these were vegetable dishes, whether raw, boiled or baked. The medieval mistrust of raw vegetables had almost disappeared.

Apple, pear and plum trees were well established in orchards, and fruits from southern Europe, including apricots, raspberries and quinces, were introduced. Dried fruits and nuts – raisins, currants, dates, figs, almonds and walnuts – continued to be imported. From his voyage to the 'Indies of Nova Hispania' in 1564, John Hawkins brought back sweet potatoes, which were considered superior to carrots and parsnips. They were also preferred to the potato, which arrived later via Spain. Drake brought some potato roots to England, and having stopped on the journey in Virginia, they became known for a time as Virginia potatoes. In the seventeenth century they were little appreciated, although by mid-century more effort was made to encourage their cultivation to provide food for the poor when the wheat harvest was low.

Sir Nathaniel Bacon, *Cookmaid with Still Life of Vegetables and Fruit,*
c. 1620–25, oil on canvas.

Probably one of the most remarked arrivals from Central America
was the turkey; in addition to putting turkey in his olio podrida,
May has a recipe for baking turkey in a pie. Another notable
import was the pineapple, which became a royal favourite with
Charles II, who was delighted by its crown of leaves.

John Evelyn was a man of many talents and interests. In addition to horticulture, he was associated with two developments
related to cooking; the first was the ice house, the second the pressure cooker. Charles II's interest in science led him to have an ice
house constructed in St James's Park; the 'digester', as the pressure
cooker was called, was invented by Denis Papin and tried out at a
Royal Society dinner, which Evelyn recorded. Several foods were
cooked in the digester, but 'nothing exceeded the Pigeons, which
tasted just as if baked in a Pie . . . being stewed in their own juice'.
He encouraged the planting of trees in England, and translated
The Compleat Gardener by Jean de La Quintinie, who created Louis
XIV's renowned potager at Versailles. In his own book, *Acetaria:*

A Discourse of Sallets (1664), Evelyn gives detailed instructions to gardeners for growing herbs and vegetables. The work includes a calendar of 35 salad plants, indicating the best times to plant and harvest them to have salad throughout the year. He tells readers to learn to 'look upon the plants themselves and judge of their vertues by their own complexions' to determine when they are ready to harvest. He gives advice on preparing and cooking vegetables, as well as successful combinations of vegetables and salad greens. When composing a salad, the plants should 'fall into their places like the notes in music, in which there should be nothing harsh or grating' and 'melt into an agreeable composition'.

The ingredients are washed, dried and assembled in a suitable dish, and the dressing, which is as important as the leaves, is prepared. Evelyn uses three parts of 'pallid olive green oil' to one part of vinegar, verjuice, lemon juice or bitter orange juice. Fine bay salt and medium ground pepper, and on occasion a little sugar, are added to the dressing. In winter the vinegar may be steeped first with

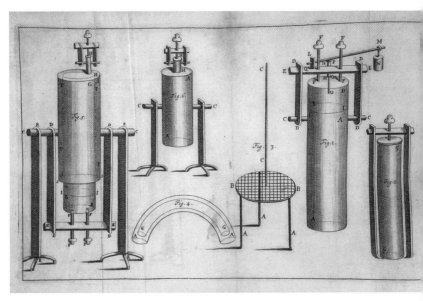

Denis Papin's digester, the first form of pressure cooker, 1681.

horseradish or with bruised guinea pepper (grains of paradise). The vinegars may be used alone or combined, and Tewkesbury or other dry mustard may be added, as much as 'will lie upon a half-crown piece'. When the salad is about to be served, two boiled egg yolks may be mashed and blended into the dressing, which is poured over and 'mingled' with the vegetables and herbs. A grand sallet also included cold roast meats – capon, veal, tongue – and capers, olives, broom buds, pickled mushrooms, raisins, almonds, Virginia potato and samphire might all be added to the salad before dressing. It was often presented in an elaborate pyramid.

The other great gardening writer of the time was John Parkinson, 'herbarist' to James I. His best-known book is his Herbal published in 1640 titled *Theatrum botanicum*; *Paradisi in Sole, Paradisus Terrestris* (a pun on his name, Park-in-Sun's Earthly Paradise) was published in 1629. The largest part of the book is devoted to garden plants, but there are sections on the kitchen garden and on starting an orchard. Much of the kitchen garden text concerns herbs 'for the pot, for meat and for the table'. Not only does he explain the best way to cultivate, and problems to be aware of, he describes flavour and uses: 'The leaves of Dill are much used in some places with Fish ... It is also put among pickled Cowcumbers, wherewith it doth very well agree, giving unto the fruit a pretty spicie taste or rellish.' His book was a work of reference and has instructions for growing beet, chicory, asparagus, carrots, cabbage, turnips, parsnips, radishes, potatoes, artichokes, beans, peas, cucumbers and more.

The rapid growth of country estates and some improvement in farming methods led to the planting of new crops, including turnips and 'great clover' brought from Flanders, and increased plantings of wheat, which brought down the price of bread. Turnips were stored and used to feed cattle in winter, which meant more fresh meat was available. Hunting and trapping wild animals and birds went on as before and venison continued to be particularly prized in winter. Meat was still the most important food for any meal for the middle and upper classes.

The new estates usually had kitchen gardens and orchards as well as elegant flower gardens, orangeries and avenues of trees. Some had glasshouses for growing vines and peaches; artificial heating was being tried out. Fishponds were maintained and many properties had farms alongside.

In his *Diary* Evelyn wrote of a visit to Swallowfield in Berkshire on 23 October 1685, where he found 'the Gardens and Waters as elegant as 't is possible'. There were 'delicious and rarest fruits', well-maintained kitchen gardens, orangeries 'but above all, the Canale and fishponds, the One fed with a white, and the Other with a black-running water, fed by a swift and quick river'. The ponds were stocked with pike, carp, bream and tench. 'We had Carps and Pike of size fit for the table of a Prince, every meale ... Carpes that had been worth at London twenty shilling a piece.' Pike was also expensive and sold by length; for example, in 1691 six 71-centimetre (28 in.) pike cost the Earl of Bedford at Woburn 12*s* apiece.

Fasting days had been abolished under Cromwell and were not restored, yet fish, particularly shellfish, remained popular. Oysters were stewed, baked or eaten raw; they were also pickled to be sent inland. Crabs and lobsters were usually boiled and served cold. Potted fish and soused and pickled fish became fashionable; they replaced salted fish for the rich, as did pickled sprats and herring for the poor. Whale and porpoise were no longer eaten as Lenten food, and sturgeon, the royal fish, became more widely available for those who could afford it.

For the middle and upper classes breakfast, taken between 6 a.m. and 7 a.m., was usually cold meats, salted or dried fish, cheese, bread and ale. On New Year's Day 1661 Samuel Pepys gave his guests a barrel of oysters, a dish of neats' (ox) tongues and a dish of anchovies, 'wine of all sorts and Northdowne ale'.[10] For a dinner two years later his guests sat down to oysters, a hash of rabbits and lamb, a 'rare chine of beef', a 'great dish of roasted fowle', a tart, fruit and cheese.[11] No vegetables are mentioned here, but vegetables may have been in the hash. By the end of the century, vegetables began to be served as accompaniments to meats.

Patrick Lamb, master cook to Charles ii, James ii, William and Mary and Queen Anne, published *Royal Cookery* in 1710. The mixture of English, French and other European dishes is similar to that in earlier books, and as is to be expected from the royal cook, many are complex and use expensive ingredients. In the preface to the second edition, he writes that there are several additional recipes 'which not being so expensive as the others, may be useful in those kitchens of private gentlemen'. There are still medieval-style dishes, but there is also a sense of a more modern approach. The recipe for 'soop de santé' is given in two versions: 'French Way' and 'English Way'. There are a variety of recipes for vegetables: artichokes, asparagus, cabbage, cauliflower, cardoons, mushrooms, peas and turnips, but the emphasis is still on meat, birds and fish. Made dishes include 'ragoos' of truffles, pullets (young hens) with truffles, olios, puddings – both sweet and savoury – and a detailed description of how to make a terrine. He has no fewer than fifteen recipes for cullis (a rich stock) to be used in 'ragoos' and 'soops'. There are cullises of capons, partridges, ducks and pigeons, a white cullis made with a pullet and almonds, a 'meagre' white cullis made with perch, another with crayfish, and vegetable cullises made with mushrooms, lentils or roots. For his general cullis he uses 2–3 pounds of lean veal, half a pound of ham, onion, carrot, parsnip and bacon dredged with flour to which broth and gravy are added. It is seasoned with cloves, leek, parsley, basil and bay leaf, minced truffles and mushrooms and the crust of two French rolls. After simmering for three-quarters of an hour, the veal is removed and the cullis passed through a sieve.

Lamb's book has fewer heavily spiced dishes, uses more herbs and more attention is given to the flavour of individual ingredients.

His monthly bills of fare are for two courses of eight to ten dishes, with some sweet dishes in the second. These are not for grand court banquets; instead of listing the dishes for those, they are set out on large folding plates. There are two for coronation dinners, one for the queen's dinner in 1704 and another in 1705; two plates to show each course of the king's dinner at Lord Ranelagh's on 20 May 1700, one for the ladies' table for an instalment at Windsor in 1704 and two for wedding suppers.

Sugar consumption increased steadily from Elizabeth I's time, when about 0.5 kilograms (1 lb) per head was consumed each year to 5–5.5 kilograms (11–12 lb) per head in the later years of the seventeenth century. The rise in sugar consumption was more than that of meat, bread or dairy products. At that time poor harvests and taxation meant high prices, but even the poor continued to buy small amounts. People had become accustomed to its taste. It was still sprinkled over meat and fish dishes before serving and was used in sauces, cakes and puddings, but it was the extravagant final sweet courses that used so much sugar. Confectioners opened shops in towns so that women who could not make their own confections could buy them.

Meals in taverns and public eating houses were generally good and inexpensive. Pepys wrote often of eating dinner out at 'an ordinary hard by Temple Gate' and at the Dolphin in Tower Street. An ordinary was a restaurant that had a set menu; as Pepys noted, 'it is very convenient because a man knows what he hath to pay.'[12] Ordinaries served a dinner of two courses, often a soup and meat or poultry, for about 1 shilling, whereas taverns were more expensive and had a menu of pies, roast meats and vegetables to choose from.

From the mid-seventeenth century dinner time was midday or later, and supper was later in the evening. The arrival of the new drinks – tea, coffee and chocolate – partly accounted for these changes as ladies entertained their friends with tea parties. Coffee and chocolate both reached England in the middle of the century, the former from the Arab world and the latter from the New World. Both were expensive to import and eventually became subject to taxation.

The first coffee-house in London was opened by the Levant Company in 1652 during the Commonwealth. They were meeting places where, while consuming the fashionable new drink, men gathered to do business or to enjoy discussions on politics, science or literature. The stock exchange and merchant banks both owe their origins to coffee-houses, as does Lloyd's brokerage to Edward Lloyd's coffee-house in Lombard Street. They were democratic places where, for the price of a penny, any man could sit, enjoy coffee and join in the conversation. Maximilien Misson, a Frenchman who was resident in London at the time, noted: 'You have all Manner of News there; You have a good fire, which you may sit by as long as you please: You have a Dish of Coffee; you meet your Friends for the Transaction of Business, and all for a Penny, if you don't care to spend more.'[13]

Chocolate houses followed a few years later. In 1648 Thomas Gage, a Dominican who had travelled widely in the Americas, reported its use in the West Indies, where, he said that all peoples rich and poor drank plain chocolate without sugar or other ingredients. In 1655 the European acquisition of Jamaica brought some established cocoa plantations on the island into English hands. The first chocolate house followed soon after. Chocolate was rarer and more expensive than coffee. The most prestigious chocolate houses, White's and the Cocoa Tree, were established later in the century.

In William Salmon's *Family Dictionary* (1710), the self-styled 'professor of physick' notes that 'cocao nuts' are grown in the West Indies and gives instructions for roasting the beans to make chocolate paste, along with three ways to drink it: with water, milk or a mixture of water and wine. Another English innovation was to add claret and egg yolk instead of or in addition to water. Sometimes arrowroot was added to counter the fattiness of the cocoa. Coffee- and chocolate houses took over from the taverns as meeting places, but while the coffee-houses were egalitarian, the chocolate houses were the gathering places of the wealthy and elite, and this continued in Georgian times.

Green tea from China was the last of the new beverages to arrive. It was brought by Dutch East India merchants who traded with the Chinese. The first advertisement for tea appeared in a newspaper in 1658, and it was sold at the Sultaness Head Coffee House on Sweetings Rents in London. Pepys noted in 1660 that he sent 'for a Cup of Tee (a China drink) of which I never had drunk before'. Tea was rare and expensive: at £3 10s a pound only the rich

Richard Collins, *Family of Three at Tea*, 1727, oil on canvas.

could afford it. In 1664 the East India Company made Charles II a present of tea; in 1689 the firm began to import tea from China, and in 1721 it was given a monopoly on the tea trade that was to last until 1833.

In 1717 Thomas Twining changed his coffee-house in the Strand into a tea shop. It was frequented by the well-to-do, both men and women, during a time when tea was becoming increasingly popular. Although it was heavily taxed and very expensive, it became a fashionable drink. There were many varieties to choose from; Bohea and Souchon were among the most popular. More tea houses opened in the city and in the new pleasure gardens, where people strolled among the pavilions, temples and grottoes.

Tea was popular with Queen Anne, who came to the throne in 1702, and ladies of the court served tea to their friends at home. It was infused briefly in boiling water and served weak. The new drink required elegant tea 'dishes' (small shallow bowls imported from China), tea caddies, sugar bowls, teapots and kettles for entertaining. Tea was served with sweet biscuits and cakes, and it became common to add sugar to the rather bitter drink.

Daniel Defoe toured England during Queen Anne's reign and described it as 'the most flourishing and opulent country in the world' in his *A Tour thro' the Whole Island of Great Britain* (1724–6). There was a sense of calm and peace after so many wars. Although little had changed in farming methods, life in towns and villages was improved by the growing prosperity of yeomen. They upgraded and enlarged their houses and farm buildings, and often set up small businesses in town for weaving or other local industries. There was more meat and wheaten bread on the table. However, the poor were still very poor and the rich richer than ever. The nobles and gentry employed Vanbrugh, Hawksmoor and other distinguished architects to design their new country houses when they were not engaged in London commissions. Their knowledge filtered down to local architects and builders, which led to a long period of good house building in towns and villages.

Industry and trade continued to develop and grow. More coal was being produced, glass and salt works were flourishing in Newcastle, new markets had been found for the cloth trade. Road travel was still very bad, so most goods continued to travel by river. Although Liverpool was fast becoming the port for the colonial trade, London was still by far the biggest and liveliest city and trading centre in the world. Sir Christopher Wren had reshaped it after the Great Fire of 1666, St Paul's was being rebuilt but the city had a growing underworld.

Tudor and Stuart recipes

To boyle spinage

Elinor Fettiplace's Receipt Book [1604] (London, 1986)

You must boil yt well with as little water as you can for the less water the sweeter your spinage wil bee, when yt is very tender part the water from it as much, as you may, then shred it very fine and put on verguice, sweet buter, and sugar then set yt on the fire and let yt stew, and when it is stewed neare enough, take the yelkes of two egges and as much Creame as the quantity of your egges and somewhat more, beate the Creame and egges together and put yt into the spinage and let them stue together, and when you serve yt strow sugar on yt.

Asparagus

John Evelyn, *Acetaria* (London, 1699)

They are sometimes, but very seldom, eaten raw with Oyl and Vinegar; but with more delicacy being so speedily boil'd, as not to lose the *verdure* and agreeable tenderness; which is done by letting the Water boil, before you put them in.

To stew turbot or holyburt (halibut)

Robert May, *The Accomplisht Cook* (London, 1685 edn)

Take it and cut it into slices, then fry it, and being half fryed put it in a stew-pan or deep dish, then put to it some claret, grated nutmeg, three or four slices of an orange, a little wine-vinegar, and sweet butter, stew it well, dish it, and run it over with beaten butter, slic't lemon or orange, and orange or lemon peel.

To roast olives of veal

Gervase Markham, *The English Huswife* (London, 1615)

You shall take a leg of veal and cut the flesh from the bones, and cut out into long thin slices, then take sweet herbs and the white part of scallions, and chop them well together with the yolks of eggs, then roll it up within the slices of veal, and so spit them and roast them; then boil verjuice, butter, sugar, cinnamon, currants, and sweet herbs together, and, being seasoned with a little salt, serve the olives up upon that sauce with salt cast over them.

To make a gooseberry fool

WM, *The Compleat Cook*, part of *The Queens Closet Opened*
(London, 1655) [*The Queen's Closet Opened* was a trilogy of
which *The Compleat Cook* was one book.]

Take your Gooseberries, and put them in a Silver or Earthen Pot,
and set it in a Skillet of boyling Water, and when they are coddled
enough strain them, then make them hot again, when they are
scalding hot beat them very well with a good piece of fresh Butter,
Rose-water and sugar, and put in the yolk of two or three Eggs;
you may put Rose-water into them and so stir it altogether, and
serve it to the Table when it is cold.

4

Prosperity and Conquest

England's prosperity continued and increased in the eighteenth century. The Duke of Marlborough defeated the army of Louis XIV in 1704 and England had a powerful presence in Europe. The sea power of Spain and Portugal was greatly diminished, the Dutch and the French were losing the race on the trade routes, and English merchant ships controlled the seas. The population increased from 5.5 million in the reign of Queen Anne to 9 million in 1801; the birth rate increased and the death rate decreased, largely due to better medical services and an improved standard of living for much of the population. The level of literacy had expanded significantly towards the end of the seventeenth century and there was great interest in reading and learning. As one historian observed, 'Addison's England was fortunate in having behind it . . . such a poet as Milton, such a physicist as Newton and such a philosopher as Locke . . . The Constitution had been established and "freedom" secured.'[1]

In the early years of the Hanoverian kings, the well-to-do were positive and optimistic, freed from the religious strife of the Stuarts and not yet caught up in the Industrial Revolution. It was a period of calm, as the rule of law prevailed and there were many opportunities for individuals to develop their potential. Education widened, and although many upper- and middle-class boys were still taught primarily in Latin, new schools with a broad curriculum were opening and lower-middle-class boys could win scholarships to attend them. Girls were still educated at home. For the lowest classes there was no education for either sex; these children worked alongside their parents.

In 1715 London's population was about 630,000; by 1760 it had risen to 750,000 and to a million by the end of the century. It was an important commercial, financial and cultural centre. The rich merchants, lawyers and bankers lived in a style comparable to that of the nobility, built grand houses run by a large staff of servants and paid handsomely for luxuries, including foods. They were relatively few in number; there were many more industrious, moderately prosperous merchants and entrepreneurs who ran successful businesses and often organized business operations in smaller towns and villages throughout the country. The country supplied London with raw materials, coal and food, and London supplied the country with imports and finished goods. Increasing overseas trade brought in new textiles and lower prices for imported foods. The city grew as a manufacturing centre, too, particularly for luxury goods such as clocks, coaches and silks, which required skilled craftsmen. A fast-growing middle class of clerks, shopkeepers, foremen and supervisors emerged.

Below the privileged and middle classes of this wealthy city were craftsmen and artisans who worked long hours for modest wages and relied on additional income from the work of their wives and children. They had a reasonable standard of living, well above the subsistence level. However, it was precarious if trade was bad. As the century progressed, the medieval guild system declined and was replaced by a free labour market and new machinery, making their livelihoods even less secure.

Below them was the largest part of the population. This underclass of unskilled, casual labourers inhabited a different universe of overcrowded slums with no sanitation, no medical services, poor food and a high mortality rate. Theirs are the faces on many of Hogarth's prints. But for resourceful and energetic men there were opportunities to escape the grinding poverty and move up the social ladder to improve their and their family's position, and eventually to own their own property and provide a better future for their children. This upward mobility occurred in London and other big towns; in rural areas long-standing traditions held and it was difficult for labourers to improve their lot, except by leaving and moving to a town.

In the first half of the century manufacturing was still part of country life; villages could provide for their own needs in buildings, tools, clothes and foodstuffs. Some villages also provided cloth for sale in the towns and for export. Towns grew larger and functioned as markets for local farmers, as well as meeting places for nearby villages, where people could shop, do business and gather for social occasions such as dances. The gentry bought many of their goods – furniture, china, books and imported foods – from London.

Throughout the country food was affordable for most labourers and workers, except in years when the harvest failed. White bread, meat and beer were their regular fare, though not all could afford meat more than once or twice a week. In the later years of the century when taxes on beer were raised, the poor took to drinking tea, even though it was expensive and less nutritious than beer. There was work, both in the country and in the new industries developing in towns, to which more and more people gravitated. Shops opened in towns and the bigger villages selling household items and imported foods such as rice, sago, spices, dried fruits, sugar and treacle.

Transport required urgent improvement to get food to towns in much greater quantities than in earlier centuries. The waterways continued to be used; at the beginning of the century the roads were still in very poor condition. Grain carts dragged along haltingly; cattle were driven very slowly to market up to 160 kilometres (100 mi.) away. In the 1720s Defoe noted that even poultry were driven on foot to London from Norfolk and Suffolk.[2]

The increased prosperity and the growth of the population created a much greater demand for food, particularly for meat and wheat. Improvements in agriculture were needed, and the first move was to reduce considerably the open-field system, where every peasant could grow what he pleased on his strip of land. On large, enclosed fields agricultural innovations could be put into practice. The country gentry and many prosperous yeomen increased their land holdings and benefited enormously from this development. Tenant farmers increased their income, if not their status; labourers were better fed, and for a while some may still have had their strip of land and small domestic industries to help them. More and more enclosures were made every decade, many on land that had never been cultivated before. By the end of the century the modern landscape with fields, hedges and farms was established.

Scientific discovery was growing fast, and it was a time to experiment with land drainage, new crops and new machines for drilling and reaping. Jethro Tull was one of the earliest to develop machinery to improve farming. His horse-drawn seed drill, introduced in the 1730s, sowed to the correct depth and spacing, and a harrow at the back covered the seeds. He also advocated hoeing to remove weeds and break up the soil, which allowed crops to flourish. A contemporary, Charles Townshend, encouraged the cultivation of turnips for winter feed, and their green tops provided grazing for sheep. He also introduced crop rotation – usually wheat, barley, turnips and clover – to improve soil fertility. Thomas Coke improved breeds of cattle, sheep and hogs and promoted better husbandry. Once it was established that healthy livestock could be kept throughout the winter, animal husbandry improved greatly. It was worthwhile to invest in improving breeds, and oxen, calves and sheep were two or three times larger at the end of the century than at the beginning. High prices were paid by buyers overseas and domestically for English pedigree animals.

Experiments were made with fertilizers and mixing soils on difficult land. The new farming methods required considerable investment for drainage, machinery and fertilizers, which could only be afforded on large properties. The larger the property the more investment could be made and the greater the profit, so many smaller farms were bought up. The wealth of the aristocracy increased, and that of tenant farmers too, though more modestly. By the end of the century, however, the life of the labourer on the land was dire. His small holding was gone, as was common grazing ground, and all that remained was his cottage garden. Rural poverty was worse than that in the towns.

There was a huge increase in the wheat crop during the century, particularly in southern England. Large new plantings were also successfully established in East Anglia. In the early years, the south grew about 60 per cent wheat and 20 per cent each of barley and rye, and the north about a third each of wheat, rye and oats. By the end of the century, the south grew 80 per cent wheat and 20 per cent barley, the north about 50 per cent wheat and 25 per cent each of barley and oats. Thanks to agricultural improvements, wheat was now cheap and the labouring classes ate white bread, once a symbol of wealth and nobility. 'Rye and barley bread, at present, are looked on with a sort of horror; even by poor cottagers, and with some excuse, for wheat is now as cheap as rye and barley were in former times.'[3] This demand for wheaten bread was widely resented by the upper classes.

England had long been a wheat-exporting country, and this continued until towards the end of the century, when demand for white bread was so great that there was insufficient to export. There were shortages during the century when harvests failed. One of the worst years was 1756, when the crop was much smaller and of worse quality than usual. Parliament authorized 'standard' bread to be made with more bran than usual, and these loaves were stamped with the letter S. It was darker than the bread people had become accustomed to, and also cheaper, but it was very unpopular because bread high in bran indicated poverty.

In years of poor harvest, the only way to make white bread was to add more alum to the flour. Alum was used as a firming agent for pickles and to preserve flour and bleach it. Bakers had used it in small amounts for many generations to make the fine white manchet of the rich. Now there was demand from the poorer classes for cheaper white bread, and the only way to achieve this with inferior flour was to increase the dose of alum. In 1758 Peter Markham calculated that alum was added to bread in the proportion of 227 grams (8 oz) per five bushels or 109 kilograms (240 lb) of flour (the standard weight of a sack of flour). Once water, yeast and salt were added to this amount of flour, it would have baked 159–63 kilograms (350–60 lb) of bread. Bread remained the staple food, and an average adult ate from 500 grams to a kilogram (1.1–2.2 lb) of bread a day. If this were alum-adulterated, the daily consumption of alum was between 0.6 and 1.2 grams (0.02–0.04 oz) per day, a relatively small amount.[4] Discussions about alum and its poisonous properties if taken in large quantities continued and, in 1758, the government banned its use in bread. Nevertheless, some bakers ignored the ban and people continued to demand white bread despite knowing that it was adulterated, and not only with alum:

> The good people are not ignorant of this adulteration, but they prefer it to wholesome bread, because it is whiter than the meal of corn. Thus they sacrifice their taste and their health, and the lives of their tender infants, to a most absurd gratification of a misjudging eye, and the miller or the baker is obliged to poison them and their families, in order to live by his profession.[5]

Potatoes had been adopted as a staple in Ireland, but attempts to persuade the English to eat potatoes rather than bread were unsuccessful. They were considered dull and insipid, and were usually eaten in a hash with onions, salt, pepper and a little meat. Cottagers with a bit of land grew a few potatoes, but it was not until the end of the century that potato cultivation became a field crop. When the corn harvest failed disastrously in 1794, the price of a standard loaf rose to 12¼*d*, compared with only 6*d* thirty years prior. William Pitt the Younger, the prime minister, urged people to make bread with potato and maize, but with little success. However, urban workers started to buy potatoes when bread became too expensive.

Cabbages were grown extensively in Scotland and spread south to the northern counties of England, where they were primarily used as cattle fodder. Market gardening expanded, particularly around London and then around other towns, and garden vegetables started to be grown as field crops.

As the century progressed, most of the rural poor no longer had land to cultivate or for grazing, nor access to forests for wood to burn. With no chickens or eggs, milk or bacon, they were reduced to bread and cheese: a poorly balanced diet. While subsistence farming was practised, rural people had managed to feed themselves, but the new, large farms with their efficient farming practices and greater crop yields needed more animal and less human labour. This caused distress and hardship in villages, and created a landless working class whose only choice was to leave the land to work in the new industries, whether the mills of Lancashire or the docks of London, Bristol or Liverpool.

In the second half of the century change came quickly, touching all levels of society. The shift from an agricultural base to an industrial one brought about huge changes in agriculture and industry and also in society. Much of the capital to start the Industrial Revolution came from agriculture. Men who had embraced the new farming methods became even wealthier, and they or their sons used some of their capital to start the mills and factories of the industrial towns. They also invested in mining, iron foundries, ship building and speculated in overseas trade. In due course much of the wealth created in industry was returned to their estates, forming a cycle of interdependent growth. For this class, there was a confident sense of agricultural, industrial and social change for the better.

As towns grew and travelling became easier owing to road improvements, villages no longer needed to be self-sufficient. Local artisans and craftsmen lost their trade as people went to town to buy goods, so they too moved to the towns. However, not all the peasants, yeomen or artisans who left the land for the cities, with little or no money in their pockets, fared badly. Many left with the spirit to succeed elsewhere, and grew into the professional, mercantile or industrial families that flourished in this new, wealthier England. This was a time of opportunity and growing prosperity.

The industrial towns grew quickly and local authorities developed, providing an administrative class that could work with the new industrial magnates to ensure efficiency and social discipline. Towns were cleaned up: rubbish was removed, streets cleaned, water provided and more hospitals built as medical knowledge increased. The overall standard of living improved, and towards the end of the century the birth rate overtook the death rate. The death rate fell even when harvests were bad. England was going through a demographic evolution; the population level was determined by industrial as well as agricultural production.

Nevertheless, for the poorest of those leaving the land, life was harsh. They and their children had to work in the mines and factories. The work was repetitive and tiring, conditions were poor and discipline was enforced. Their living conditions were bleak, and loss of work meant even greater poverty and starvation. Their diet suffered; they lived on bread, cheese and vegetables and occasionally a bit of bacon. When the harvest was bad, they could scarcely afford even a meagre meal of bread, jam and sweet tea – a poor replacement with little or no vitamins or protein.

In the early eighteenth century, iron was smelted by charcoal, but the forests were limited and as more iron was needed, experiment led to smelting by coal and coke and mechanization increased. Water power was also harnessed to drive machinery in the cotton mills, and a greater transformation came with James Watt's invention of the steam engine, patented in 1769. However, industrial development was still held back by inadequate transport until, towards the end of the century, there were significant improvements. Cheap Irish labour was brought in to dig a network of canals, which reduced the cost of production and resulted in lower prices as goods were transported more speedily. There were radical improvements in road building to create turnpike roads, and a network of stagecoaches was established, though travel by coach was slow and expensive. Docks and shipyards were extended to keep pace with local and international trade. There were improvements in industrial organization, and technological inventions brought dramatic changes to the textile industry, metallurgy, mining and engineering.

International trade was booming, most notably the slave trade from London, Bristol and particularly from Liverpool. The Liverpool 'slavers' took cotton goods from Lancashire to Africa, embarked slaves and took them across the Atlantic, returning with sugar, tobacco and raw cotton. In 1771, 50,000 enslaved people were transported to the American mainland and the Caribbean. Little thought was given to the lives of these people, who were torn from their homelands and forced to undertake arduous and dangerous journeys to new lands, where, if they survived the voyage, they were coerced into a system of punishing labour. It was not until 1792 that William Wilberforce led the campaign that resulted in the Commons abolishment of the slave trade. This finally happened when George III signed the Act for the Abolition of the

Slave Trade in 1807. By this time, England had a population of about 15,000 Black people, mostly in the port cities and working in domestic service – in great houses having Black servants was fashionable and displayed wealth – while others worked in trades or business.

Noblemen, city businessmen and rich merchants continued to build new country mansions. Many now had a kitchen and some of its offices incorporated into the house; others had a separate kitchen block nearby, and the grandest of these were linked to the house by an underground passage, so the food was not spoiled in transit and the servants were not seen. Some still-houses remained, but many were reduced to stillrooms near the kitchen; the bake-house, dairy, brewhouse and some larders, particularly that for game, remained in the courtyard around the kitchen.

The owners spent some of their wealth and leisure time shooting and hunting, but no longer for deer because there was enough meat and many had deer enclosures on their land: fox hunting was now the sport. They also laid out grand parks and gardens with fishponds fed by running water, and created orchards, orangeries and kitchen gardens. The kitchen gardens were planted with many varieties of vegetables, herbs and fruits. Grapes, melons, peaches, figs and eventually pineapples were grown in glasshouses, and orchards had a wide variety of nut and fruit trees.

Anxious to keep up with the fashions at court, the nobility had ice houses built on their country estates if they had lakes from which ice could be gathered. By the mid-eighteenth century ice houses were common and using ice to cool drinks and fresh fruit was a well-established practice. In towns, there were commercial ice merchants who sold ice to be kept in ice boxes.

Charles Carter published *The Complete Practical Cook; or, A New System of the Whole Art and Mystery of Cookery* in 1730. Carter was cook to the Earl of Albemarle and other nobles; his preface entreats his noble employers to recognize the cook as an artist:

no Occupation in the World is more oblig'd to *Invention*; every Year and every ingenious Artist constantly producing *New Experiments* to gratify the Taste of that Part of Mankind, whose splendid Circumstances make them emulous to excel in the Delicacies of this Mystery, especially when they exert their Wealth and their Magnificence to entertain their Friends with *grand* and *sumptuous* Repasts.

He continues that his words may seem vainglorious, but his concern is to ensure the noble reader will never be misled into employing a 'Tavern-bred Dabbler in the Science'. He finishes by acknowledging the quality of Leadenhall Market and others in the city, but on a country estate, however good the gardens, farms and fishponds, the cook-artist will be essential to create, invent and diversify. Carter's recipes use expensive ingredients, as befit his employers' status. The first recipe is a simple one for a strong broth of flesh, and this is followed by an olio podreda with even more and grander ingredients than Robert May's.

The rich landowners who spent several months of the year on their estates enjoying the produce of the land may well have had Carter's book in their new kitchens, which had improved greatly since the seventeenth century. Coal had started to be used alongside wood as fuel in the late sixteenth century, and now a new long fire basket on legs was developed to fit into the back of the kitchen chimney. Spits, operated by a clockwork mechanism, rested on the front legs. Roasting remained the preferred way of cooking meat. The sides of the range were fitted with metal plates from which trivets to support pans could swing out over the fire. Eventually iron plates were fixed at either side of the front of the range to serve as hobs. Gentle heat for simmering and sauce-making was still provided by charcoal stoves; the best kitchens had brick platforms to hold one or more small fire baskets for burning charcoal. Until the middle of the century earthenware ovens, heated by building a fire inside, continued to be used for baking. Then a new oven was invented made of iron with a fire grate beneath it; this was a great improvement because the heat could be controlled. Some years later, the oven was incorporated into one side of the range and on the other was a boiler for hot water fitted with a tap. Much of the heat was still lost up the chimney until, following the suggestion of Count Rumford, recently arrived from Bavaria, a range was devised in which the fire was covered with another iron plate. Dishes could be simmered on this plate and charcoal stoves became redundant, which was much better for the health of the cook. In poorer houses the cauldron hanging over the fire was still the main cooking utensil; if there was a piece of meat to roast, it was hung on a chain over the fire or sent to be done in the baker's oven.

In the 1776 edition of *The Experienced English Housekeeper*, Elizabeth Raffald included a folding plate of a new stove she had invented. Stove fires burned coal or embers, which were cheaper

Unknown artist, *The Business of the Kitchen*, 1813, etching.

Elizabeth Raffald's design for three stoves, engraving from *The Experienced English Housekeeper*, 5th edn (1776).

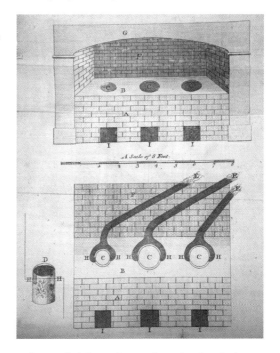

and 'less pernicious to the cooks' than charcoal, and a flue led into the chimney. The cooking pots covered the fires completely, ensuring that no fumes went into the kitchen. Large and small stewpans, frying pans, saucepans, sieves and colanders, chafing dishes, bowls, baking tins, ladles, wooden spoons, knives, forks, pestle and mortar, pudding cloths, whisks, toasting irons, pots and jugs would have been the basic tools in most large kitchens. In some of these new mansions changes were made in the kitchen staff. The clerk of the kitchen was still in place in the grandest establishments, ordering food and equipment and distributing them to the cook and his staff. However, if the cook was a highly paid professional French chef, he probably was in full charge of the kitchen, the staff and provisioning. In some houses the clerk was replaced by a house steward who shared the responsibility for ordering food and setting menus with the cook. The senior kitchen maids worked with the cook and did much of the basic cooking. Other maids cleaned

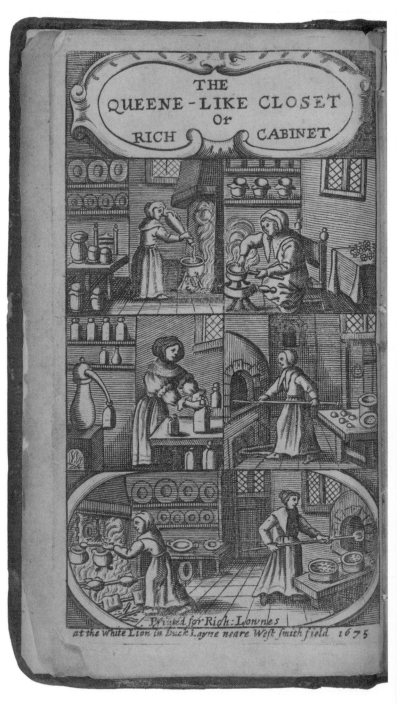

Frontispiece to Hannah Woolley, *The Queen-Like Closet; or,
Rich Cabinet*, 3rd edn (1675).

and dressed poultry, cleaned and filleted fish, prepared meat and cleaned vegetables. The scullery maid, who cleaned all the pots and pans, was on the lowest rung of the kitchen staff. Very grand houses also had pastry maids to prepare desserts.

In more modest houses women took on responsible positions as housekeeper and as cook. The housekeeper had a supervisory role throughout the house, and for the kitchen she bought provisions, made menus and distributed ingredients to the cook. She was also usually in charge of the stillroom for distilling medicinal waters, making preserves, pickles and, later, ice creams. The women eventually employed as cooks had often worked as senior kitchen maids to a male cook in a grand house. In contrast to Carter's 'artist' was Hannah Woolley's job description of the cook in such a house:

> The Cook, whether Man or Woman, ought to be very well skilled in all manner of things both Fish and Flesh, also good at Pastry business, seasoning of all things, and knowing all kinds of Sauces, and pickling all manner of Pickles, in making all manner of Meat Jellies; also very frugal of their Lords or of their Masters, Ladies or Mistresses Purse, very saving, cleanly and careful, obliging to all persons, kind to those under them, and willing to inform them, quiet in their Office, not swearing nor cursing, nor wrangling, but silently and ingeniously to do their Business, and neat and quick about it; they ought also to have a very good Fancy: such an one, whether Man or Woman, deserves the title of a fit Cook.[6]

Woolley's *The Queen-Like Closet*, published in 1670, was the first successful cookery book written by a woman for other women. It was addressed 'To all Ladies, Gentlewomen, and to all other of the Female Sex who do delight in, or be desirous of good Accomplishments'.

On his income of £400 a year, a cook such as Woolley describes would have been too expensive for the Revd James Woodforde and for many other country parsons and squires. Woodforde employed two maids, two manservants and a boy. These rural families ate better than much of the urban middle class. They had their kitchen gardens and orchards, and many families had a poultry yard and kept a cow or sheep or pigs. They didn't have the garden staff employed on big estates and often did some of the work themselves. Woodforde wrote in his diary of pruning his apple trees, sowing grass seeds and cutting weeds in his garden. He also noted that after 'brewing a vessel of strong beer' two of his pigs drank some of the beer grounds from a barrel and 'got so amazingly drunk by it, that they were not able to stand'.[7]

Most of the entries in his diary have some reference to food, whether how much he paid for ingredients, the fact that green tea for breakfast had upset his stomach, or what he served when guests came to stay. When entertaining at home on 11 December 1787, he served his guests boiled leg of mutton with capers, roasted chickens, a tongue, a Norfolk plain batter pudding, tripe, tarts and four sorts of cheese. When he dined with the Bishop of Norwich on 4 September 1783, they were twenty at table and had two courses of twenty dishes each and a dessert of twenty dishes, with Madeira, red and white wines. Carp, tench and a haunch of venison were in the first course; turkey, partridges and pigeons in the second; and for dessert mulberries, melons, currants, peaches and grapes. The centre of the table held a beautiful artificial garden. Dinner started at 3 p.m. and lasted until 6.30 p.m., when the company retired to the library for tea and coffee.

Woolley's recipes are similar to those in earlier books, but less grand. Spices, wine and sometimes sugar are still among the main flavourings, and many call for more butter than was used before. The first recipes are for waters, including traditional medicinal waters for plague, melancholy or palsie (palsy), as well as fruit cordials.

'Leg of mutton with oisteers' and 'Roast a pig with a pudding in his belly' are two of the dishes for large cuts of meat. Hashes, collops (slices of meat), pasties, chickens, turkeys and game birds are well represented, and she gives recipes for fruit preserves, desserts, salads and vegetables, breads, broths, pies, puddings and pottages.

Her bills of fare are for modest occasions: 'for lesser feasts, for Gentlemens houses of lesser quality, without feasting, or for Familiar times'. The two courses for lesser feasts consist of thirteen and twelve dishes, mostly meat or birds with 'a dish of custards in little China Pots' in the first and 'a warden (a type of pear) or quince pie' in the second. That for 'Familiar times' in the summer season has two courses each of seven dishes:

The First Course in Summer season.

1. A Boiled Pike or Carp stewed.
2. A very fine Pudding boiled.
3. A Chine of Veal, and another of Mutton.
4. A Calves head Pie.
5. A Leg of Mutton rosted whole.
6. A couple of Capons, or a Pig, or a piece of rost Beef, or boiled Beef.
7. A Sallad, the best in season.

The Second Course to the same.

1. A Dish of fat Chickens rosted.
2. A cold Venison Pasty.
3. A Dish of fryed Pasties.
4. A Joll of fresh Salmon.
5. A couple of Lobsters.
6. A Dish of Tarts.
7. A Gammon of Bacon or dried Tongues.
After these are taken away, then serve in your Cheese and Fruit.

Woolley was followed by several other successful women writers: Eliza Smith, Elizabeth Moxon, Elizabeth Raffald, Sarah Harrison and Hannah Glasse. They wrote for women of the middle to upper ranks of society who were careful about household expenditure, but certainly not poor.

A rift was opening between English and French styles of cooking. English food was considered to be straightforward and centred on large servings of prime roast meat, whereas French was more sophisticated with complex dishes and elaborate sauces. In *The London Tradesman* (1747), R. Campbell complained,

> in the days of good Queen Elizabeth, when mighty roast beef was the Englishman's food; our cookery was plain and simple, as our manners; it was not then a science or a mystery . . . But we have of late years refined ourselves out of that simple taste, and conformed our palates to meats and drinks dressed after the French fashion.[8]

French food remained fashionable with the aristocracy; the families to whom the new women writers' books were addressed followed fashion to some extent, but they were also pragmatic.

Many women writers denounced the French culinary tradition as being too wasteful and focused on luxury. In England, there was a move towards a simplified style of cooking, away from the rich sauces and refinements of French haute cuisine. Recipe books condemned the 'cullis' (coulis), a rich stock 'for the thickening of all sorts of Ragoos and Soops and to give them an agreeable Taste'.[9] For the most extravagant cullises, large quantities of veal or other meat and vegetables were cooked down to produce a small amount of very rich stock. Eliza Smith maintains in her preface to *The Compleat Housewife* of 1727 that her recipes are wholesome and natural ways of preparing 'such Provisions as are the Product of our own Country, and in such a Manner as is most agreeable to *English*

Palates'. She notes that disgracefully there has been too much enthusiasm for all things French, but she will nevertheless include some French dishes which she thinks 'may not be disagreeable to *English* palates'.

Hannah Glasse was writing *The Art of Cookery Made Plain and Easy* at the time of the Jacobite rebellion. The Jacobite army had marched as far south as Derby in 1745. If the Stuarts were restored, Catholicism and French fashions were likely to return, which may partly explain her stand against French cooking. She was vehement in her condemnation of extravagant French cooking: 'I have heard of a Cook that used six Pounds of Butter to fry twelve Eggs, when every Body knows, that understands Cooking, that Half a Pound is full enough, or more than need be used. But then it would not be French.' In spite of this vigorous protest, she included some French dishes in her book. The heading for Chapter Three says: 'Read this chapter and you will find out how expensive a French cook's sauce is'. It also gives eight recipes for cullises and essences.

The Art of Cookery, published anonymously as 'by a Lady', was reprinted many times and was the most influential book of the period. Although she claimed that all the recipes were original, many had been already published elsewhere; about a third were lifted from Hannah Woolley. Plagiarism was common at that time and continued through the nineteenth century. The anonymous writer's aim was to teach literate servant girls how to cook, and the book is written in a direct, simple manner. There is more detail than in earlier works: more precise quantities are given, and clearer indications of cooking time are provided instead of the typical instruction 'until it is done'. The chapter headings specify the type of dish or cooking method; one of the longest has dishes for fasting days which range from roast lobsters to mashed parsnips. This heading seems surprising given that fast days were abolished under Cromwell, but she adds that the dishes may be used at other times. Catholic families that continued to observe fasting days

To make a Currey *the* India *Way.*

TAKE two Fowls or Rabbits, cut them into small Pieces, and three or four small Onions, peeled and cut very small, thirty Pepper Corns, and a large Spoonful of Rice, brown some Coriander Seeds over the Fire in a clean Shovel, and beat them to Powder, take a Tea Spoonful of Salt, and mix all well together with the Meat, put all together into a Sauce-pan or Stew-pan, with a Pint of Water, let it stew softly till the Meat is enough, then put in a Piece of Fresh Butter, about as big as a large Walnut, shake it well together, and when it is smooth and of a fine Thickness dish it up, and send it to Table. If the Sauce be too thick, add a little more Water before it is done, and more Salt if it wants it. You are to observe the Sauce must be pretty thick.

'To make a Currey the India Way', recipe from Hannah Glasse, *The Art of Cookery Made Plain and Easy*, 3rd edn (1748).

did so very discreetly. Pickling, potting, preserving, cakes, creams and jellies are covered thoroughly; the 'Made Dishes' chapter includes 'Mutton Kebob'd', a 'Currey' and a 'Pellow' (pilau/pilaff) the Indian way. Officers of the East India Company returning home had brought recipes with them. One chapter is addressed to the captains of ships and includes a ketchup to keep twenty years made with stale beer, anchovies, spices and mushrooms. Pickled mushrooms, mushroom powder and portable soup (soup boiled down to a 'glew' and cut into pieces to be rehydrated) are foods that would keep for a long voyage, but many others would only last for a relatively short time. A short chapter at the end covers seasonal marketing. Lists of foods in season now replaced monthly bills of fare in many books.

Elizabeth Whitaker was in service and worked her way up to be housekeeper at Arley Hall in Cheshire, but when she married John Raffald in 1763 she had to leave because servants in great houses were not permitted to be married. She and her husband moved to Manchester where they opened a shop selling sweet-meats, desserts, cakes, pickles, ketchup, portable soups and potted meats as well as tea, coffee and chocolate. The business flourished, and she published *The Experienced English Housekeeper* in 1769.

Elizabeth Raffald was not caught up in the discussion about the extravagance of French food; her recipes are a record of the foods she had known as a housekeeper and those she made to sell in her shop. The range is wide, from 'Venison pasty' and 'Beef steaks' to broil to 'Picalillo' and 'Walnut Catchup'. The recipes are clear and concise, often containing bits of practical detail, which indicate that she would have made the dishes herself and passed on information that would have been of use to the reader. Most chapters start with practical observations relevant to the dishes: as a basis for any soup, she recommends putting the meat and a piece of butter in the bottom of the pot, followed by the chopped herbs and roots. The pot is covered tightly and simmered gently 'to draw all the virtue out of the roots or herbs' and only then is water added. When making creams and custards, she advises that the pan must be well tinned and to add a spoonful of water to prevent the cream sticking to the bottom.

Europeans in India discovered that Indians ate pickles and chutneys with their meals. Many of them were made fresh for each meal, but others were preserves of fruit and vegetables layered with salt and spices, packed into jars with oil or water and left to ferment in the sun. Sailors and merchants were grateful for these pickles to accompany their meals on board ship and so they arrived in England, where vinegar was used to do the pickling. Lacking the same foods, English writers created recipes such as 'mango cucumbers' or 'mango melons'. Another example was Mrs Raffald's 'Indian Pickle or Picalillo'. The first recipe in *The Compleat Housewife* by Eliza Smith is 'To make English *Katchup*', which she recommends is 'good to put into Fish Sauce, or any savoury Dish of Meat'.

English and French cuisines remained somewhat intertwined; for both, meat was the prime ingredient and in constant demand, whether dressed simply or in a rich sauce. Cattle breeding continued to improve, more cattle were kept through the winter, and more fresh meat was available. There had long been a trade in meat animals between the upland northern parts of England and the lowland south, and in the eighteenth century many Scottish cattle and sheep were sent south to be fattened. Roast joints, basted with butter or dripping, retained their popularity. Although the meat was plain, it was served with mustard, horseradish or a ketchup or pickle. Collops, ragoos, fricassees, stews, hashes and allowes (slices of beef or veal stuffed with herbs and egg yolks) were similar to those of the past, but the spices were more muted. Sometimes a batter pudding was baked in the dripping pan while the meat roasted. Hannah Glasse included a recipe for Yorkshire pudding in *The Art of Cookery*. Boiled suet puddings were filled with oatmeal, rice, bread, salt fish, cabbage, carrots and spinach; some sweet puddings, mostly those made with cream, were boiled in a cloth, but those filled with fruit and nuts were baked in a puff paste case. Roast meat and a pudding were considered a good dinner by the middle classes.

Soused and pickled meats were widely enjoyed; a boned and rolled joint was cooked in salt water with vinegar, herbs and spices and left to cool in the liquid. Hams and sides of bacon hung in the larder. The country poor made their soused meat from the pig's chitterlings (intestines), ears and head. Pies and puddings using meat and dried fruits were still made, although the tendency was towards savoury rather than sweet flavours. Beef, ham and tongue were minced and mixed with spices and butter and potted.

Some fish was still salted before being sent inland, but quite early in the century the trade carrying fresh pike, perch, tench and eels in barrels of water between the Fens and London was established. The water was changed each evening of the journey. Salmon salted or pickled in vinegar was regularly transported from Scotland to London, but at the end of the century there was a dramatic change. Alexander Dalrymple, an official of the East India Company, had seen how Chinese fishermen took ice to sea to preserve their catch and also packed fish in ice to send inland. He persuaded a Scottish fish merchant to pack salmon in boxes of pounded ice and send it to London by sea. The voyage took six days and the salmon arrived in excellent condition. The country estates had their ice houses; in towns ice was available from merchants and the sale of fresh salmon flourished. Ice houses were built on the Scottish lochs and greater supplies of salmon were shipped south.

Fish were cooked in a well-flavoured broth with spices, often mace and pepper, salt, vinegar and verjuice. Salmon, mackerel and other oily fish were served with grated horseradish or mustard. Salmon, eel and lobster were potted and served with toast. Orange and lemon were used more frequently in sauces for fish than in the past. Salt cod was served with a sauce made with chopped hard-boiled egg stirred into a lot of melted butter. Shellfish were widely

Scottish ice house, Balnagown Estate, near a loch from where salmon was shipped south in the 18th century.

enjoyed and began to be used as garnishes for meat. Hannah Woolley's leg of mutton with oysters has already been mentioned; capons were stuffed with oysters and beef marrow, while mussels were served with duck. Pickled oysters, herring sprats and other small, pickled fish were popular with the urban poor. Anchovies were boiled with neats' (ox) tongues, and John Nott adds a little minced veal or ham, pepper and vinegar to his anchovy sauce to serve with meat.[10]

Butter consumption increased enormously among the rich. As before, it was used in cakes and pastry, to fry fish or baste meat and in pottages, but now it was added to boiled foods as they cooked or poured over them before serving. Nott has recipes to clarify, burn and draw butter; for the latter he stirs 2 pounds of butter into half a pint of strong broth over a fire, then adds 2 to 3 pounds more, and more liquid if needed. He continues: 'stir it continually till it be all dissolv'd, and that it looks white: If it turn yellow, it is curdled, and you will hardly recover it.' To correct an oily butter, he recommends heating half a pound of butter in a pipkin (an earthenware pot) over a low fire, and when it is white to add some of the oily butter slowly while stirring, but to be careful not to add too much. Roast mutton or beef was served with a sauce made of the basting butter mixed with the juices from the dripping pan. Boiled puddings were eaten with butter, and butter went into the fillings for hot pies; a layer of butter also protected potted foods.

Recipes for potted cheese were included alongside those for meat and fish. Hannah Glasse's recipe uses Cheshire cheese pounded with butter, flavoured with mace and a little 'Canary wine' (similar to Madeira), and sealed with clarified butter. She wrote: 'A slice of this exceeds all the Cream-Cheese that can be made.' Cheese started to be used more in cooking, following the French usage of serving braised vegetables with a topping of grated cheese browned with a cheese iron. It was grated over macaroni and added to hashes. Parmesan, which had long been imported, and Cheshire were the most commonly used. Both Cheddar and Cheshire cheese were made cooperatively with the milk from all the houses in the village, and they slowly acquired a fine reputation. According to Defoe, Cheddar was 'without dispute the best Chese that England affords, if not, that the whole World affords'.[11]

Salads continued to be eaten regularly, both simple and grand versions. Lettuces, herbs and flowers made a simple spring or summer salad, while winter salads used cabbage or corn dressed with grated horseradish. A grand salad was very similar to Evelyn's (see Chapter Three) with a mixture of seasonal herbs and cresses, flowers, pickled ingredients like capers and olives, dried fruits, and sometimes cold capon breast. Vegetables introduced from Europe were widely accepted and kidney beans arrived from Peru. Fresh fruits were now viewed with less suspicion and eaten raw, but more were cooked for tartstuff, creams and fools, or candied and preserved.

William Walker, after James E. Doyle, *A Literary Party at Sir Joshua Reynolds's*, 1848, engraving. Samuel Johnson is second from left.

Charles Philips, *Tea Party at Lord Harrington's House, St James's,*
1730, oil on canvas.

As the century progressed, mealtimes changed. People rose
early and workers breakfasted early, but the leisured classes had
breakfast about ten o'clock in the morning. The meal included
bread and butter, rolls, buttered toast, a variety of cakes, perhaps
cold meat, and coffee or chocolate. Tea came to replace drinking chocolate on the breakfast tables of the gentry and was soon
adopted by the middle classes. Dinner time had been moving
steadily backwards from 1 p.m. since the mid-seventeenth century,
and by the 1720s the meal was usually taken between 2 and 3 p.m.,
with supper at 8 or 9 in the evening. By the 1780s, 4 p.m. dinner was
usual. Dinners had become occasions to invite witty, lively people
for the pleasure of their company rather than family members or
people who had to be impressed. Samuel Johnson was a frequent

guest at private dinners and expected extra trouble to have been taken in preparing the meal. According to Boswell:

> No man ate more heartily than Johnson or loved better what was nice and delicate. Mr Wilkes was assiduous in helping him to some fine veal. 'Pray give me leave Sir: – it's better here – A little of the brown – Some fat, Sir – A little of the Stuffing – Some gravy – Let me have the pleasure of giving you some butter – Allow me to recommend a squeeze of this orange; or the lemon, perhaps, may have more zest.'[12]

Such dinners often lasted for several hours, with many bottles of wine; then the ladies withdrew and the men drank their port. About 8 p.m. there was tea, coffee and cake, and a supper of cold meats, sweets, fruit and wine followed between 10 p.m. and

Thomas Rowlandson, *An Eating House*, 1815, hand-coloured etching.

midnight. Le Duc de la Rochefoucauld's account of being invited to such a dinner 'at 4 o'clock precisely' tells how tiring he found it:

> the first two hours are spent in eating . . . the servants disappear. The ladies drink a glass or two of wine . . . and all go out together. It is then that the real enjoyment begins . . . conversation is as free as it can be, everyone expresses his political opinions with as much frankness as he would employ on personal subjects . . . At the end of two or three hours a servant announces that tea is ready and conducts the gentlemen from their drinking to join the ladies in the drawing-room . . . After taking tea, one generally plays whist, and at midnight there is cold meat for those who are hungry.[13]

Eating out in taverns, pastry shops and chop-houses increased. While Johnson enjoyed dinners with close friends, he often preferred to dine in a tavern rather than a private house, where he felt there was always some anxiety about not offending the host. In taverns, 'You are most sure of a welcome; and the more noise you make, the more trouble you give and the more good things you call for, the welcomer you are.'[14]

Ralph Rylance's *The Epicure's Almanack*, published after the turn of the century, gave a clear idea of the eating establishments in London at the end of the eighteenth century. 'This book is designed to direct any man with a delicate stomach and a full purse, or any man with a keen strong stomach and a lean purse, where he may dine well, and to the best advantage, in London.' It describes eating establishments district by district, whether they have rooms for travellers, dining rooms or only offer a takeaway service, and who the usual clientele are – magistrates, merchants, lawyers, masons or 'theatrical gentlemen'. The streets around St Mary Axe offered predominantly kosher fare; Brick Lane and its market provided Jewish 'sugar sticks and peppermint drops' along with tripe shops and vendors of eel and meat pies. Birch in Cornhill belonged to Alderman Birch, who served soups and pastry 'in a superior style', and set out lemons, cayenne and other condiments, with toasted French bread for diners. In 1814 Birch became Lord Mayor of London, the only cook to attain the position. *The Epicure's Almanack* finishes with advice on kitchen ranges that are economical to use and on the best Italian warehouses importing foreign foods; of London markets he singles out Covent Garden for the quality of its vegetables. In contrast, Ned Ward's *The London Spy* (1703) gives a clear picture of the life of the lower classes, how they made ends meet and where they ate. Of the cookshops around Smithfield, he wrote: 'We soon deliver'd our squeamish Stomachs from the Surfeiting Fumes, that arose from their Rotten-Roasted Diet.'

One of the smartest eating houses was the London Tavern in Bishopsgate, with grand public rooms suitable for meetings, lectures, concerts and balls. It was patronized by the directors of the East India Company and also by radical politicians. John Farley, author of *The London Art of Cookery* (1784), was the chef. This is a thorough book, probably intended for apprentice cooks in his own or a similar tavern. The chapters are arranged by cooking method, not by ingredient. The first covers shopping and how to inspect meat, birds and fish to ensure buying the best quality. Much of the fruit, vegetables, butter and cheese sold in London was neither fresh nor of good quality. Adulterated food was still common – grit or sand was found in sugar, alum in flour, and milk was often watered. He also includes an appendix on culinary poisons, and especially poisons resulting from using untinned copper vessels and lead-glazed pottery. In this he was ahead of his time.

William Verral, master of an inn in Lewes in Sussex, was another author-cook. His book, *The Cook's Paradise: A Complete System of Cookery*, was published in 1759. Verral inherited the White

Hart Inn from his father, who had been in charge while William was apprenticed to St Clouet, a French chef who served the Duke of Newcastle, minister of state to George II. Verral acknowledges that he learned many of his dishes from St Clouet, yet at the same time he has a practical English approach to cooking. Sometimes he finds French dishes too fussy, but on other occasions notes how inferior to the French some English dishes are. His food is restrained compared to that of many professional cooks of the day. He includes one recipe for cullis, a modest one using only bacon, veal, ham and vegetables. At the end he notes: 'Be sure great care is taken of this, for on it the goodness and beauty of all the rest depends.' Most books by professional chefs include cullises, and most are more extravagant, using a wider variety of meats and larger quantities. Many of Verral's dishes include vegetables – mutton with cucumber and celery, mutton with carrots, lamb's ears with sorrel, calves tongue with cauliflowers, sweetbreads with mushrooms. This is good, unpretentious food. Verral adapted the skills learned with St Clouet to produce the kinds of dishes the inn's clientele of local gentry and travellers would expect and enjoy.

Grand desserts in the style of Tudor banquets disappeared quite early in the century, but the appetite for sweet foods did not. Sugar was now much cheaper too. In *The Art of Cookery*, Hannah Glasse did not neglect sweet dishes, including those meant for display before being eaten, as were 'sotelties' in earlier times. Her 'Hedge-Hog' is made with crushed almonds, orange flower water, eggs, cream and sugar heated in melted butter until it is stiff enough to be formed into a hedgehog; this is stuck with blanched almonds, 'slit and stuck up like the Bristles of a Hedge-Hog'. It is placed in a dish surrounded by a sauce of cream, egg yolks and sugar. When cold, 'it looks pretty in the Middle of a Table for Supper'.

In 1760 she published her *Compleat Confectioner*, in which she gives instructions for clarifying sugar, preserving fruits, flowers and herbs, and making creams, custards, jellies, cakes and biscuits.

Hero's recruiting at Kelsey's; — or — Guard-Day at St James's.

Two officers eating sweet treats inside a London confectioner's, 1797, hand-coloured
etching by James Gillray. The younger one (left) is eating 'sweet plumbs', while the
older soldier is eating ice cream or jelly.

She includes a recipe for making ice cream coloured with 'any sort of fruit, saffron or cochineal . . . the white wants nothing but orange-flower water and sugar'. The earliest recipes in English for ice cream were in translation in Massialot's *Court and Country Cook* (1702). Glasse also suggested buying ice cream from a confectioner, indicating that it was easily available.

In *The London Tradesman*, published in 1747, R. Campbell recorded the arrival of this new trade:

> The confectioner is a sweet-tooth'd tradesman: He makes all manner of sweet-meats, preserves all manner of fruit . . . he makes sour things sweet and sweet things sour . . . he coveres the products of summer with artificial frost and snow, and delights the eye as much with the arrangement of his pyramids as the taste with the delicious flavour of his wet and dry sweet-meats. It requires no small knowledge to compleat a confectioner, though I never esteem him one of the most useful members of society.

Confectioners may not have been considered useful members of society, but they were certainly much in demand by the rich. Several confectioners were running successful businesses, and one of the most important was Domenico Negri, an Italian pastry cook. In 1757 he opened his shop, The Pot and Pineapple, in Berkeley Square, where he sold 'all Sorts of English, French and Italian wet and dry'd Sweet Meat, Cedrati and Bergamot Chips . . . all sorts of Biskets & Cakes . . . all Sorts of Ice, Fruits & Creams in the best Italian manner'. Negri was the most renowned confectioner of his time. He served the royal dukes and the best houses in the city. In 1784 he took in a partner, James Gunter, who went on to establish a family business. Gunter's became confectioners to Queen Victoria and the business continued for a century and a half. Frederick Nutt, who was apprenticed to Negri, published his *Complete Confectioner* anonymously in 1789. It has recipes for homemade wines, cordials and liqueurs as well as biscuits, cakes, jellies, sweetmeats, creams, ice creams and water ices, preserved and dried fruits and fruit cheeses. He also included many folding plates of table settings for desserts for large parties.

Edward Kidder's *Receipts of Pastry and Cookery* had appeared much earlier, in circa 1720. He ran a cookery school six days a week at two venues in central London, and the book was intended for his 'Scholars'. The title page also states that 'Ladies may be taught at their own Houses.' It is a small book which provided the student with a range of meat and fish dishes as well as recipes for pies, puddings, cakes, custards and creams. These are dishes to be cooked in middle- and upper-class houses, so it is likely that servants were sent to the school. The other entry into cooking was to be apprenticed to a chef.

Tea consumption increased throughout Georgian times; in 1700 about 9,000 kilograms (20,000 lb) were imported and in ten years the amount trebled. It was expensive because it was highly taxed. Adulteration and smuggling were rife: dust and other substances were mixed with it, and used leaves were dried and sold again. The worst fake 'teas' were not tea at all, but sloe or white-thorn leaves, boiled and baked on an iron plate, then rubbed to curl them to look like tea leaves. They were coloured with logwood to make black tea, and with verdigris to make green. It took until the early nineteenth century for cases such as these to be brought to court. Friedrich Accum, a German chemist living in London, was appalled at the amount of adulteration that was tolerated in England and struck out against it.[15] In spite of so much adulteration, tea was the fashionable drink. It remained popular throughout the century and continued to be the drink of choice of the working class in spite of the likelihood of adulteration and the expense.

By the end of the century, tea imports had grown to 9 million kilograms (20 million lb), about 0.9 kilogram (2 lb) per person.

In addition, huge quantities were smuggled from France. James Woodforde noted in his diary on 27 March 1777: 'Andrews the Smuggler brought me this Night about 11 o'clock a Bagg of Hyson Tea 6 Pd Weight, He frightened us a little by whistling under the Parlour Window just as we were going to bed. I gave him some Geneva and paid him for the Tea at 10/6 Per Pd.'[16] Tea smugglers only sold to the upper and middle classes, since no one else could afford to buy it in large quantities. It was considered normal for an upright citizen like Woodforde to have dealings with a tea smuggler as he would with any other tradesman. A few years later in 1784, legal tea merchants brought pressure on the government to lower the tax to stop smuggling. It was reduced from 119 per cent to 12.5 per cent. Tea became more affordable, smuggling stopped, and consumption rose fast, as did imports of sugar to sweeten it. Sweet tea was consumed at all levels of society.

The amount spent on tea through the year by labouring families was substantial; it was £2 a year out of an annual income of about £40, and sugar, which was now cheap, was bought to go in it. But the tea of the poor was 'spring-water, just coloured with a few leaves, and sweetened with the brownest sugar . . . To this they recourse of necessity . . . Tea-drinking is not the cause, but the consequence of the distresses of the poor.'[17] Tea became the drink of the poor because malt was highly taxed and beer became too expensive: 'In short, we are so situated in our commercial and financial system, that tea brought from the eastern extremity of the world, and sugar brought from the West Indies, and both loaded with the expense of freight and insurance . . . compose a drink cheaper than beer.'[18] In 1797 Sir Frederick Eden noted: 'in poor families, tea is not only the usual beverage in the morning and evening, but is generally drunk in large quantities at dinner. Whether this exotic is more palatable or nutritious than home-raised barley converted into broth, I leave the Medical Gentlemen to determine.'[19] Alongside this, annual consumption of sugar rose to 9 kilograms (20 lb) per person at the end of the century.

For the urban poor who had forgotten how to make pottages, or lacked the fuel to do so, tea was the only warm element in their diet. By the end of the century, annual consumption of tea also reached 9 kilograms per person. Sweet tea was far less nutritious than the beer or ale it replaced, and water was still not safe to drink unless boiled.

For the rich there were many different green and black teas to try in their elegant teapots and 'dishes'. Their tea was usually sweetened with refined sugar. Coffee drinking continued to be popular in the middle and upper classes, but drinking chocolate disappeared, eventually to be replaced by eating chocolate in the nineteenth century.

In addition to the large amount of tea consumed, huge quantities of alcohol were drunk in all classes of society, particularly in London and the growing industrial towns. The sale of beer and ale was restricted to licensed premises in the sixteenth century. At the end of the seventeenth century, taxes on ale and beer were increased and consumption declined, which led to a decrease in brewing. However, in the early years of the eighteenth century, London brewers developed a new darker, richer and more complex beer: porter. Porter was fermented for longer than normal beer and was more alcoholic. It became hugely popular and was soon made in other parts of the country.

Many more people, particularly the poorest, turned to drinking spirits, which were only minimally taxed. During the reign of William and Mary (1689–1702), large quantities of gin or genever (it was sometimes called by its Dutch name) were imported into England and taxed at 2*d* per gallon.

It has been estimated that the consumption of real gin, that is spirit on which duty had been paid and which was probably more or less drinkable, rose from half a million gallons in 1700 to more than five million gallons in 1735, when the authorities began to take steps to check the evil.[20]

The government raised taxation in 1736, but it had little effect. Acts of parliament in 1690 and 1703 had removed the monopoly of the Distillers' Company and opened distilling to anyone. In 1726 there were more than 6,000 places in London where gin was sold. This huge increase in distilleries led to the sale of crude spirit or cheap 'gin' often distilled from almost anything that would ferment. One recipe, published in the *Publican's Daily Companion* in 1794, listed oil of vitriol (sulphuric acid), oil of almonds, oil of turpentine, spirits of wine, lump sugar, lime water, rose water, alum and salt of tartar as ingredients for gin.[21]

In the back streets of London and other cities, hundreds of 'gin' shops and other illegal establishments sold dubious spirits to the poor, who drank to escape their misery: this was Hogarth's Gin Lane. Drunkenness was a common state. It is thought that by the middle of the century 1.1 litres (2 pt) of gin were consumed each week for every man, woman and child living in London, and more than 9,000 children a year died from drinking spirits. In 1751 taxation on spirits was increased significantly and again in 1783. This, and the sharp rise in the price of grain, closed many distilleries and gin dens, and people turned back to drinking cheaper beer and tea.

Cider and perry were still drunk. Punch, a traditional Indian drink, was introduced at the end of the seventeenth century. A long drink made with citrus juice, brandy, sugar, spices and water or wine, it was often served in a large bowl. It was brought by the East India merchants and remained very popular with them and with seafarers. Dutch genever, French brandy and rum from West Indian plantations were the most popular spirits. Large shipments of wine arrived too: sack from Jerez, malmsey from Madeira and hock from the Rhineland. Pepys had enjoyed the 'good and most particular taste' of Château Haut-Brion, as he recorded on 10 April 1663, but as relations with France deteriorated, fewer Bordeaux wines were imported, and more table wines from Portugal were brought in as well as large quantities of port.

Woodforde's diary has more entries about drinking in his early years in Oxford than in later years. In December 1759, as a scholar he was given eight bottles of wine; he drank one on the 24th, two on the 27th, one on the 28th, two on the 29th and two on the 31st. Although he occasionally noted that someone else was drunk, he seems to have moderated his own drinking subsequently. Throughout the diary he mentions wine or porter when dining in company and he brewed barrels of mild table beer at home. As the century drew on, red wine or, more usually, port was drunk throughout the meal and the evening, and three or four bottles an evening was considered normal by many well-heeled men. Drinking to excess was a problem in all social classes and it continued into the nineteenth century.

Eighteenth-century recipes

To dress a salt cod

Elizabeth Raffald, *The Experienced English Housekeeper* (London, 1769)

Steep your salt-fish in water, all night with a glass of vinegar, it will fetch out the salt and make it eat like fresh fish; the next day boil it; when it is enough pull it in flakes into your dish; then pour egg-sauce over it, or parsnips boiled and beat fine with butter and cream; send it to the table on a water-plate, for it will soon grow cold.

To make egg sauce for a salt cod

Elizabeth Raffald, *The Experienced English Housekeeper* (London, 1769)

Boil your eggs hard; first half chop the whites, then put in the yolks, and chop them both together, but not very small; put them into half a pound of good melted butter, and let it boil up, then put it on the fish.

Des Cervelles de veau au riz (Calves' brains with rice)

William Verral, *The Cook's Paradise: A Complete System of Cookery* (London, 1759)

The brains of two heads is enough for a good dishe, but as an Hors d'oeuvres in particular, blanch them, and take off the bloody little fibres, cut into two pieces each, and soak them in a marinade of white wine and vinegar etc for an hour, put them into a stewpan with some cullis and gravy, and stew them softly about half an hour; boil your rice in water a few minutes, strain it off, and stew it in broth till it is tender, with a little salt and a bit of mace, dish up the brains, and pour some of the sauce to the rice, squeeze in a lemon or orange and pour over for serving at table.

To roast a fillet of beef

Martha Bradley, *The British Housewife*, vol. II (London, 1758)

Mix together some Pepper, Salt, Nutmeg, Crumbs of Bread, and grated Lemon-peel, and shred some Thyme, Parsley and Sweet Basil, mix all these very well together into a good and well relished Seasoning.

Cut out the Inside of a large Sirloin of Beef, take it out clean and entire, take off the Skins that are about it, and then gash it a little everywhere with a sharp Knife, but don't cut it too deep; pour upon it a quarter of a Pint of red Wine, rolling it about: Then dust it very well over and over with the Seasoning, and tie it around several Times with Packthread to keep it tight.

Spit it carefully upon a small Spit, and lay it down to a moderate Fire to roast.

Put into a Dripping-pan a Quart of Milk, and a Quarter of a Pound of Butter; baste it with this as it roasts, and when it is enough, lay it handsomely in a Dish, untying the Strings; and pour over it some rich Gravy.

A Fillet of Beef this plain Way, is a very agreeable Thing.

A Yorkshire pudding

Hannah Glasse, *The Art of Cookery Made Plain and Easy* (London, 1747)

Take a Quart of Milk, four Eggs and a little Salt, make it up into a thick Batter with Flour, like a Pancake Batter. You must have a good Piece of Meat at the Fire, take a Stew-pan and put some Dripping in, set it on the Fire, when it boils, pour in your Pudding, let it bake on the Fire till you think it is nigh enough, then turn a Plate upside-down in the Dripping pan that the Dripping may not be blacked; set your Stew pan on it under your Meat, and let the Dripping drop on the Pudding, and the Heat of the Fire come to it to make it a fine brown. When your Meat is done and set to Table, drain all the Fat from your Pudding, and set it on the Fire again to dry a little; then slide it as dry as you can into a Dish, melt some Butter, and pour into a Cup, and set it in the Middle of the Pudding. It is an exceeding good Pudding, the Gravy of the Meat eats well with it.

Ginger ice cream

Frederick Nutt, *The Complete Confectioner* (London, 1789)

Take four ounces of ginger preserved, pound it and put it into a bason, with two gills of syrup, a lemon squeezed and one pint of cream; then freeze it. Put it into the freezing pot and cover it; put the freezing pot into a pail and some ice all around the pot; throw a good deal of salt on the ice in the pail, turning the pot round for ten minutes; then open your pot, and scrape it from the sides, cover it up again, and keep turning it for some time, till your cream is like butter, and as thick; put it in your moulds, put them into a pail, and cover it with ice and salt for three quarters of an hour, till you find the water has come to the top of the pail; do not be sparing of salt, for if you do not use enough it will not freeze: dip your mould into water and turn it out on your plate and send to table.

NOTE: 1 gill is 150 ml (5 fl. oz).

5

The Birth of the
Industrial Nation

———

Over the course of the nineteenth century England changed from being a predominantly agricultural country with a fairly large rural population to a predominantly urban and industrial one. The population doubled from 9 million in 1801 to 18 million in 1851, probably partly due to a fall in the death rate, particularly in infant mortality. These changes meant that instead of being largely self-sufficient in food, imports were essential.

The early years of the century were good for the large land-owners, farmers and new industrialists, but catastrophic for the poor. The Napoleonic Wars disrupted the economy, creating a difficult environment for all the social and industrial changes that were proceeding so rapidly. Trade and therefore employment were interrupted; people left the land in ever increasing numbers and moved into hastily and badly built urban areas: instant slums with no sanitation, amenities, civic structure or social controls. London had long had its slums, but the newly created slums of the northern industrial towns were even worse, and a stark contrast to the villages of the countryside.

The wars cut off supplies of European corn, which had become necessary to feed the growing population; with three bad harvests in succession in 1809–11, prices tripled from those of the 1790s, causing great hardship and near-starvation among the poor, though yeomen and tenant farmers who adapted their cultivation to take advantage of these high prices grew rich. When the market collapsed at the time of the Battle of Waterloo in 1815, these same farmers faced ruin but were saved by the Corn Laws, which placed taxes on imported grain from 1815 to 1846, and so restored their prosperity at the expense of the consumer.

The laws were violently opposed by both the urban poor and the middle classes, creating new grievances: urban against rural communities as well as rich against poor. Discontent and distress spread, and the condition of the poor grew steadily worse; in the country more cottagers lost their meagre strips of land under the Enclosure Acts and foraging for wild foods became more difficult. The cost of living had risen steeply, but farm labourers' wages barely increased in the first 25 years of the century. 'The standard of life from 1800 to 1834 sank to the lowest possible scale ... and insufficient food has left its mark in the degeneracy of the peasantry'.[1]

If the poor were to be fed, a cheaper alternative to bread had to be found and that was the potato. It enabled

the workers to survive on the lowest possible wage. It may be that in this way the potato prolonged and encouraged for another hundred years, the impoverishment and degradation of the English masses; but what was the alternative, surely nothing but bloody revolution. That England escaped such a violent upheaval in the early decades of the nineteenth century, and more than once we were within an ace of such disaster, must, in large measure be placed to the credit of the potato.[2]

Nevertheless, bread remained their preferred food, and by far the largest weekly outgoing was for bread; after this came rent, potatoes, then coal and wood. Much smaller amounts were spent on tea, sugar, soap, butter, cheese and candles. In the 1840s the typical weekly expenditure for a family with four working members and two smaller children was 13s 9d – exactly their weekly income. This family was in East Anglia; in the northern counties the diet was more varied, where in addition to bread, potatoes and tea, there were milk, oatmeal and broth, pies and bacon.[3]

After the war unemployment rose, food prices increased and wages still declined, leading to widespread unrest in both rural and industrial communities. In his *Rural Rides* William Cobbett noted derelict farms and deserted villages and the misery of the poor in stark contrast to the grand estates of the rich – often absentee – landlords. The farm workers were 'the worst used labouring people upon the face of the earth. Dogs and hogs and horses are treated with more civility, and as to food and lodging, how gladly would the labourers change with them.'[4] These were day labourers, many of whom took their families and went in desperation to the slums of the industrial towns of the North and the Midlands. Skilled labourers fared better, as they were essential to the smooth running of large farms and had annual employment arrangements with the farmer. The last remnants of village industries such as weaving disappeared.

Scientific farming practices begun in the eighteenth century spread further and faster; soil analysis was widely adopted to determine the minerals present and artificial manuring was introduced. The new chemical fertilizers increased crop yields, and new winter feeds for animals were developed, including cottonseed and linseed cakes. New machinery was invented; crop rotation was practised more widely. Nevertheless, food imports remained essential. After a poor corn harvest and a potato disease in 1845, starvation loomed and revolt threatened, but the Corn Laws were repealed, which reduced the price of bread and other staples, and imported corn made up the loss. Potato planting increased: potatoes were an invaluable crop because they would grow where wheat would not, and survived weather that destroyed grain harvests. In some areas small amounts of potato started to be used in bread-making, particularly in home and village baking, but labourers were still unwilling to change their bread-based diet for potatoes unless they were desperate. Cobbett feared that a diet based on Ireland's 'lazy-root' would reduce Englishmen to the level of an Irish peasant, whom he considered a slave living in a hovel.

A few farm labourers still had a bit of land to grow potatoes, but they had to find wood to light a fire to cook them and to boil water for tea, which became even more popular as the century progressed, replacing beer, which eventually became a social drink. Poaching was ever more dangerous; it was illegal to sell or buy game, gamekeepers patrolled the woodlands, and a poacher could be hanged or deported to Australia or America.

In 1844 Friedrich Engels described the working-class diet:

The better-paid workers, especially those in whose families every member is able to earn something, have good food as long as this state of things lasts; meat daily and bacon and cheese for supper. Where wages are less, meat is used only two or three times a week, and the proportion of bread and potatoes increases. Descending gradually, we find the animal food reduced to a small piece of bacon cut up with the potatoes; lower still, even this disappears, and there remains only bread, cheese, porridge and potatoes until, on the lowest round of the ladder, among the Irish, potatoes form the sole food.[5]

In her *Cottage Cookery* (1859), Esther Copley set out to instruct poor wives to be clever managers and good cooks to wean their families away from meals of bread, potatoes and tea.[6] Her recipes for broths and stews, pies and puddings are more nourishing and, she claims, not more expensive if the ingredients are chosen carefully. Small amounts of ox cheek and tail, mutton neck and head are the meats for her stews, and rice, barley, peas or oats provide the thickening ingredients. Root vegetables, parsley and thyme add flavour. Her rich pastry is made with lard or marrow and butter; for 'common pies' dripping or lard will suffice. The chapter on 'Frugality and Cheap Cookery' combines practical suggestions to send children out to gather wild fruits in season and to dry young strawberry leaves or herb leaves to make tea, with admonitions to cut down on sugar consumption to have money for more nourishing foods. There are many sensible suggestions and no doubt the book was written with good intentions, but as the daughter of a silk manufacturer, Copley had no experience of the struggle to feed a family on a few shillings a week with minimal cooking facilities, and sometimes even no fire. In those conditions, bread and a cup of hot tea made a warm meal.

As Dorothy Hartley noted in *Food in England*: 'With the Industrial Revolution the people are driven off the land; they are cut off from their natural food supply, and are compelled for the first time to *buy* food. The cruelty of the Industrial Revolution was that it made money a necessity of *life*.'[7] It changed forever the national diet. In the past, although the rich feasted and the serfs ate minimally, the poor could manage to provide for themselves from the land. In the towns they could not. All of life – housing, clothing, fuel and food – depended on a monetary economy, and the foods that were available and affordable (bread, potatoes and tea) provided little sustenance.

The poor were constantly confronted with the rapid increase in prosperity of the landowners and owners of collieries, mills and factories. Vast increases in exports and shipping led to the accumulation of wealth along with the new slum towns and the degrading poverty of most of their population. The working class was distinctly downtrodden as the gentry and the upper levels of the middle class moved aggressively upwards at their expense. Wages did not keep pace with the cost of living, and the labourer

– whether on the land or in industry – was close to subsistence level throughout the first half of the century, whereas all around him were indications of wealth, partly a result of his own labour which benefited his employer. In his landmark *Making of the English Working Class*, E. P. Thompson noted: 'His own share in the "benefits of economic progress" consisted of more potatoes, a few articles of cotton clothing for his family, soap and candles, some tea and sugar.'[8] In these circumstances it is not surprising that the potato acquired its nickname: 'the root of misery'.

In the earlier rural economy, women and children were employed in weaving and other cottage industries to contribute to the family budget, but there were always other daily tasks to be done to relieve the repetition and monotony. As these rural industries disappeared, the women and children worked on the land to supplement the husband's wages. For those who moved into towns, work in factories and mines was repetitive and dulling, and they were required to do it for twelve hours a day or more. In a 'good' mill the workers had half an hour for breakfast, an hour for dinner at midday and a further half hour in the afternoon. They often started at 6 a.m. and finished at 8 p.m., and ate standing where they worked. Work was no longer small scale when it could be organized to suit family routines; the speed, regularity and length of time worked were controlled by the machines and factory owners. The requirements of the steam engine created the industrial working class and, within it, different levels of skill and competence.

The workers' living conditions were appalling; Engels described one of the slums of Manchester:

> it is a disorderly collection of tall, three or four-storied houses with narrow, crooked, filthy streets ... The houses are occupied from cellar to garret, filthy within and without ... But this is nothing in comparison with the dwellings in

the narrow courts and alleys between the streets, entered by covered passages between the houses, in which the filth and tottering ruin passes all description.[9]

Charles Dickens gave a similar description of a London slum: 'Crazy wooden galleries common to the backs of half-a-dozen houses, with holes to look upon the slime beneath; windows broken and patched ... rooms so small, so filthy, so confined ... every loathsome indication of filth, rot and garbage.'[10]

Two of the biggest problems since the explosive growth of the towns was the lack of clean water and the disposal of sewage. The mid-century outbreaks of cholera were eventually linked to drinking contaminated water. It was discovered that water from the town wells was contaminated by percolation through the soil, and charcoal filters were introduced to purify domestic water. A Commission of Sewers was set up in 1848, and in collaboration with a newly appointed medical officer for London, the unhygienic cesspools were abolished and underground sewers installed. Liverpool had taken this step before London, and other towns followed. Improvements continued through the second half of the century, but it was only in 1902 that the Metropolitan Water Board bought up the old water supply companies and took scientific control of the capital's supply.

Industrialization was relentless and it would be many more years before social concerns for the standard of living of the workers would be addressed. Huge long-term investment in canals, railways, factories, mines and foundries was essential, and this is where the emerging industrialists focused their objectives, rather than on the workforce.

The demand for quality English goods was overwhelming, both within the country and for export. Great advances were made in developing machinery to speed up the production of cotton and woollen goods, to increase iron and steel production and in engineering and mining. The eighteenth-century canal network was extended, roads were macadamized, and in 1825 the Stockton & Darlington Railway opened. The transport networks were important for exporters, and also essential for getting food supplies to the bustling cities. There was no concern about protecting the environment; rivers were polluted by dyes from the textile industries, towns blackened by smoke and the air quality poor.

In the 1770s about half of the working population was engaged in agriculture; by 1800 it had dropped to about 35 per cent, and by 1851 was only 16 per cent. The number employed in industry increased to 35 per cent by 1851, but not all were in fully mechanized factories; trades such as tailors, cobblers, shoemakers and seamstresses continued, as did domestic service: the second largest occupation of all.[11]

The wages of urban workers varied more widely than those of farm labourers because there were so many categories of work. For a small number of the working class, industrialization brought sudden wealth, while for many it made little difference, and many more were substantially poorer than they had been. In the early days of industrialization there were rapid shifts between prosperity and poverty; even skilled workers could find themselves without employment from one week to the next. Food prices fluctuated widely too, which caused anxiety, particularly if the price of bread rose since the average worker's family spent half of its income on bread.

Preparing food changed greatly in town too. Domestic cooking facilities were minimal, and with everyone away from the home to work for long hours, there was little time or energy for cooking. Bakers and other food retailers provided most of their needs. Food that was ready, quick to prepare and preferably to eat hot was essential: bread, potatoes baked in their jackets, bacon and tea were the daily staples, and broths or puddings might be made on Sundays when there was more time.

The growing urban population had to be fed, and thanks to the railways fresh food could reach the cities from longer distances. In London markets were opened near the railway terminals for fruit and vegetables to be brought in to supplement the crops from market gardens surrounding the city. Nevertheless, Covent Garden remained the best fruit and vegetable market in spite of being some distance from any terminal. Steamships brought fish to the coastal towns quickly, and it was then taken by canal or rail to inland towns. Livestock markets in town centres were moved to the outskirts; London's Smithfield was closed and rebuilt as a meat market, improving hygiene and eliminating the stench of the slaughterhouses.

In the early years of the century milk was supplied by 'milk walks'; dairies on the outskirts of the city employed women twice a day to milk their cows, and the milk was taken to small traders who sold the milk from door to door. Tobias Smollett described, in *The Expedition of Humphry Clinker* (1771), the women as verminous drabs masquerading under the respectable denomination of milkmaid. Milk sellers were notorious for watering their already less than clean milk, and when milk started to be taken into London by train it was sent in sealed cans. At the depot, it was decanted into smaller cans, which were also locked 'to ensure that which is somewhat rare in the metropolis – pure milk'.[12] In the early days of its development, Manchester was supplied by dairies within a 16-kilometre (10 mi.) radius to prevent sour milk being dispatched. By 1825 milk was sent twice a day by canal, a smoother journey into the city centre, and by the middle of the century much greater quantities were transported by rail from further afield. However, raw milk was a carrier of infection, including bovine tuberculosis. Only at the end of the century was pasteurization introduced, originally to prolong the life of milk reaching the towns after a long rail journey. Pasteurization killed the bacteria that would have turned the milk sour. Some years later it was realized that it also provided protection from milk-borne disease.

Adulteration of tea, alcohol and bread had been common for many years, but now there was more cause for concern. Food production was no longer local but was prepared increasingly in industrial surroundings and could not be traced back to a farm or other source. As Sam Weller remarked in *The Pickwick Papers*: 'Wery good thing is a weal pie, when you know the lady as made it, and is quite sure it ain't kittens.'[13]

The use of additives to increase profit became a serious health problem. Accum exposed in his *Treatise on Adulterations of Food* (1820) some practices that were truly poisonous, such as mixing vinegar with sulphuric acid to increase its acidity and using a colourant with a high copper content to make garishly coloured green sweets. He also drew attention to the use of copper pans in the kitchen and copper vessels for brewing beer. Others were less harmful, such as the adulteration of tea with dust or dried leaves of local trees or of coffee with powdered dried peas and beans. Brewers were frequently convicted for adulteration of ale and porter. Hartshorn shavings, caraway and coriander seeds were among the ingredients used as cheap substitutes for malt and hops; they diluted the beer by giving it a false appearance of strength and flavour. Aged beers were popular, but ageing in vats was expensive, so some publicans added sulphuric acid to age new beer. As Accum tartly noted: 'the man who robs a fellow subject of a few shillings on the highway is sentenced to death; while he who distributes a slow poison to a whole community escapes unpunished.'[14]

Inevitably, the poor suffered most; they bought their food from street hawkers and costermongers because their prices were lower, but many were persistent swindlers often selling adulterated foods and cheating on weight. Their weights were usually some ounces light, their liquid measures short, and they used boxes with

John Thomson, 'Strawberries. All ripe! All ripe!' and 'Seller of Shell-Fish', 1877, photographs from *Street Life in London* (with Adolphe Smith).

John Thomson, 'Cheap Fish of St Giles's', 1877, photograph from *Street Life in London* (with Adolphe Smith).

false bottoms. Adulteration continued apace, but it took until 1875 for the government to pass the Sale of Food and Drugs Act.

Henry Mayhew gave vivid accounts of the costermongers in his articles for the *Morning Chronicle* in the late 1840s.[15] They were a significant part of the London population; they bought food wholesale, mostly fruit and vegetables but also fish, and sold them retail on the streets. Most costermongers were as desperately poor as their customers. Both knew that, perhaps with the exception of some local seasonal fruit and vegetables, the quality of the food was poor, and all were striving to get enough to eat. Costermongers had a dress code: corduroy trousers and waistcoats and silk neckerchiefs, which they treasured. Many started out as children of costermongers: the girls sold flowers or watercress from the age of six, while the boys worked with their fathers. Some had barrows, and others walked with handcarts or trays on their heads, shouting their wares. A great range of foods was available – cooked eel, soups, trotters, baked potatoes. Trade was seasonal and bad weather brought them close to starvation. Spring through to autumn was fine as they sold seasonal crops – cherries, soft fruits, plums, pears, apples, oysters and sprats. The coster dwellings Mayhew visited were abysmal, just as squalid as those of their customers, but they spent most of their lives on the streets.

Soup kitchens to feed the poor had been started in Britain at the end of the eighteenth century by Count Rumford, the renowned physicist and humanitarian. Although it was later recognized that his soup had insufficient nourishment to sustain someone in employment, it was nonetheless better than starving. They continued into the nineteenth century, and Alexis Soyer, the flamboyant French celebrity chef of the new Reform Club, who was also a social reformer, started to teach charitable ladies how to make nutritious soups to feed the poor. He eventually set up a soup kitchen in London to feed two to three hundred people a day.

John Thomson, 'Halfpenny Ices', 1877, photograph from *Street Life in London* (with Adolphe Smith).

Charles Elmé Francatelli, another grand London chef, opened a similar enterprise. Soyer started to work on designs for a soup boiler that could feed many more people a day and a kitchen that could serve thousands. In 1847, the worst year of the Irish potato famine, the English government asked Soyer to open a soup kitchen in Dublin. This had a huge 1,100-litre (242 gal.) steam cauldron, an enormous bread oven and coal fires. It served more than 8,000 meals a day. Once established, Soyer left Dublin for his next challenge: the field kitchens of the Crimean War, which he radically improved.

Soyer was a remarkable inventor; when invited to be chef of the new Reform Club in 1837, he accepted on condition that he could design the kitchens in collaboration with the architect. He installed gas stoves, a great innovation, as well as coal and charcoal stoves, and the ovens had adjustable temperature controls. In the meat and game larder were slate dresser tops and lead-lined ice drawers. Fish was kept on a marble slab and cooled by a constant

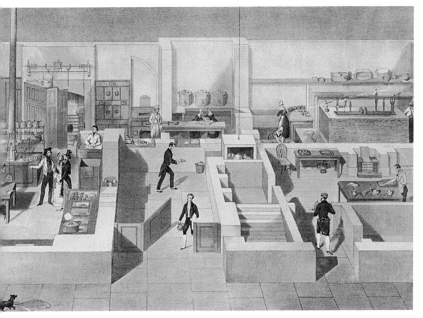

Alexis Soyer's kitchens at the Reform Club, London, 1842.

flow of iced water. The kitchens gained such renown that there were guided tours. He constantly produced novelties, from new bottled sauces to steamers and multi-egg poachers; from a portable tabletop stove to a gas-fired apparatus for roasting a whole ox. For Queen Victoria's coronation breakfast on 28 June 1838, Soyer prepared a breakfast for 2,000 people at the club.

His first cookery book, *The Gastronomic Regenerator*, was published in 1846; this was intended for the chefs of the upper class, and many peers and gentlemen who were Reform Club members were among the original subscribers. The first section is 'The Kitchen of the Wealthy', which deals with carving and has classic French sauces, fish, hors d'oeuvres, first and second courses, and entremets (small dishes served between the main course and dessert) or sweets. His instructions are detailed and easy to follow, and he explains what the texture and appearance of the end result should be. The final part of the book, after describing the kitchens of the Reform Club, is 'My Kitchen at Home', where he offers plainer recipes 'that the industrious classes of society may partake freely of them at very moderate expense'. He followed this book a few years later with *The Modern Housewife*, addressed to the 'Fair Daughters of Albion': middle-class rather than wealthy young women. It contained breakfasts, nursery food, invalid dishes, beverages for evening parties, and 'minute directions for family management in all its branches'. In 1855 he followed this with *A Shilling Cookery for the People*. Soyer's recipes for the poor could all be made with the most basic kitchen equipment: gridiron, frying pan, iron pan and black pot.

He did not expect his readers to be so poor that they existed only on bread, potatoes and tea; there are several recipes for meat, mostly offal and cheap cuts but also steak, and fish from mackerel to turbot. He deals at length with potatoes: how to choose between different varieties and how to cook them nutritiously. He noted that the poor did not eat enough vegetables and urged those with a bit of land to plant more. He also suggested commercial condiments – chilli vinegar, anchovy sauce, Soyer's relish and Soyer's mustard sauce – to boost flavours. Ever the showman and opportunist, the final chapter describes the benefits of using his baking stewing pan and his kitchen timer. All of his books sold thousands of copies.

Francatelli, the second most renowned chef of the period, was born in England but trained under Marie-Antoine Carême in France. He worked for several noble families before becoming chef to Queen Victoria from 1840 to 1842, and eventually also cooking at the Reform Club in the 1850s. He wrote *The Modern Cook* for the well-to-do, and later *A Plain Cookery Book for the Working Classes*. Francatelli hoped, as he wrote in the book's introduction, that 'industry, good health and constant employment' would have enabled his readers to set aside some money so that they could purchase 'a cooking-stove, with an oven at the side ... and a boiler at the back of the grate ... to have hot water always at hand'. He also advised his readers to have a range of pans, a gridiron and a copper for washing or brewing, and gave the price item by item of the whole shopping list of equipment with a total of £6 12s 4d. In the middle years of the century, wages kept pace with price rises, and food prices, including tea and sugar, were fairly stable, so it was possible for some poor families to save.

Many recipes for soup, meat, fish and vegetables are similar to Soyer's. He includes a simple fish curry: fried onions are topped with sliced green apples, then pieces of fried fish, the whole sprinkled with curry powder, the pan covered and cooked slowly for a further half hour, when it is ready to serve with boiled rice. A bouillabaisse soup sounds less authentic, but his suggestion to serve salt fish with boiled parsnips, a butter and vinegar sauce and chopped hard-boiled eggs seems a good way to reduce the lingering salt.

787. CHARTREUSE OF VEGETABLES, GARNISHED WITH PARTRIDGES.

Chartreuse of vegetables, garnished with partridges, from
Charles Elmé Francatelli, *The Modern Cook* (1846).

His Christmas plum pudding is boiled in a cloth and served, 'if you can afford it', with a butter, sugar and flour sauce made with 'half a gill of any kind of spirits'. It is probably equally unlikely that his readers could afford to use his recipes to bake a goose or a suckling pig.

Even if they had the equipment to cook, many of the poorest lacked even basic cooking skills and were ignorant about nutrition, as Soyer noted in *A Shilling Cookery for the People*. Removal to an urban environment and dependence on bought foods, often from necessity, had led to loss of the knowledge and practice. As the century progressed, groups of middle-class women intent on improvement and reform volunteered to teach working-class women how to get the best from the food they could afford. Some girls' schools introduced cooking classes about the basic methods with recipes for pies, soups and cakes, but not all families could afford the ingredients. Other women continued to cook what their mothers had cooked.

The population grew as rapidly in the last fifty years of the century as it had in the first. It had doubled to 18 million by 1851, and then doubled again to 36 million by 1911. Now more attention was given to the health and welfare of industrial workers and their families. Slum improvements were undertaken. Trade unions began to provide some employment protection and the demand for labour grew as industries expanded. Wages increased and the standard of living improved, since food prices did not rise excessively, and for the first time some workers had a margin of income over essential expenditure.

From medieval times England had always had a small class of merchants and professionals, but the Industrial Revolution increased their number hugely with manufacturers, engineers, industrialists, bankers and others. Their influence swelled with their numbers; they were the innovators who led Victorian social and economic development. In the 1850s and '60s all classes benefited,

but profits grew faster than wages and many middle-class fortunes were made. However, the national income remained very
unequally distributed; the poorest were still three-quarters of the
population. The wealthiest had at least £1,000–£5,000 a year; the
middle class £300–£1,000; the lower middle class, skilled labourers, unskilled labourers and agricultural workers under £100.[16] The
rich became ever richer, and for the first time the lowest paid were
emerging from the dire poverty of the early part of the century.
Many of the poor moved up the social scale by acquiring new
skills that enabled them to take on clerical or administrative jobs
within the industrial system. The desire for scientific and technical
knowledge among some of the working class led to the opening of adult education institutes. Education for poor children had
been neglected and left to religious charities, but by mid-century
state-aided schools received larger grants. Upper-class sons continued to receive a classical education at the public schools; the
middle classes sent their children to private academies, where they
received a more modern and scientific education. Some old grammar schools still remained but they had been neglected after Stuart
times. As the century progressed, the public schools were opened
to the sons of the nouveau riche industrialists.

Life in the towns and cities was becoming slowly more democratic, but the countryside was still mostly in the hands of the
wealthy upper class. Their tenant farmers continued to increase
output with better machinery, drainage and manuring and
improved livestock breeding. With an ever-increasing population
to feed, these improvements were essential.

While Louis-Eustache Ude, Soyer and Francatelli were
chefs catering to the rich and to the poor with their publications,
women writers were following Hannah Woolley, Elizabeth
Raffald, Hannah Glasse and others who wrote for middle-class
families in the previous century. Glasse was the most successful
eighteenth-century writer, and her book remained in print until

the 1840s. Maria Rundell's *A New System of Domestic Cookery* appeared in 1806 to challenge that success, and it sold half a million copies in her lifetime. Unlike earlier women writers who had usually spent some time in service, she was the daughter of a barrister and the widow of a surgeon who wished to pass on advice to her married daughters about how to run a household well. Her 'Miscellaneous Observations' are about how to do that: keeping account of expenses, avoiding waste, setting aside feathers from poultry to stuff cushions, know-how on storing different foods, and ensuring there is always food prepared for 'noonings' (luncheons) and suppers in case unexpected visitors arrive.

Her recipes are clear, with measures given for all ingredients, and for many she gives cooking times. Most are for traditional dishes that are found in books from earlier centuries, but some belong to this era of colonial expansion. In the eighteenth century a few books included a curry or other Indian dish, but Rundell's book is more comprehensive. Standard kitchen pepper is included, and so is chetna sauce: a blend of vinegar-soaked shallots, walnut and mushroom ketchups, soy, cayenne and chilli vinegar boiled together for five minutes and bottled. Several recipes for curry follow: a standard one, the King of Oude's curry, Dopeeaza curry, Madras curry, Bengal curry, Lord Clive's curry and even a Malay curry. There are also several different curry powder blends. This awareness of regional and personal dishes suggests that she knew people who had lived in India. Her tomato sauce, one of the earliest in an English cookery book, is made with baked tomatoes, chilli vinegar, garlic, salt and ground ginger – ingredients from both West and East. Her desserts and cakes are very English: gooseberry fool, stewed pears, trifle, floating island, gingerbread, seed cake and macaroons.

After Rundell came Eliza Acton, whose *Modern Cookery, for Private Families*, first published in 1845, was distinctly modern in tone. Her writing is clear and elegant, her directions concise and sensible; her great innovation was to list ingredients and cooking time at the end of each recipe. Wherever you dip into Acton, you have a sense of someone who appreciates good food for itself and wants the reader to share that pleasure through cooking her dishes. Her book is more clearly directed to urban middle-class women than were those of her predecessors. She assumed her readers would easily be able to buy ingredients for foreign dishes, and also that they would direct their cooks to ensure the food was wholesome and well prepared: 'Good cookery is the best and truest economy, turning to full account every wholesome article of food, and converting into palatable meals, what the ignorant either render uneatable, or throw away in disdain.'[17] In order to provide her readers with a greater variety of daily staple dishes, she avoided 'elegant superfluities or luxurious novelties', remarking that if they were required, they could be bought from an 'able confectioner'. The publication of the second edition in 1855 was influenced by the English publication of Justus von Liebig's *Chemistry of Food*. Her other concern in the second edition was the appalling level of adulteration in basic everyday foods. Her solution to this was to make as much as possible at home, including jams and preserves, but particularly bread. Acton published her bread book in 1852, and she added a chapter on breadmaking to the revised edition of *Modern Cookery*. Thirty years later, Sir Henry Thompson, an eminent doctor and writer on diet, was still complaining that bakers' bread was unpalatable and indigestible; he did not suppose that any thoughtful or prudent consumer would, unless compelled, eat it habitually.

After Acton came Isabella Beeton. She grew up in a large family with many stepchildren and as one of the eldest spent much of her youth helping with the housekeeping. At twenty she married Sam Beeton, a bright young publisher who immediately set her to work for him. In four years she collected and compiled recipes, wrote and edited the general information and instructions that eventually became *The Book of Household Management* (1861).

Many of the recipes were published in Sam's *Englishwoman's Domestic Magazine*, and were tested in the family kitchen. Others were taken from earlier books, and from Acton she also took her innovation of setting out the quantities of ingredients and timing for the recipes, to which she added the likely cost of the dish. Originally published in monthly parts from 1859 to 1861, which were very popular, the book was published in 1861. It was an astonishing achievement to complete this thorough and detailed volume of over a thousand pages in four years in addition to writing articles for her husband's magazine, running her household and leading an active social life. The book was a huge success. In January 1865 she finished writing a dictionary version of it, but she died a few weeks later at the age of 29.

Beeton's book was written not only for the urban middle-class woman but also for the lower middle-class. It starts by explaining the role of the mistress. The mistress of the house should rise early, practice frugality, as well as know how to cultivate good temper, pay and receive morning calls and host dinner parties. It provides a guide to the role of housekeeper, the number of domestic servants required, their tasks, and how much they should be paid. Each chapter in the cookery section starts with general information about the subject, followed by the recipes in alphabetical order. Much of the book is devoted to meat cookery; the beef chapter starts with 'cold meat cookery', a selection of dishes for using up leftovers, and the mutton and pork chapters have more. At the end of a recipe for braised breast of mutton, she adds a note on Saxon names of animals and Norman names of meat:

> The names of all our domestic animals are of Saxon origin; but it is curious to observe that Norman names have been given to the different sorts of flesh which these animals yield. How beautifully this illustrates the relative position of Saxon and Norman after the conquest. The Saxon hind

had the charge of tending and feeding domestic animals, but only that they might appear on the table of his Norman Lord. Thus 'ox', 'steer', and 'cow' are Saxon, but 'beef' is Norman; 'calf' is Saxon, but 'veal' Norman; 'sheep' is Saxon, 'mutton' Norman; so it is severally with 'deer' and 'venison', 'swine' and 'pork', 'fowl' and 'pullet'. 'Bacon', the only flesh which, perhaps, ever came within his reach, is the single exception.

Her chapter on sauces is very thorough, and also includes recipes for preserves: dried mushrooms, pickled red cabbage, pickled oysters and various stuffings and forcemeats. Puddings, creams and jellies are covered extensively, from 'Monday's Pudding' made with leftover plum pudding and a 'Plain Christmas Pudding for Children' to 'Indian Trifle' and the 'Hidden Mountain', a thick pancake with slices of citron. For each month she gives menus for plain family dinners and for dinner parties from six to eighteen people, shows the table settings and explains the etiquette. Mrs Beeton epitomized the Victorian middle classes; she provided inspiration and also reassurance for their domestic life, for social occasions and for moral virtues.

Country house life was taken up with hunting, shooting and entertaining. The aristocracy continued to live on their property for much of the year, moving to London for the season; they were still the leaders in fashion and society. The rapid growth of the upper middle class created manufacturers and merchants who rivalled the nobles in wealth; they acquired country estates and married their daughters into aristocratic families and adapted to their way of living. Members of the gentry – knights, squires and independent farmers – maintained their position below the aristocrats in rural society. The nobility continued to enjoy classic French cuisine and could afford the expensive smuggled wines and foods from France. The prestige attached to employing expensive French chefs remained throughout the war with France and beyond. Even the Prince Regent briefly employed Carême, the leading French chef of the day; Soyer, Francatelli and Ude were the most renowned chefs in London.

Significant improvements were made in country house kitchens; cast iron was the material of the age and it was used extensively to create new closed kitchen ranges. Some of them had a hot water boiler installed to one side. In the smartest ranges each section had its own fire pit with a door and a drawer below to collect the ashes. Fires of different intensity could be set to allow slow and rapid cooking, grilling and simmering to be done at the same time. The roasting oven devised by Count Rumford had a cylindrical iron oven with a shelf a little below the centre to hold a dripping pan, on which the meat was placed on a raised grid. Two blow pipes went into the bottom of the oven and a steam pipe went out at the top. Shortly before the meat was ready, the blow pipes were heated by a small fire and the additional heat in the oven browned the meat and finished the cooking. Joints cooked in this oven lost much less weight than those turned on a spit and were more juicy and better flavoured. Flues rose above the ranges to take smoke and fumes away through the chimney. Boilers to create steam were introduced and the steam travelled through lagged pipes to steaming kettles and hotplates and also to insulated cupboards near the dining room so that food could be served hot. Gas plants for lighting and cooking were introduced by the 1840s, and electricity generating plants followed in the 1880s as older equipment was replaced. These new kitchens made feeding large households and their guests considerably easier.

New equipment came with the new kitchen ranges: pans were flat-bottomed and had shorter handles and were made of tin-plated cast iron rather than copper or brass. New pans were created to meet the needs of elegant entertaining: fish kettles for round and flat fish, omelette pans and sauté pans. Tinware pastry and biscuit cutters, jelly moulds, raised pie moulds and tongue presses were followed by more labour-saving tools: graters, potato peelers, bean slicers and marmalade cutters.

From Jane Austen's novels we have a sense of middle-class country life in the late eighteenth and early nineteenth centuries. The daughter of a country parson, she and her sister Cassandra learned from their mother about housekeeping and took over as their mother aged. The family kept cows, pigs, sheep and hens; they had a vegetable garden and fruit trees. Their maids made bread, butter, cheese, preserves, pickles and home-made wine and cured ham and bacon. Tea, coffee, sugar and other foods were bought, but they provided much of their daily food themselves. Their brother Henry had a French cook, and Jane wrote to her sister about how much she enjoyed his food. She also liked to try out new dishes, and in another letter to Cassandra wrote: 'My mother desires me to tell you that I am a very good housekeeper . . . I always take care to provide such things as please my own appetite, which I consider as the chief merit of housekeeping.'[18] Food and entertaining are in the background in all her novels. In *Northanger Abbey* Catherine Morland is impressed by the elegance of General Tilney's breakfast set, in which she finds that the tea is 'as well flavoured from the clay of Staffordshire, as that from Dresden or Sêve'. But apart from the tea we don't learn what else was served. Mrs Bennett is particularly concerned to impress when Bingley and Darcy are to be the family's guests for dinner in *Pride and Prejudice*. Intent on maintaining the family's standing on the social ladder, she is certain that nothing less than two full courses would 'satisfy the appetite and pride of one who had ten thousand a year'. *Emma*'s hypochondriac father, Mr Woodhouse, tries to persuade his guests not to eat asparagus or roast pork, which he finds 'unwholesome', but to have lightly boiled eggs and gruel, and perhaps a 'little bit of tart, a very little bit. Ours are all apple-tarts. You need not be afraid of unwholesome preserves here.'

In the early years of the century breakfast was still a leisurely meal taken at about 10 a.m. for the fashionable, but workers, and increasingly managers in industry, had a much earlier, quick breakfast. It then became customary to have a snack in the middle of the day at a coffee-house or pastry cook's, or at an inn in the country. This was called nuncheon or luncheon. Dinner moved to 6 p.m. and might be followed by tea for the ladies and cards, and a late supper for those who were hungry, as at the end of the seventeenth century.

By mid-century breakfast was taken earlier, at 8 or 8.15, to allow the man of the house to leave for his office early enough. Now there were books devoted to breakfast dishes. *The Breakfast Book*, published in 1865, gave four kinds of breakfast: the family breakfast, the *déjeuner à la fourchette*, the cold collation and the *ambigu*. The family breakfast consisted of side dishes, hot or cold; the *déjeuner à la fourchette* had dishes served in sequence; cold collations were cold dishes prepared for the meal to produce an ornamental effect, and an *ambigu* was similar to a dinner, except that all the dishes were put on the table at once. The author, Georgiana Hill, noted that everyday breakfasts were mostly *ambigu*, since 'broiled fish, cold pasties, devilled bones, boiled eggs, cold ham etc, all appear together.'

Tea was the usual drink, but at country house breakfasts coffee was often offered as well. These were more leisurely meals and could still be as late as 10 a.m. Major L . . . suggested:

> fish, poultry, game, if in season; sausages, and one meat of some sort, such as mutton cutlets, or fillets of beef; omelets . . . bread of both kinds, white and brown, and fancy bread . . . jam, orange marmalade, and fruits when in season; and on the side-table, cold meats, such as ham, tongue, cold game, or game pie, galantines, and in winter a round of spiced beef.[19]

Luncheon remained a snack. Mrs Rundell, who used the word 'nooning', wrote that this was an informal, light meal similar to a supper.[20] Mrs Beeton's luncheon dishes were 'the remains of cold joints, nicely garnished, a few sweets or a little hashed meat, poultry or game ... with bread and cheese, biscuits, butter etc'. She also noted: 'it should be a light meal but its solidity must of course in some degree be proportionate to the time it is intended to enable you to wait for your dinner and the amount of exercise you take in the meantime.'[21] Lunch at 12.30 or 1 p.m. became established as a family meal at home and as a light, regular meal rather than a snack. Leftovers from dinner the night before were often reheated and served. Major L ... was enthusiastic about hunting luncheons and travelling luncheons, which required special cases fitted to hold meat cutlets or a meat pie, bread, cake and bottles of water or wine. Business and professional men did not usually lunch because it broke up the working day; at best they had a snack and a glass of wine to keep them going. Their clerks either had a substantial breakfast or took a snack from home.

Ladies still had afternoon tea about 4 p.m.; as in the eighteenth century, this was a social occasion to display fine china and eat delicate small cakes. By mid-century high tea was introduced, an hour or two later. It was most popular in the north of the country and was a substantial family meal with meat, fish, cheese, bread and butter, preserves, baked goods and sweets. Sweet and savoury foods, mostly cold, were put on the table at the same time and people chose what they preferred. It was, of course, accompanied by tea. Originally, it was probably a working-class meal timed for the early evening when labourers returned home and the family relaxed together. It extended to be the early evening meal for provincial middle-class families too, while upper-class children continued to have tea in the nursery and their parents dined at 7 or even 8 p.m.

Dinner parties were the most important form of entertaining for the upper and middle classes, probably once or twice a week for the former, once or twice a month for the latter. At dinner parties, the mistress of the house and other ladies were seated at the head of the table, the master and the male guests at the bottom. Early in the century dinners were usually of two courses with removes (side dishes). Dishes for the first course were put on the table and diners helped themselves. If there was meat or fish to carve for the second course, it was done by the host, and servants passed the plates to guests. Other dishes for the second course were set out and again guests helped themselves. If there was a cheese course, it was arranged in the same way, then the table was cleared completely and dessert was served. Throughout the meal for wealthy families the butler and his staff served wine and other drinks.

After dessert the ladies withdrew, and the men enjoyed their port. This style of dining, called *service à la française*, was standard among the middle and upper classes; the menu differed according to the finances of the host. By the second half of the century in the most fashionable and wealthiest households, it was replaced by *service à la russe*. This style of dining required many more staff because all dishes were offered by servants instead of guests helping themselves. It required more china and cutlery, and much more space for servants to work. As dishes were no longer put on the table, displays of flowers in silver or glass épergnes took their place. *Cassell's New Universal Cookery Book* (1896) gave lengthy advice on which colours of silk best offset different colours of flowers for the table decoration.

Seating at dinner changed as well; now each gentleman escorted a lady in to dinner and sat next to her. In this intensely class-conscious society, precedence was strictly observed. Little books of etiquette were published to tell young women how to behave on these social occasions and how to organize them.

On evenings when there was a ball or other social entertainment after dinner, guests were offered an elegant supper of cold dishes. Cold meats were garnished with herbs, raised pies with chopped aspic, while fish and poultry were coated in aspic for a glossy appearance. People helped themselves and sat at small tables with other guests. Mrs Beeton suggested dishes she considered suitable for a standing supper, which included 'beef, ham, tongue sandwiches, lobster and oyster patties, sausage rolls . . . galantine of veal . . . custard in glasses, compôte of fruits, several dishes of small fancy pastry, dishes of fresh fruits'.[22] For families who had high tea, her supper recommendations were a slice of cake and a glass of wine or bread and cheese and a glass of beer.

Many of the working class still had dinner in the middle of the day and a light supper in the evening; others had a snack at midday and high tea or more filling supper when they arrived home. Domestic servants almost always had their main meal at midday and a supper of bread and cheese or something similar. The kitchen staff in the country and town houses of the rich continued in the same roles as in the past.

As in the eighteenth century, taverns and chop houses provided much of the food for town dwellers with no or few cooking facilities. Standards varied, but one tavern retained its high standards: businessmen, politicians and other influential men continued to hold meetings and dine at the London Tavern in Bishopsgate, as they had in Farley's day. Its clientele could also be found in the new clubs of the West End, some of which came to owe their celebrity to their chefs. George Dodd noted in 1856 that clubs brought economy into fashion because an excellent dinner at a club cost no more than a mediocre dinner at a dining room. He also observed that clubs had helped eliminate 'the once fashionable vice of drunkenness'.[23] The other place to find good food was in the private hotels around Piccadilly and St James's; Francatelli ran one for some years. These hotels were only open to residents and there was no dining room, at least initially. Residents took a suite of rooms and their meals were sent up.[24]

Lower down the scale were the dining rooms frequented by shopmen and clerks. Dodd found most to be much cleaner and nearly as economical as the cookshops: 'The provisions are uniformly good; the cookery and serving are fairly managed.'[25] A constant stream of customers from midday until 6 p.m. enabled them to keep the charges down. He was critical of cookshops: 'the meat purchased is cheap and common, the soups and puddings are of questionable character; the charges made are exceedingly low; and the demand, about twelve or one o'clock in the day, is immense.'[26]

Many of Dickens's characters took their dinner home from the cookshop; David Copperfield served his friends a three-course meal all bought from the pastry cook. In *Oliver Twist*, describing the thieves' market frequented by Fagin, Dickens wrote: 'Confined as the limits of Field Lane are, it has its barber, its coffee-shop, its beer-shop, and its fried-fish warehouse.'[27] Fried fish shops were emerging as people realized that, once fried, the fish would keep a bit longer. Mayhew also wrote of an itinerant vendor who hawked fried fish with bread around the public houses. It is possible that fish coated in batter and fried was introduced by Sephardic Jewish immigrants from Spain and Portugal – they had a tradition of frying fish in oil – but it may also have originated with someone like Mayhew's vendor who had worked as a servant in a gentleman's house and fallen on hard times. Fried fish shops were established in the industrial towns of Yorkshire and Lancashire at about the same time. English cooks usually used lard rather than oil.

Soyer includes a recipe for 'Fried Fish, Jewish Fashion' in *A Shilling Cookery for the People*. He uses halibut or flounder and fries it in fat or lard in a frying pan – it is not deep fried – noting that Jews would use oil, and recommends serving it with salt and lemon. He also notes that it is good cold with cucumber, oil and vinegar. He adds that Jewish families told him that the fish will keep for several days.

Sir Shirley Murphy, London's Medical Officer of Health in 1906, recorded that there were a few fried fish shops in 1851, the year of the Great Exhibition. He noted that the fish was usually sold with baked potatoes or bread, and it was in the 1870s that the practice of selling fried fish *à la mode*, that is with chips, was introduced from France.[28] There are earlier English recipes for potatoes sliced thinly, but not chips. In *The Cook's Oracle*, William Kitchiner shaved the potatoes round and round 'as you would peel a lemon', fried them in boiling lard and served them with salt. Fifteen years later, Eliza Acton made crisped potatoes or potato-ribbons to serve with cheese. The potatoes were pared into long ribbons and fried in butter. Her plainer recipe for fried potatoes is perhaps nearer to chips: the potatoes were sliced thinly or pared in ribbons and thrown into boiling butter or clarified dripping. She observed: 'this is an admirable way of dressing potatoes, very common on the Continent, but less so in England than it deserves to be.'[29] Gerald Priestland tracked down a very old customer of a shop in Bethnal Green who remembered getting daily orders of fish and unpeeled chips for his parents and siblings in 1884.[30] As cooking facilities in poorer households remained limited and both men and women worked long hours, dinner from the fish and chip shop became a regular feature of working-class life.

More technical innovations changed the English diet. Preservation was one of the most significant. A French confectioner, Nicolas Appert, started to experiment with preserving foodstuffs at the end of the eighteenth century. He put foods in partially closed glass jars, placed them in boiling water to expel air, and then sealed them with cork and wax. Napoleon was impressed by his work and saw this as a useful way of supplying an army. A few years later, an English merchant, Peter Durand, conceived the idea of using tin for the same purpose, and was granted a patent in 1810 to can vegetable and animal foods. A few years later he sold the patent to Donkin and Hall, who set up a canning factory to supply the British army and the colonial service. By the 1820s tinned foods were widely accepted in Europe and the United States.

Tinned meats developed rapidly, and soon they were imported from Australia and America. *Cassell's New Universal Cookery Book* noted that tinned meats had much improved since the first arrivals, and recommended that the meat should be taken from the tin in good-sized lumps so that it did not get stringy, and be used in a dish such as Irish stew.

Tinned fruits from America came soon after. In 1871 the Fray Bentos canning factory was established in Argentina and large quantities of Fray Bentos Corned Beef reached England a few years later. At home, sweetened, condensed milk was canned and was cheap enough to be sold to the poor instead of fresh milk. It was not until the early years of the twentieth century that tinned baked beans in tomato sauce, invented by H. J. Heinz in the 1890s, were rather unenthusiastically tried in England. The essential tin-opener was introduced in the kitchen.

Margarine arrived in England from France in the 1870s; it was created by French chemists charged with finding a cheap butter substitute. Initially, it was made from beef tallow, then from a combination of vegetable oils. Cheap jams were made from vegetable pulp, colouring, sugar and artificial flavouring – another food of the poor without nourishment.

Bread lost much of its vitamin content with the shift to roller-milling in the 1860s. The flour passed through a series of rollers that eliminated the bran and wheatgerm and produced a white flour with few nutrients and which was also chlorine bleached. If a little bran was added back to the processed flour, the bread could be sold as brown or wheatmeal; it was not wholemeal.

The use of additives had continued throughout the century in beer, bread, tea, pickles and many other processed foods. The 1875 Sale of Food and Drugs Act required that additives be named on the packaging so that consumers knew what they were buying;

public analysts were appointed to check foods and, if necessary, prosecute the producers.

Improvements in refrigeration led to fitting out the holds of ships to carry frozen mutton and beef from Australia in the 1880s; this meat was affordable to the working classes once or twice a week as their wages had risen and prices were cheap and stable. More frozen meat was imported from America, Argentina and New Zealand.

Another development in the rapidly growing food industry was the expansion of sweet biscuit making. Originally, biscuits were hard and dry, made only with flour and water, to be taken to sea. Some confectioners had started to make batches of sweet biscuits with butter, eggs and flour. By the middle of the century, when machinery for cutting and stamping biscuits was developed, factories opened making a variety of biscuits with different flavours. Huntley & Palmers, Peek Frean, Carr, McVitie & Price were among the first companies to develop this profitable business.

In the eighteenth century several confectioners had established successful businesses in London. James Gunter's enterprise was certainly flourishing into the nineteenth century, given that Jarrin, his confectioner, had preserved more than 2,000 bottles of fruit by the Appert system in 1820. A few years later Jarrin published his own book, *The Italian Confectioner*, a thorough treatment of all aspects of sugar work, chocolate, marmalades and jellies, fruit preserves, creams and ices. He was skilled in moulding ices into fruit shapes and colouring them. He also noted that fruits preserved without sugar under the Appert system were well suited to making ice cream. Jarrin's speciality was in making table ornaments, both edible (*pièce montée*) and inedible (*assiette montée*), reminders of the 'banquetting stuffe' of the past.

His book also includes table layouts for desserts for four to thirty persons; given the wide choice that was deemed acceptable, if a dinner was to be given for more than ten people, the hostess would have been well advised to follow Eliza Acton's advice and buy all or most of her desserts from a reputable confectioner. London had many to choose from. Early in the century the most renowned was Monsieur Parmentier, 'the celebrated confectioner to the Prince Regent and to the Dukes of York and Kent'.[31] Elaborately moulded ices and jellies were expected at all fashionable dinner parties. The London confectionery business required huge amounts of ice. Frequent shipments arrived from Norway on a massive scale, and later from Greenland. All grand houses had to have their ice houses to chill the desserts, just as they needed bain-marie cases to keep sauces and garnishes warm.

Another person whose business depended on a continuous supply of ice was Mrs Agnes Marshall, a formidable entrepreneur renowned for her ice creams and chilled desserts, and many other accomplishments. She and her husband opened the Marshall

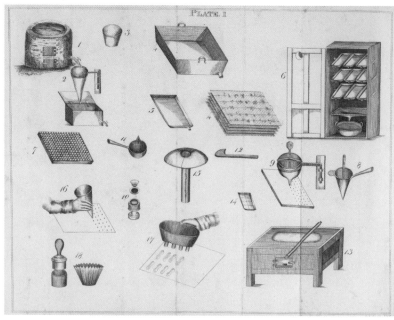

Confectionery equipment, engraving from G. A. Jarrin,
The Italian Confectioner (1820).

Bill of fare for 24 to 30 persons, from G. A. Jarrin, *The Italian Confectioner* (1829).

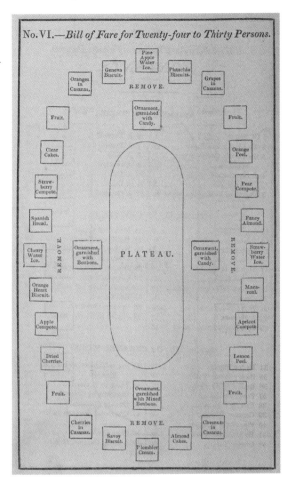

School of Cookery in 1883 offering a variety of courses to thousands of students; they employed specialist teachers for some topics: a colonel who had served in India taught curries, and a Cordon Bleu graduate, haute cuisine. The Marshalls also opened an agency for domestic staff, a shop that sold foods made in the school along with spices and flavourings sold under their own name. Another shop sold cooking utensils: fancy moulds for ices and desserts, her patent freezer and ice cave, cabinet refrigerators and ice tools. In 1886 they started a weekly magazine, *The Table*.

Spinning sugar, illustration from Agnes B. Marshall, *Larger Cookery Book of Extra Recipes* (1891).

Her first cookery book, *The Book of Ices*, came out in 1886, and three more followed: two general books that were used in the school and *Fancy Ices* in 1894. She invented the handheld edible ice cream cone; the recipe is in her 1888 *Mrs Marshall's Book of Cookery*, and ice cream in a cone was sold in the shop. In 1885 she was granted a patent for an ice cream machine that could freeze a pint of ice cream in five minutes. She also recommended using liquid nitrogen to make it.

As the Victorian era neared its end, although the diet of many working-class people had improved, it was often inadequate for the work they did, and many families still survived on tea, bread and potatoes. However, some employers were beginning to recognize a social responsibility for their workers, and among the foremost were the Lever Brothers, who took over a small soap works in Cheshire, where they invented a new form of soap. In 1888 the brothers built a 'model village', Port Sunlight in the Wirral, to house their workers and set up a new factory alongside. They were very concerned with industrial welfare and provided schools, a church and a meeting hall to use for events as well as simply for socializing. The main chocolate manufacturers, most of them Quaker families – Rowntree, Cadbury and Fry – opened kitchens and dining rooms for employees to heat their own foods or buy ready-prepared meals at cost. Jacobs, Huntley & Palmer, Colman's mustard and others followed their example. Many other businesses made kitchens and dining rooms available to their staff to bring and heat their own food or buy a meal at a fair price.

By the end of Victoria's reign England had acquired a great empire and huge wealth, which enhanced the country's standing worldwide. What soon became clear was that the commercial and

Fry's Chocolate, postcard, 1912, illustrated by Tom Browne.

Staff dining room at Cadbury's chocolate factory in Bournville, 1930s.

industrial successes of the last seventy years had been achieved in appalling conditions, with great neglect and suffering. The physique and health of the working classes had deteriorated dramatically. B. Seebohm Rowntree's 1901 study of living conditions in the city of York was largely concerned with housing and the need for pure water and good drainage, but also drew attention to the role of diet in health. Most families lived on white bread and many went hungry. In most cases dire poverty was the cause.[32]

The government and the upper and middle classes appeared to be indifferent: 'It is no exaggeration to say that the opening of the twentieth century saw malnutrition more rife in England than it had been since the great dearths of medieval and Tudor times.'[33] The government paid little attention to Rowntree's study until a year later, when the director general of the Army Medical Service reported that there were insufficient men of satisfactory physique to recruit for the South African War. A committee was set up to examine his findings and it became clear that nothing Rowntree had stated was exaggerated; overcrowding, bad sanitation and factory conditions were contributing factors, but semi-starvation due to poverty was a root cause of ill-health and poor physique. Boys aged ten to twelve who were students at private schools were 12.7 centimetres (5 in.) taller than those at council schools.[34]

Nineteenth-century recipes

Cauliflower with parmesan cheese

Eliza Acton, *Modern Cookery, for Private Families* (London, 1845)

Take all the green leaves from two or three fine white cauliflowers, and cut the stalks off very closely, so that they will stand upright in the dish in which they are served; boil them tolerably tender, but not sufficiently so as to hazard their breaking; drain them well, and dish them, so as to give the whole the appearance of one cauliflower; pour a little good white sauce equally over the tops, and on this strew grated Parmesan cheese, drop over it a little clarified butter, add another layer of cheese, and cover the whole with the finest breadcrumbs; moisten these with more clarified butter, and brown them with a salamander, or set the dish into the oven, to give them colour; pour white sauce round the cauliflowers and send them very hot to table.

The Poet's Salad

To make this condiment your poet begs
The pounded yellow of two hard-boiled eggs;
Two boiled potatoes passed through the kitchen sieve,
Smoothness and softness to the salad give.
Let onion atoms lurk within the bowl
And, half-suspected, animate the whole.
Of mordant mustard add a single spoon,
Distrust the condiment that bites so soon;
But deem it not, though man of herbs, a fault
To add a double quantity of salt;
Four times the spoon with oil of Lucca crown,
And twice with vinegar procured from town
and lastly over the flavoured compound toss
a magic soupçon of anchovies sauce.
Oh green and glorious! Oh, herbaceous Street!
Twould tempt the dying anchorite to eat;
Back to the world he'd turn his fleeting soul,
And plunge his fingers in the salad bowl!
Serenely full, the epicure would say,
'Fate cannot harm me, I have dined today.'

NOTE: Revd Sydney Smith (1771–1845) often preached on the virtues of a sensible diet in his sermons. He was a good cook and turned this salad recipe into a poem for his friends. Versions were quoted in contemporary cookery books, including Eliza Acton's and Charles Herman Senn's. Make it with robust greens – watercress, chicory, rocket and cos lettuce.

Stewed duck and peas

Alexis Soyer, *The Modern Housewife* (London, 1850)

Procure a duck with the legs trussed inside, which put into a stewpan with two ounces of butter and a quarter of a pound of streaked bacon, let it remain over a fire, stirring occasionally until lightly browned, when add a tablespoon of flour (mix well) and a quart of broth or water, stir round gently until boiling, when skim and add twenty button onions, a bunch of parsley, with a bay-leaf and two cloves, let simmer a quarter of an hour, then add a quart of nice young peas, let simmer until done, which will take about half an hour longer, take out the duck, place it on your dish (taking away the string it was trussed with), take out the parsley and bay-leaf, season the peas with a little pepper, salt and sugar, skim the fat, reduce a little if not sufficiently thick, pour over the duck and serve.

Savoury soufflé omelet

Charles Herman Senn, *Recherché Side Dishes* (London, 1899)

Separate three yolks of eggs from the whites, put the yolks in a basin, work well, and add a teaspoonful of chopped parsley, half a teaspoonful of chopped shallots, and a salt spoonful of dried savoury herbs. Whip the white of egg to a stiff froth, mix gradually with the yolks, season with a little salt and a pinch of cayenne. Dress neatly in a buttered gratin dish, sprinkle with grated Parmesan, and bake in a moderate oven for about fifteen minutes.

English macaroons

G. A. Jarrin, *The Italian Confectioner* (London, 1823)

One pound of sweet Almonds, one pound and a quarter of Sugar, six whites of Eggs, and the raspings of two Lemons.

Pound the Almonds very fine with six whites of eggs, or a few more if required, as this depends on the size of the eggs; feel the almonds, and if there be no lumps in them they will do, then add your powder sugar, and mix it well with the lemon raspings. Dress them on wafer paper, of what size or shape you please; the general shape is oval; bake them in a moderate heat; when done let them stand till cold, then cut the wafer paper around them, but leave it on the bottoms of the cakes.

To make a trifle

Isabella Beeton, *The Book of Household Management* (London, 1861)

INGREDIENTS – For the whip, 1 pint of cream, 3 oz of pounded sugar, the whites of 2 eggs, a small glass of sherry or raisin wine. For the trifle, 1 pint of custard, made with 8 eggs to a pint of milk; 6 small sponge cakes or 6 slices of sponge cake; 12 macaroons, 2 dozen ratafias, 2 oz of sweet almonds, the grated rind of 1 lemon, a layer of raspberry or strawberry jam, ½ pint of sherry or sweet wine, 6 table-spoonfuls of brandy.

Mode – The whip to lay over the top of the trifle should be made the day before it is required for table, as the flavour is better, and it is much more solid than when prepared the same day. Put into a large bowl the pounded sugar, the whites of the eggs, which should be beaten to a stiff froth, a glass of sherry or sweet wine, and the cream. Whisk these ingredients well in a cool place, and take off the froth with a skimmer as fast as it rises, and put it on a sieve to drain; continue the whisking till there is sufficient of the whip, which must be put away in a cold place to drain. The next day, place the sponge-cakes, macaroons and ratafias at the bottom of a trifle-dish; pour over them ½ pint of sherry or sweet wine, mixed with 6 tablespoonfuls of brandy, and should this proportion of wine not be found quite sufficient, add a little more, as the cakes should be well soaked. Over the cakes put the grated lemon rind, the sweet almonds, blanched and cut into strips, and a layer of raspberry or strawberry jam. Make a good custard by the recipe above, using 8 instead of 5 eggs to the pint of milk, and let this cool a little; then pour it over the cakes etc. The whip being made the day previously, and the trifle prepared, there remains nothing to do now but heap the whip lightly over the top: this should stand as high as possible, and it may be garnished with strips of bright currant jelly, crystallized sweetmeats, or flowers; the small coloured comfits are sometimes used for the purpose of garnishing a trifle, but they are now considered rather old-fashioned.

Average cost, with cream at 1s per pint 5s 6d
Sufficient for 1 trifle.
Seasonable at any time.

Ingoldsby Christmas puddings

Eliza Acton, *Modern Cookery, for Private Families* (London, 1845)

Mix very thoroughly one pound of finely grated bread with the same quantity of flour, two pounds of raisins stoned, two of currants, two of suet, minced small, one of sugar, half a pound of candied peel, one nutmeg, half an ounce of mixed spice, and the grated rinds of two lemons; mix the whole with sixteen eggs well beaten and strained, and add four glasses of brandy. These proportions will make three puddings of good size, each of which should be boiled six hours.

Bread-crumbs 1 lb; flour 1 lb; suet 2 lbs; currants 2 lbs; raisins 2 lbs; sugar 1 lb; candied peel ½ lb; rinds of lemons 2; nutmegs 1; mixed spice ½ oz; salt ¼ oz; eggs 16; brandy 4 glassesful: 6 hours.

Obs. – A fourth part of the ingredients given above, will make a pudding of sufficient size for a small party: to render this *very rich* half the flour and bread-crumbs may be omitted, and a few spoonsful of apricot marmalade well blended with the remainder of the mixture.*

*Rather less liquid will be required to moisten the pudding when this is done, and four hours and a quarter will boil it.

AUTHOR's NOTE: this has been our family
Christmas pudding for many years.

6

From Edwardian Picnics
to the Microwave

I n the early years of the twentieth century the stark contrast between the lives of the rich and the poor continued. In 1901 Edward VII inherited the crown from Queen Victoria. As Prince of Wales for more than forty years, he had performed ceremonial duties and undertaken diplomatic missions and was immensely popular. He was known for his taste for opulence, comfort, mistresses, clothes, good food and wine. Edwardian high society indulged in extravagance in everything: country house parties, balls, dinners, racing and hunting picnic luncheons.

Picnics in the country had been enjoyed for many years, particularly in attractive places. Towards the end of Victoria's reign and into Edwardian times, grand picnic parties became extremely popular. Mrs Beeton had given bills of fare for different numbers of people. They included many bottles of wines, brandy and non-alcoholic drinks and huge quantities of the best foods. In addition, the 'Things not to be Forgotten at a Picnic' included 'a stick of horseradish, a bottle of good mint sauce, well corked, a bottle of salad dressing, a bottle of vinegar, made mustard, pepper, salt, good oil and pounded sugar'. There is also a list of the china and cutlery, tumblers and wine glasses needed, which ends with 'Take three corkscrews'. An army of servants must have been needed to get everything to the picnic spot and to serve the meal. By the time Mrs Leyel wrote *Picnics for Motorists* in 1936, the quantities of food

George Goodwin Kilburne, *Picnic Party on the Lagoon*, *c.* 1877,
watercolour and gouache.

and the equipment required had been restricted to what would fit
in the boot and serve the number of people in a car. She suggested
suitable picnic baskets and fittings, and gave sixty menus with
three to five courses, with beer or white wine to drink.

The Edwardians added more courses to lunches and dinners,
and French cuisine once more predominated. In London the aristocracy and the rich dined in clubs and restaurants. In his *Dinners
and Diners* (1901) Lieutenant Colonel Nathaniel Newnham-Davis
included more than a hundred restaurants with their style of cooking; many were French or Italian, a few old English, two German,
one Jewish, one fish and tripe, and a couple were vegetarian. Some
offered haute cuisine, others table d'hôte, grill or à la carte. His
personal knowledge of the place and the cooking in each restaurant is evident, as are many of his descriptions of the menus and
meals. He describes a dinner at Kettners in Soho to which he took
an elderly lady whom he had known in India. He requested a small
private dining room and this menu:

Caviar

Consommé à la Colbert

Filets de sole à la Joinville

Langue de boeuf aux champignons

Epinards Pommes Anna

Poulet à la Parmentier

Salade

Asperges Sauce mousseline

Biscuits glacées

Dessert

It was accompanied by a bottle of Moet '89, just chilled.
The bill: two dinners, £1 1s; one Moet, 15s; two cafés, 1s;
two liqueurs, 2s; total, £1 19s

On another occasion he describes dinner at the Savoy Hotel under Maître Escoffier. Newnham-Davis went to the Savoy the morning of the dinner to discuss the menu with the maître d'hotel and they agreed on hors d'oeuvre, borscht (a speciality of the Savoy), a mousse as entrée, poulet de grain polonaise, parfait de foie gras, English asparagus and pêches glacées vanille. He notes that Escoffier insisted on his hot dishes being scrupulously una-dorned, and that the cold dishes gave the opportunity to 'M. Escoffier and his staff to show what they could do in the way of decoration'. The bill: two couverts, 1s; borscht, 3s; sole Savoy, 6s; mousse jambon, 6s; poulet polonaise, 8s; salade, 2s; foie gras, 6s; asperges verts, 7s 6d; pêches glacées vanille, 7s; one bottle champagne 15s; café, 2s; liqueurs, 2s; total £3 5s 6d.

In his later book, *The Gourmet's Guide to London* (1914), Newnham-Davis tried the newly opened Cathay restaurant. He had eaten some Chinese food when stationed in the East, and after describing some of his experiences elsewhere, both good and bad, he decided on the set luncheon. The soup, with strips of bamboo and morsels of chicken flesh, 'tasted very much like the chicken

SPECIMEN BILL OF FARE

Of a Vegetarian Dinner at

THE 'ALPHA,'

"The First Food Reform Restaurant,"

23, OXFORD STREET, LONDON, W.,

OPPOSITE THE "OXFORD,"

Thursday, July 18th, 1889.

SOUPS.		PORRIDGES.	
Lentil		Oatmeal	With Sugar
Vegetable	3d.	Wheaten	or 3d.
Tapioca Milk	BREAD	Maize Mush	Syrup.
Green Pea	EXTRA.	Anglo-Scotch	

SAVOURIES.

Lentil Cutlet, Sauce, and Beans	3d.
Lentil Cutlet, and Green Peas	3d.
Lentil Cutlet, and Vegetable Marrow	3d.
Savoury Pie and Parsley Sauce	4d.
Green Peas, Mint Sauce, and New Potatoes	4d.
Vegetable Marrow, Parsley Sauce, and New Potatoes	4d.
Macaroni and Tomato Omelette	4d.
Tomatoes and Macaroni	4d.

EXTRA VEGETABLES.

Green Peas	2d.	Mashed Potatoes	1d.
Vegetable Marrow	2d.	Tomatoes	2d.
Runner Beans	2d.	Haricots	2d.
New Potatoes	2d.	Macaroni	2d.

SWEET PUDDINGS.		PASTRY.	
Sago Custard	3d.	Apple Tart	3d.
Cold Rice	3d.	Peach Tart	3d.
Bread and Butter	3d.	Black Currant Tart	3d.
Maize and Fruit	4d.	Red Currant Tart and Custard	4d.
Wheat and Fruit	4d.		
Macaroni and Jam	4d.		

STEWED FRUITS.		SUNDRIES.	
		Tea or Coffee	2d.
Black Currants		Chocolate	2d.
Red Currants		Cocoa	2d.
Peaches		Mineral Waters	1d. & 2d.
Prunes		Soda and Milk	2d.
Pine Apple		Cheese	1d. & 2d.
		Cake	2d.
		Mixed Salad	3d.
		Iced Lemonade	2d

FREDK. TARRANT & SON, Camberwell Printing Works, 110 Camberwell Road.

An 1889 menu from The Alpha, considered London's first vegetarian restaurant.

Auguste Escoffier and his staff at the Carlton in London, 1899–1920.

Customers enjoying afternoon tea at Lyons' Corner House on
Coventry Street, London, 1942.

broth that one is given when one is ill and on a low diet'. The fried
chicken and vegetables were 'quite good eating, and the taste of
the bamboo shoot in it was particularly pleasant to the palate'.
He declined the roast pork, but enjoyed a plate of 'chow chow,
an admirable sweet' and enjoyed his excellent Chinese tea without sugar or milk. He paid 2*s* 6*d* for his lunch and described it as a
pleasant experiment. He advised readers who would like to explore
Chinese food in comfort to follow his lead.

The Dickensian cookshops of the last century were replaced
by snack bars and cafeterias as more of the less wealthy ventured
to eat out and not rely on the fish and chip shop. Milk bars, with
their high bar stools and smart décor, were enormously popular.
Their frothy milk drinks with exotic names had great appeal. The
tea shops of J. Lyons and Co., launched in the last years of the
nineteenth century, were meeting places to have a cup of tea and

a cake or ice cream. They became reliable places for shoppers and office workers to have a quick snack or a cheap, bland meal. The tea shops remained popular until 1981, when the last one closed. Lyons produced their own bread, cakes and other baked goods, which were also sold at retail counters. In 1909 they opened their Corner Houses, with a food hall on the ground floor and restaurants and other services upstairs, that were smarter and more expensive than the tea shops. It was now becoming acceptable for women to go to restaurants without a male escort and Lyons opened the opulent Trocadero in 1903 to attract them. It had several restaurants, some with space for dancing, private dining rooms, an orchestra in the great hall and 'glittering comfort' throughout.

The many wealthy American visitors to London in the early decades of the century brought with them the new rhythms of jazz and their love of cocktails, which were quickly adopted by the smart crowd. Cocktail bars sprang up, often in hotels, serving these glamorous new drinks. Tea dances often meant dances where cocktails were served. Jazz became as fashionable as cocktails. The early 1920s financial boom marked a release from austerity, and the rich intended to enjoy themselves dining and dancing. The Savoy Hotel installed a dance floor in the restaurant. Cabaret and dinner became another way to spend an evening for the well-to-do. London was a vibrant city that attracted people from all parts of the globe. This was also a time of technological innovation; electricity had been used in a limited fashion in the nineteenth century, but now there were street lighting, the new telegraph system, cars and motorcycles, faster trains, ocean liners and cargo ships, and by the 1920s, radio.

It was also the time when women finally won the franchise. Women's suffrage societies had submitted many bills to parliament towards the end of the nineteenth century, but they were rejected because Queen Victoria was opposed to the movement. The Women's Social and Political Union led by Emmeline Pankhurst became involved in protests, which were followed by hunger strikes in prison. Finally, in 1918 an Act of Parliament was passed giving the franchise to women over thirty years old who met a property qualification. In 1928 the age was lowered to 21 to be on an equal footing with male voters. The dominant role of the House of Lords was broken by the Liberal government in 1911, and the land-owning class no longer had a commanding role in determining how the country was run.

While the wealthy were feasting and partying, most of the population continued to live a very different life. At this time the

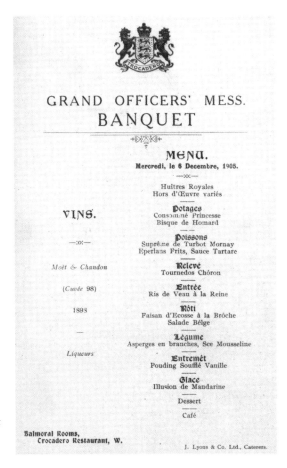

Menu for a banquet at Trocadero Restaurant, 1905.

middle classes spent about 40 per cent of their income on food and drink, and the working classes about 70 per cent. At the outbreak of the First World War in 1914, wages were little higher than they had been twenty years earlier, but the cost of living was much higher, which led to many strikes. The report of the committee set up to examine Rowntree's findings was published in 1904, and while it focused on appalling housing conditions and the lack of sanitation, it also emphasized the inadequate diet of poor families. They were severely undernourished, surviving on a basic diet of white bread and tea. Very few babies were breastfed because their mothers were too undernourished to produce milk; most were raised on sweetened condensed skimmed milk. Poor children were given bread and jam to eat and little else. Thousands of young children, often shoeless and dressed in little more than rags, were close to starvation; rickets and bad teeth were common. The government had to acknowledge that these children must be properly fed before they could benefit from attending school. An Education Act was passed to provide school meals, and by 1911 more than 200,000 poor children were fed under it. It would be some years before the newly recognized science of nutrition was used to determine the best foods to feed the poor affordably. Some improvements were slowly made in housing, but the city slums remained overcrowded, smelly and squalid. The condition of the poor had not improved greatly some thirty years later when George Orwell wrote in *The Road to Wigan Pier* (1937):

> The miner's family spend only tenpence a week on green vegetables . . . and nothing on fruit; but they spend one and nine on sugar (about eight pounds of sugar, that is) and a shilling on tea. The half-crown spent on meat might represent a small joint and the materials for a stew; probably as often as not it would represent four or five tins of bully beef. The basis of their diet, therefore, is white bread

and margarine, corned beef, sugared tea and potatoes – an appalling diet.[1]

The medical establishment was slow to accept that bread made solely from roller-milled flour was not nutritious. It was digestible and so was thought unlikely to be damaging to health. Several years elapsed before the absence of vitamins and mineral salts in the flour was recognized; the first vitamins were chemically defined in 1926.

The war effort demanded that more men and women work long hours in foundries, munitions and armaments factories, and they had to be properly fed if they were to work efficiently. Industrial canteens were established where people paid a minimal sum or nothing. On 20 September 1916 *The Times* reported, 'The provision of proper meals for the workers is, indeed, an indispensable

Children eating their school meals, 1943.

condition for the maintenance of output on which our fighting forces depend, not only for victory but for their very lives.' The diet considered necessary for a worker should contain:

A sufficient quantity of nutritive material in proper proportions.

Suitably mixed.
Easily digestible.
Appetizing and attractive.
Obtainable at low cost.

An average factory canteen menu consisted of 'soup, meat and two vegetables, made-up dish, pudding, tea'.[2] A made-up dish was a stew or pie or something similar.

During the first two years of the war, there were no acute food shortages, even though the country relied on significant supplies of imported food, especially flour, but at the end of 1916 the government appointed a Food Controller. Initially, his role was to supervise food imports and stocks, particularly of flour and sugar. However, in 1917, as the situation worsened, all essential supplies of food and beverages, whether imported or home produced, were bought by the Food Controller at fixed prices. Households were registered so that fair distribution could be made; the price of bread dropped thanks to a government subsidy, and a scale of prices for meat was established. Sugar had been rationed since early 1916, and general rationing was decreed early in 1918. It continued until late 1920.

Wartime feeding had a far-reaching effect on developments in the medical awareness of the significance of different foods in the diet, and in the preparation of food, its storage and transportation. It became widely accepted that the lack of physical fitness was the result of inadequate nutrition, and medical research programmes were established to investigate the link. Research was also conducted into food technology – how to prepare, preserve and store perishable foods. Surveys of different regions of the country showed that in general people were getting enough to eat, but for the poorest the quality of the food was very low.

After many years of semi-neglect, during the war British agriculture was required to increase production, especially of wheat, meat, vegetables and dairy products, in order to reduce imports. Farming was subsidized and prices were regulated. After the war, when standards of living had improved somewhat, there was demand for 'better' foods: eggs, butter, fruit, vegetables and meat could easily be produced locally. Wheat, flour, rice, sugar and animal foodstuffs continued to be imported.

For well-off families the variety of foods increased, both those imported and those produced locally. A wider range of cheeses, more canned foods and a variety of biscuits filled the shelves, and most fresh foods were still weighed and wrapped for each customer. Canned foods continued to be imported, but in the 1920s more British companies started to can British fruits and vegetables; peas were particularly popular. As the urban populations grew, multiple grocers developed, buying goods more cheaply in bulk and selling through several outlets. In 1869 the first Sainsbury's, run by a husband and wife, had opened in London in Drury Lane, then a poor part of the city. Early in the twentieth century it expanded into a multiple business, alongside Home and Colonial, Liptons and the newly formed co-operative societies, which rapidly acquired members in the 1920s and '30s. These stores provided food of reasonable quality more cheaply, and daily fresh supplies became the norm. As competition increased, branding started with eye-catching packaging and advertisements to entice the shopper. Packaged breakfast cereals arrived from America, while powders to make custard, blancmange and other desserts made life easier for the cook, and flavoured chocolate bars offered more choice. There was still room for independent grocers, butchers, greengrocers and bakers, but increasingly many grocers sold packaged, branded goods.

Many of the women shoppers had very little knowledge about cooking. The *Daily Mail* spotted a market here and commissioned Mrs C. S. Peel to write the *Daily Mail Cookery Book* (1919). Cooking methods are explained, and the recipes are economical and nutritious and interspersed with lively advertisements. They did not require more than basic kitchen equipment and could be cooked on a coal range as well as the new gas cookers. By the 1930s and '40s the manufacturers of gas cookers gave away their own cookery books with purchases.

A short-lived boom came after the war, followed by the Great Depression, which caused mass unemployment throughout the

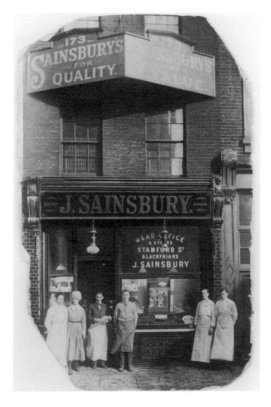

Exterior of the Sainsbury's branch at 173 Drury Lane in Holborn, London, *c.* 1919. This was the first shop opened by John James and Mary Ann Sainsbury in 1869.

industrialized world. Provision for social security and unemployment relief was minimal; in Britain only about half the labour force were covered by it. Between 1929, the year of the great crash on Wall Street, and 1932 global trade fell by 60 per cent and national protectionism took over. Social considerations became as important as economic ones; resolving large-scale unemployment was a key issue. The demand that the incomes of fully employed workers would generate was relied upon to have a stimulating effect on the economy, but this goal was some way off.

In 1929 more than 2 million people were unemployed, and many could only afford what their grandparents and great-grandparents had lived on: white bread, jam, margarine, tea and fried fish. Meat, milk and fresh produce effectively disappeared from their diet. In the early 1930s the Ministry of Health published a list of 'protective foods' – milk, fresh fruit and vegetables – that should ideally form part of the daily diet, to which oily fish such as herring should be added once a week. Milk was provided daily for poor school children at a nominal price, and later became free for all. By 1933 the British Medical Association provided advice on the foods needed for sufficient nourishment and estimated the cost to be 5–6 shillings per man per week.[3] What they had not reckoned with was that this sum was far too high for many families, particularly among the unemployed. A 1934 survey compared data with consumption and cost a hundred years earlier. It showed that tea and sugar had fallen by more than half in price and consumption had increased fivefold per head; meat and fats had fallen in price and consumption doubled, bread consumption had declined and the amount of milk drunk had remained the same, but that was about half of the amount recommended. The diet of the poor might have improved marginally, but they were still underfed.

In the inter-war years the middle class grew as the number of professionals and office workers increased, but they were generally less affluent than at the beginning of the century. Inflation hit hard and they had to make economies, which meant managing with fewer servants, who went to find work at factories and offices. Memories of the difficulties faced during wartime rationing lingered. Grand dinners in the Edwardian style disappeared; lunch and dinner were usually reduced to three courses, except on formal occasions.

Drinking habits changed somewhat too. Wine continued to be served with dinner in upper-class and some wealthier middle-class households. In London cocktails and champagne continued to be the fashion with the lively party crowd, and barmen competed to invent new cocktail mixtures. Poorer families would send out for a jug of beer for a special dinner, but increasingly beer drinking became a social occasion, mostly for men, who met in the pub.

In the introduction to her *Book of English Food*, Arabella Boxer wrote:

> English food of the 1920s and '30s is curiously hard to define, partly because it is understated. It lies at the other end of the spectrum from robust peasant cuisines for it is basically bland in flavour, although the accompanying sauces and garnishes are often sharp, sour, or spicy. Since a contrast of flavour was often the aim, the individual foods were almost always cooked and served separately so that they met for the first time on the plate.

She noted that meals became less formal and the dishes lighter, but good English food still demanded a skilled cook who could prepare quality ingredients needing precise timing without fault, and also produce an elegant presentation.[4]

Breakfasts for the well-to-do were scaled down too. Lady Jekyll recommended aiming for simplicity and, within that, perfection, which meant that breakfast must be hot:

That long metal food-warmer with spirit lamps known as the 'Sluggard's Delight' whereon porridge, coffee, hot dishes can be kept palatable, is a great help. Insist on a water kettle of real efficiency, on a tea-caddy which will contain a delicate as well as a pungent blend of tea, more than one tea-pot, and a small saucepan over a spirit lamp for boiling eggs, with an hour-glass standing sentry near by.[5]

Breakfast for the working class was very different: it consisted of bread and margarine, or very occasionally butter, taken with a cup of strong tea early in the morning. Porridge was eaten in some middle-class households, as were breakfast cereals, eaten with cold milk.

The midday meal was called lunch or dinner depending on class and which part of the country you lived in. Northerners had dinner at midday and high tea in the early evening, which was a substantial family meal with tea and hot meat, fish or vegetables. Afternoon tea resembled the teas of the seventeenth century, when tea was taken alone or with cake or biscuits. Dinner followed in the evening.

At that time all upper-class and upper-middle-class households had a cook, although not all were very skilled. There was much less variety in the dishes eaten than there is today. Most families, even the grandest, had a fairly small selection of meals that they ate regularly.

In her essay 'Kitchens and Their Cooks', Elizabeth David, born in 1913, described the work of the kitchen staff in the manor house where she and her sisters grew up:

There were four sets of meals to be prepared every day: breakfast, lunch, tea and dinner for the dining room; lunch and supper for the nursery (nanny made breakfast and tea);

lunch, tea, a supper tray for the governess for the school-
room, and breakfast, lunch, tea and supper for the servants'
hall. The cooking was done on a coal-burning range. Cups
of tea and cake were always available for outdoor staff
and anyone making a delivery, whether the grocer or the
telegraph boy.

She reflected that the kitchen staff only got through the day at
all because the food was very basic:

> We ate a lot of mutton and beef plainly cooked, with plain
> vegetables. The boiled potatoes were usually put through a
> device called a ricer so that they came up to the nursery in
> dry, flaky mounds ... Puddings weren't much better. Junket
> was slippery and slimy, jam roly-poly greasy, something
> called ground rice pudding dry and stodgy.[6]

A Frenchman who made his mark on English meals at this
time was Marcel Boulestin, who had moved to London earlier
in the century. Before the First World War he had a decorating
business, but when he returned to London after serving in the
French army, there was no demand for decorators and he turned
to cookery writing. His *Simple French Cooking for English Homes*
was published in 1923, with an attractive jacket design and frontispiece by his friend J. E. Laboureur. His is bourgeois family cooking,
not the extravagant table d'hôte menus offered by restaurants. He
points out that French home cooking is economical because all
the 'remnants' are used; there is no waste. His book is directed
to 'people who have a good cook, to those who only have a plain
one, and to those who have not got one at all'. His writing is fresh
and clear; his easy, economical recipes were well received, and the
book was reprinted frequently. The blurb for the first edition of
the book states: 'M. Boulestin dispels the prevalent belief that

French cooking is wasteful and expensive. Nearly all his recipes are well within the reach of a small household. Economy, variety and attraction will be gained by following his methods. His general remarks on food and wine contain much novel and sound advice.' Boulestin wrote several more books, all dealing with family cooking, and articles for *Vogue*, the *Manchester Guardian*, the *Daily Express* and *The Spectator*. In 1925 he opened a London restaurant with a Parisian chef. It had a high culinary reputation thanks to his exacting standards. He was also the first television chef, broadcasting for some of the BBC's earliest experimental programmes in the late 1930s.

Other English food writers were looking at our diet from a different perspective. One was the herbalist Mrs Leyel, who founded the Society of Herbalists and opened Culpeper House in 1927. In 1925 she and Olga Hartley published *The Gentle Art of Cookery* for 'those who appreciate the fact that good cooking is one of the attainable amenities of life if extravagance is eliminated'.[7] Many chapters are arranged by main ingredient so that menus can be devised according to what is available; one has dishes that appeal to children, another caters for cold Sunday suppers, and yet another has recipes for flowers – nasturtium salad, eggs cooked with marigold, primrose vinegar. The final chapter, 'The Alchemist's Cupboard', covers what is required in the store cupboard: bottled sauces, different vinegars, spices, essences, dried fruits, rice, pasta and flour. Through the 1930s Mrs Leyel published 'The Lure of Cookery', a remarkable series of small cookery books on different topics from *Picnics for Motorists* to *The Complete Jam Cupboard*.

At about the same time Florence White, a food journalist who feared that traditional English dishes were being forgotten or lost, founded the English Folk Cookery Association. In her articles she wrote about regional dishes – Stilton cheese, Yorkshire pudding, Melton Mowbray pork pie, Cornish cream – and she asked readers to send in family or regional recipes from all parts of the country. The response was very positive, and in 1932 she published *Good Things in England*, a collection of some eight hundred English recipes 'containing traditional and regional recipes suited to modern tastes'. White felt that French food was becoming dominant in England and wanted to preserve the best English dishes: 'There is no reason why the famous French cuisine and our fine traditional English cookery should be bitter rivals. Both are absolutely distinctive, but equally good in their different ways, and there is plenty of scope . . . even in England, for both.'[8]

In the 1930s more kitchen appliances were available. Even the poorest families had a gas ring, and the more affluent a gas cooker. The heat of the gas rings could be adjusted easily, and dishes could be left to cook in the oven. The cookery books provided by the manufacturers of the new cookers were hugely popular; the recipes were clear and had temperatures and timings for dishes. Time spent cooking could be reduced. Gas, and later electric, refrigerators were installed in wealthier households, and later still came electric kettles, toasters, irons and water heaters. The other great benefit of the gas cookers was that they were easy to clean and no labour was required, unlike fetching wood or coal for a range.

The diet was becoming more varied and the consumer more demanding. Refrigerated apples and pears were imported from the southern hemisphere and also some tropical fruits. Eating out was becoming a more regular occurrence, although the heights of Edwardian dining were gone for good. The wheatlands of Australia and Canada expanded; improvements in refrigeration meant more beef arrived from Argentina, lamb and butter from New Zealand and bacon from Denmark. Competition was fierce. British farmers specialized in vegetables, fruit, milk and eggs for the local market. They became more efficient, adopting more mechanization and fertilizing, and were assisted by government subsidies.

At the outbreak of the Second World War in 1939, the government brought back the Ministry of Food and introduced ration books for the nation. Residents established themselves with a grocer and a butcher who became their regular suppliers. Coupons from the ration books were handed over to the shopkeeper as well as cash. Sugar, butter and bacon were the first foods rationed, soon followed by meat, margarine, cooking fats, preserves and tea. Prices for food were fixed, and the ministry developed a nutritional policy to keep standards as high as possible and to ensure everyone had access to good food. Domestic food production increased significantly: arable acreage increased by 50 per cent, supported by the Dig for Victory campaign. More wheat and vegetables were grown, and fewer animals kept, except cattle for their milk. In some villages families reared a pig to be slaughtered and shared. Many families had allotments where they grew vegetables and sometimes kept hens. It was essential to reduce as much as possible the quantity of food arriving by sea. By 1945 Britain was producing 80 per cent of its own food.

The science of nutrition had advanced significantly and dietetically sufficient rationing schemes were developed. Professor Jack Drummond (who was later knighted) became scientific adviser to the ministry. The link between poverty, poor diet and poor health was now well understood. Bread had to be of a higher nutritive value, so wholemeal flour was used; margarine was fortified with vitamins A and D, eating more oats and green vegetables was recommended, and children and nursing mothers were given a pint of milk a day. Dried eggs, milk powder and dehydrated vegetables were introduced, helping to reduce the tonnage imported, as did importing more canned, boneless meat like corned beef and spam.

Rationing policy allowed a certain amount of choice; meat, bacon, fats, cheese, tea, sugar and preserves were rationed, but bread and potatoes were not, and price controls ensured they were affordable for all. A points scheme was introduced for foods that were considered luxuries and would contribute beneficially to the diet. These included canned salmon, sardines, fruit, dried fruits, biscuits, rice and condensed milk. Adventurous cooks enhanced their meals with foraged wild foods. The diet was very dull and meals were repetitive, but it was fairly healthy. For the poorest undernourished third of the population it brought a big improvement; for the first time they had an adequate diet. Infant mortality rates decreased, as did adult diseases caused by a poor diet.

The Food Advice department of the ministry put out a wide range of information, gave recipes using dried foods and tips on how to eat healthily on the radio, in posters and booklets and in the press. Publishers and newspapers contributed too. One cutting from a London paper is for Corned Beef Cake for 'those who are sick to death of the corned beef in their meat ration'. Bacon fat is melted in a frying pan, a chopped onion added, and it is seasoned with salt, pepper and curry powder. The corned beef is chopped up and added with three times as much cold cooked potato and a dash of Worcester sauce. All is chopped together while slowly cooking and it is shaped into a cake. The cake is turned and cooked on the other side – with practice it can be flipped like a pancake – and served with a lot of fried parsley.

Penguin published a *Wartime 'Good Housekeeping' Cookery Book* compiled by the Good Housekeeping Institute. It had lots of practical information on the best and most economical ways to cook different foods. The recipes range from wartime pastry, noodle steaks with bacon, mystery pie and marmalade made with the skins of sweet oranges, to chocolate shortbread and (perhaps rather optimistically) chestnut stuffing for turkey. Marguerite Patten, a home economist who worked for the Ministry of Food, broadcast a radio programme called the 'Kitchen Front' from 1947, and then presented 'Cookery Club' on television from 1956. She went on to write many successful cookery books.

Housewife surrenders coupons for her supply of bacon, 1943. Consumers
could purchase no more than 4 oz of bacon per week and not more
than 23 pence worth of other meats.

Canteens were established in schools and factories to provide one well-balanced and inexpensive – or free in the case of
poor children – meal a day. British Restaurants were set up in
areas where there were several small factories that did not have
their own canteen so that workers could be assured of a midday
meal. They were open to the public too, but workers had precedence. Other restaurants remained open, but were restricted to a
maximum charge of 5s, which priced out game and some fish and
seafoods, although some managed to include expensive foods by
increasing the price of wine to compensate.

At the end of the war, the population was generally healthier
than it had been at the beginning. The poor ate more and better
than they had in the past, and the rich probably ate less. Fewer
mothers died in childbirth or had stillborn babies; children were

taller and stronger, and rickets and tooth decay were less prevalent. Rationing did not end in 1945; it continued for many foods until 1953, and finally stopped in 1954 when meat and cheese were removed and ration books thrown away.

'In Defence of English Cooking', an article for the *Evening Standard* published on 15 December 1945 and written by George Orwell, argued that many of the best English foods could not be found elsewhere: 'kippers, Yorkshire pudding, Devonshire cream, muffins and crumpets . . . Christmas pudding, treacle tart, apple dumplings'. He cited many more English dishes but noted sadly that foreigners coming to England would be unlikely to taste them because good English cooking was seldom found outside a private house. Restaurants imitated French cooking. He finished: 'It is not a law of nature that every restaurant in England should be either foreign or bad, and the first step towards an improvement will be a less long-suffering attitude in the British public itself.'

The Labour government elected after the war moved towards a 'post-capitalist society' in which the power of the state was greater than that of market forces or any one class. National income redistribution was a political decision; the national minimum wage was revised. In 1945 wages councils regulated pay in the main industries, and major welfare services were put in place. There was much to be sorted out: bombed towns, cities and factories had to be cleared; there was a severe housing shortage, many cities still had appalling slums and many people were homeless. In 1947 the exceptionally cold winter brought the whole country to a standstill. Coal stores froze and could not be moved, while roads and railways were under snowdrifts. Factories closed; there was insufficient fuel for heating, and ice floes appeared off the coast of East Anglia. Crops of wheat and potatoes were ruined, and cattle and sheep died in the deep snow. Rivers flooded with the thaw, inundating much of lowland England. Food supplies were as low as during the war, and bread had to be rationed.

Slowly life improved throughout the country; at this period the population was about 30 million, mostly working class. People continued to work in the pre-war industries: mining, factories, engineering and ship building. The middle class expanded quickly, as staff for the new health service and welfare state were needed. More teachers were needed as the number of grammar schools increased and the school-leaving age was raised to fifteen. Some working-class children attending these schools would be the first from their families to go to university.

Slums were cleared, and towns and cities were rebuilt with new roads and houses, many of them terraced houses with small gardens. Blocks of flats, new parks and new schools were part of the rebuilding process, and the first self-service shops (not yet on the scale of today's supermarkets) were introduced. More houses now had washing machines, refrigerators and television sets.

The National Food Survey in 1959 found that convenience foods – that is, instant coffee, tinned, dehydrated and frozen foods – were increasingly popular, particularly with young families. Soups were top of the list of tinned foods, though sales of packets of dehydrated soup were increasing. Breakfast cereals were eaten regularly and sugared versions were being introduced to the market. Food advertising on television started at around the same time.

In the 1950s and '60s the country opened to people from the empire, particularly from India, Pakistan, Bangladesh, Hong Kong and the Caribbean, initially to fill gaps in the labour market. Many of them found work in the textile towns of Lancashire and Yorkshire, and in manufacturing in the Midlands. Many more worked in the NHS as doctors and nurses. Later migrants came from Africa. They all brought their culture, including their food, with them to cities and towns throughout the country, and some opened restaurants, initially for their fellow immigrants. Gradually, English people ventured to try their food.

Wages and salaries kept pace with, or were a little higher than, the cost of living. Families were smaller, with one or two children, and more women went out to work. They had more labour-saving devices in the kitchen and around the house. Many more convenience foods were on the market: sales of tinned and frozen meat, fruit and vegetables increased, as did sales of chicken. Fresh fish was less popular, but fish and chips flourished, although at higher prices than before.

In 1950 the 5*s* limit on restaurant charges was lifted, so if you had money, you could go out and eat whatever you wanted. Prawn cocktail, steak and chips and Black Forest gâteau became popular standards in restaurants like the Berni Inns, which catered largely for lower-middle-class and working-class people who had probably never eaten out before, except for snacks in the local pub or fish and chips.

Advertisement for Berni Inn, 1983.

In 1951 Raymond Postgate published the first *Good Food Guide*. He deplored the badly cooked food and poor service in many hotels and restaurants, which they excused by referring to the Ministry of Food regulations. It had five hundred entries for restaurants all over the country written by people who had eaten in them. This annual guide soon set standards for restaurants to aspire to if they wished to be included. It became popular and successful as more people contributed recommendations.[9]

Elizabeth David spent the war years working for the Ministry of Information in Cairo and returned to rationing and a bleak winter in London in 1946. She had no idea of the deprivation or of the appalling food offered in restaurants; in Cairo food was plentiful and varied. It was escapism, distress and protest at what she found that made her write in the introduction to *A Book of Mediterranean Food* (1950):

> The ever-recurring elements in the food throughout these countries are the oil, the saffron, the garlic, the pungent local wines; the aromatic perfume of rosemary, wild marjoram and basil drying in the kitchen; the brilliance of the market stalls piled high with pimentos, aubergines, tomatoes, olives, melons, figs and limes.[10]

Her recipes for pilaff, lamb kebab, salad of aubergines, and orange and almond cake could not be made then. Almost every ingredient essential to Middle Eastern or Mediterranean cooking was rationed or unavailable, but she hoped reading about such food would help to relieve the drudgery and frustration of coping with the weekly rations. Later she wrote that she had come to realize that these were 'dirty words' to people who had gone through years of deprivation. Four more books followed in quick succession: *French Country Cooking*, *French Provincial Cooking*, *Italian Food* and *Summer Cooking*, as well as articles for newspapers and magazines.

For David, writing on food was not just about cooking, but about memory, place, people and history. She evoked places, tastes and aromas in a direct and elegant style that immediately drew the reader in, and she soon had a huge following. She was criticized by some writers for attracting readers to Mediterranean dishes, yet many of these foods were part of our meals in the Middle Ages, and they slowly became available again. She transformed the way post-war England approached food, and influenced restaurateurs, other food writers and shopkeepers selling food and cooking equipment.

In the past only the rich had travelled widely in Europe, but it soon became affordable for the less affluent too. Travel now included visits to markets, charcuteries and cheesemongers as well as churches, museums and beautiful landscapes. During the 1950s and early 1960s demand for imported foods grew: garlic, courgettes, aubergines, saffron, lemons, dried fruits, pistachios and almonds from southern Europe appeared first in Italian and French shops in Soho and slowly spread to grocers, greengrocers and supermarkets in other parts of the country.

David's enthusiasm for Mediterranean and Middle Eastern food continued throughout her life, but she also had a fine collection of English cookery books. She read them and cooked from them regularly, and they formed the background of her later books on English food. In *English Bread and Yeast Cookery* (1977) she attacked the big millers and factories making industrial bread with the texture of 'boiled wool'; readers scoured the shops for yeast and wholemeal flour to make their own. Factory bread still exists, but England now has many more independent bakeries and home bakers. Her books and her eloquent, honed journalism made David the most influential food writer of the twentieth century.

Jane Grigson, Elizabeth David's contemporary and friend, was also a fine writer and cook. Her books encouraged people to try new ingredients and cooking methods, as well as to gain knowledge and confidence in the kitchen. Grigson and her family spent half the year in rural France, and her first book, *Charcuterie and French Pork Cookery* (1967), was the result of her own exploration of charcuterie-making in the small towns of their region. The following year she became the food writer for *The Observer*, a role that she kept until her death in 1990.

David and Grigson had similar concerns about the selection and quality of food available in English shops: 'Tomatoes have no taste. The finest flavoured potatoes are not available in the shops. Vegetables and fruit are seldom fresh . . . "Farm fresh" means eggs that are no more than ten, fourteen or twenty days old. Words such as "fresh" and "home-made" have been borrowed in commerce to tell lies.'[11] Good-quality ingredients may at times have been lacking, but in *English Food* Grigson guides readers to the best traditional dishes selected on the basis of quality. Her *Vegetable Book* and *Fruit Book* are authoritative reference works as well as books to inspire the reader to try new ideas; *Good Things* and *Food with the Famous* are collections of lively articles written for *The Observer*. During the long years of rationing and deprivation, shoppers had become accustomed to accepting what was on offer; producers' standards needed to be improved, and David and Grigson encouraged shoppers to aim higher and demand better-quality food.

The third writer to make her mark on English food at this time was Claudia Roden, whose *Book of Middle Eastern Food* was published in 1968. David's *A Book of Mediterranean Food* had introduced some dishes from the Middle East, but Roden's book deals comprehensively with the food of the region. Forced into exile from Egypt, she and her family settled in London, where she set about gathering recipes for 'food that was a constant joy of life in a world so different from the Western one'.[12] The dishes are primarily Turkish, Egyptian, Syrian, Iranian, Lebanese, Moroccan and Israeli. Many are simple, easy to prepare and inexpensive, although they may need time for slow cooking. The demand for vegetables, fruits and seasonings from warmer climates continued to increase and the market responded.

Middle Eastern restaurants, primarily Lebanese, opened in London and other cities as more people developed a taste for their dishes. The taste for Indian food had already been established two centuries earlier, and during the 1960s many Chinese people arrived via Hong Kong to escape Mao's China. Small restaurants and takeaways sprang up, primarily in the dockland areas of London and Liverpool, serving southern Chinese food for these new immigrants. Eventually, modest Indian and/or Chinese restaurants spread to towns throughout the country, usually offering a short, simple, somewhat anglicized menu. Some years elapsed before they began to specialize in the foods of different regions and had more knowledgeable customers ready to eat more adventurously. Now there are 'Chinatowns' and 'Indian suburbs' in most large cities, with restaurants offering excellent food.

Chinese restaurant in Limehouse, London, 1932,
offering both English and Chinese food.

Veeraswamy, the UK's first Indian restaurant, pictured in 1962. It opened in 1926 at 99 Regent Street, London, where it is still located.

Soho was the hub of Italian food in London, and Lina Stores, which opened in 1944, was the best place to find Italian and other Mediterranean ingredients. The shop (and now restaurant) was, and still is, renowned for its handmade pasta. Italian trattorias joined the more upscale French restaurants in the cities. The most famous trattoria of the Swinging Sixties was La Terrazza in Soho. It served authentic traditional dishes. Unlike other restaurants which only admitted men wearing jackets and ties, La Terrazza had a relaxed dress code and informal but efficient service. It marked a change in the way restaurants would be designed and run in future.

At about the same time new fast food restaurants were opening in England. The American Wimpy burger chain granted a licence to Lyons to open burger restaurants in England in 1954, but there were few in the early years. Pizza Express opened its first London restaurant in 1965, the same year that the first Kentucky

Fried Chicken opened, in Preston. In 1971 the first McDonald's opened in Woolwich, east London. All quickly became popular because they were inexpensive and informal. Competitors soon arrived – Burger King, Pizza Hut, Nandos, Chicken Shack and many more. The cheap battery chicken boom fuelled the expansion

Burridge Bros fish and chip shop in Tottenham, London, 1965.

of fast food outlets, providing high profit margins for the franchise holders, for little is spent on the welfare of the chicken or the quality of the meat used in burgers. Fish and chip shops survived this new invasion, although there are currently only about 10,000 in the country compared with 20,000 or more at the end of the war. Many raised their sights, offered a wider variety of fish, and catered to a middle-class market. Fish and chip shops are more likely to offer better-quality food than the chicken outlets.

Coffee-houses were popular in England in the seventeenth century, but by the end of the 1800s most had disappeared as more tea was drunk. Coffee bars emerged in the late 1950s when the espresso coffee machine spread to England from Italy. They were places for young people to socialize, replacing the milk bars and tea shops of earlier years. Starbucks had opened espresso bars in Seattle in the 1970s, selling a range of Italian coffees with pastries and cakes in attractive, comfortable surroundings. In 1998 the chain opened in London, and was soon followed by Costa Coffee, Caffè Nero and more. Coffee bars became the social spaces for people of all ages who did not want to go to a pub.

By the 1960s life was changing dramatically throughout the country; there was a sense of liberation and liberalism after long years of deprivation. Just as English tastes in food were expanding, so were popular culture and music. The decade saw the rise of satire, starting with *Beyond the Fringe*, which opened at the Edinburgh Festival in 1960. The show transferred to London and continued a successful run. It was followed by *That Was The Week That Was*, another clever satire show on television, and *Private Eye*, the weekly satirical paper, was launched at about the same time. Satire was revived in 1984 with the television puppet show *Spitting Image*, which continued until the mid-1990s and was more recently revived.

The 1960s also saw the BBC launch *Top of the Pops* on television in response to the arrival of the Beatles, the Rolling Stones, the Who and many other British bands. Some bands were influenced by American music, but others, most notably the Beatles, had a local focus. Lennon and McCartney wrote their own music and lyrics, often with Liverpudlian references and containing some of their favourite foods: honey, strawberries, rice, marshmallow pie and, of course, tea. As small boys they lived through wartime and post-war rationing, so the references to food, and particularly sweet food, are not surprising. Much of this new music emerged from working-class and lower-middle-class young people; in the past it is unlikely they would ever have experienced such success and power. Pop pushed its way into traditional English social and cultural life and quickly became an integral part. Soon after these new groups were established, Bob Marley brought reggae from Jamaica. Jazz clubs, most notably Ronnie Scott's in Soho, flourished and had celebrity artists perform. There was innovation everywhere, not only in music and how it was listened to – on transistor radios, cassettes and juke-boxes. There were more telephones and televisions, more cars and motorways and more tourism; Mary Quant and others revolution-ized fashion. The goods and services of the upper and middle classes increasingly became mass market. More people ate out, whether in a fast food outlet or a stylish restaurant. The deprivations of war had finally gone; it was the time of a wide-ranging social revolution, in which the young had a more significant role than in the past. It was also the age of consumerism when celebrities became the new 'aristocrats'.

The death penalty was abolished, abortion legalized, the divorce laws reformed, homosexuality between consenting adult males legalized, and the immigration laws improved. The jury at the Old Bailey found in favour of Penguin Books in declaring that D. H. Lawrence's *Lady Chatterley's Lover* was not obscene under the Obscene Publications Act. More children were in secondary and higher education, and overall incomes increased. Women's role in society moved upwards as they were better educated and were offered more challenging jobs.

For families who had more leisure now, breakfast returned as a grander meal, at least at weekends. Porridge remained popular, especially in winter; a wider range of breakfast cereals was available, and the cooked breakfast made a reappearance. The 'fry-up' or 'full English' could include bacon, sausages, black pudding, fried eggs, mushrooms, tomatoes and potatoes. It became so popular that it is often available in cafes all day.

Frozen food took off in England in the early 1970s when more homes acquired freezers. Fish fingers and peas were the most popular choices in the early days, and frozen food ranges extended quickly, especially with the introduction of frozen food stores such as Bejam, later taken over by the supermarket chain Iceland. In 1985 Marks & Spencer introduced the first chilled ready meals; Felicity Lawrence described in detail in *Not on the Label* (2004) the contents of the lamb dish she bought.[13] The ingredients list on the back included those she expected to find – lamb, potatoes, peas, carrots, onion, red wine and water – but in small type were many more, including eight sweetening agents, seven fats, four preservatives, three chemical flavourings and starch thickeners. There was also 5.9 g of salt (the Food Standards Agency recommends a maximum per day of 6 g for an adult). The vegetarian lasagne she also checked had a similar unhealthy concoction of ingredients, and the main ingredient of the dish, by weight, was water.

Ultra-processed foods continue to sell in ever larger quantities; in July 2021 the *Daily Telegraph* recommended downloading the Open Food Facts app to scan the barcode on a product to learn the extent of the industrial processes it has been through, and it urged readers to look out for claims such as 'made with wholegrains' and 'high in iron' which are often used to 'give a healthy whitewash' to ultra-processed foods. It also pointed out that ultra-processed foods have high profit margins, so manufacturers are likely to spend more on fancy packaging and tv advertising.

Vending machines have existed since the end of the nineteenth century, and those for food and drinks increased greatly in the later years of the twentieth century. Some dispense hot food, others are chilled for ice creams, and many more dispense packs of crisps, chocolates or fizzy drinks such as Coca-Cola and Fanta. In recent years we have become a nation of snackers. In the post-war period, fish and chips and ice cream were almost the only foods eaten in the street, but now many children expect a snack after school – crisps, chocolate, biscuits, nuts and fizzy drinks. Supermarkets and corner shops are filled with snacks, both savoury and sweet. Snacking is firmly established in most households, at least occasionally, and in some poorer households it replaces meals. Snacks are relatively inexpensive and may be satisfying to eat, but they aren't filling, and the high sugar and salt content leads to obesity and health problems. This is now one of the biggest public health issues in the country.

In the mid-1970s a severe depression hit Western economies, including the UK. Oil supplies to Western countries were cut after the war between Israel and Egypt in 1973 and prices soared. The miners also put in a huge pay claim which was rejected and led to a strike; the two together meant the government faced severe economic problems. There were no coal stocks; petrol was rationed, and from 1 January 1974 the three-day week was introduced because of fears over power shortages. Food prices increased, wages decreased. From the 1950s to the early 1970s people's disposable income had grown, but from 1974 it fell sharply. Unemployment reached a million in 1975, rose to more than 3 million in 1980, and did not drop back to the lower level until 2000.

From the 1950s agricultural employment decreased throughout Europe as mechanization increased, and people moved to live and work in towns. Farming became ever more mechanized and depended on companies making processed feed and fertilizers. Factory farms tend to produce foods of poor quality, such as the battery chicken. Mechanized production lines became standard in slaughterhouses and other 'food factories'. The industrialization of food did not improve its quality but it did increase production and make food cheaper.

Many men, especially the unskilled or semi-skilled, were the victims of advanced industrialization, and England lost 25 per cent of its manufacturing industries between 1980 and 1984.[14] High inflation and unemployment continued until the late 1980s; then slowly the country climbed out of unemployment and moved towards an upward spiral of prosperity. This led to a demand for better housing and services, cheaper travel abroad and cheaper food. Holidays were taken further afield, and at home food was affordable, even if the quality was sometimes questionable; there were more television channels, more ways to listen to music, and it was the start of the computer age.

More people from across a broad spectrum of society started to eat out regularly because they could afford it. New restaurants opened, less formal than the traditional ones that were decidedly

The Eagle, Clerkenwell, 2011.

upmarket. Many were opened by immigrants from Asia – Thailand, China, India and Japan – and there was a surge in European restaurants too, particularly Italian trattorias, French brasseries, Greek souvlaki cafes and Spanish tapas bars.

In the early 1990s gastropubs developed. The Eagle in Clerkenwell, London, was the first. These were pubs renowned not only for their beer, but for the quality of their food. They had at least one chef as a member of the staff. Often the pub had a bar on the ground floor and a restaurant upstairs. Not only did they serve beer, but they introduced wines to serve both up- and downstairs. Now there are good gastropubs in all parts of the country. Traditional English dishes are often served in pub restaurants: roast beef with roast potatoes, Yorkshire pudding and at least one green vegetable; fish and chips; shepherd's pie; Lancashire hotpot (a stew). Now, as demand has changed, the cooking is increasingly more adventurous and varied.

At about the same time, takeaway meals began to be offered in city neighbourhoods, and now they thrive as many people use them regularly. People's palates had become more sophisticated, and many of these restaurants offer regional specialities from India, China, Korea and Thailand. Pizzerias thrive on takeaway meals, as do sandwich bars. It is easy to ring and order what you want from most local restaurants and then go and collect it or get it delivered.

A fashion of recent years is afternoon tea turned into an 'event' in smart hotels. Tea (there are several varieties to choose from) or sparkling wine is accompanied by sandwiches, scones, pastries and cakes in elegant surroundings, and in some places it is offered from late morning until early evening.

Artisan cheese-making had almost disappeared after the war, but it revived slowly in the 1970s and '80s, largely due to the cheesemonger Patrick Rance, and later to Neal's Yard, La Fromagerie and other cheesemongers up and down the country. The Milk Marketing Board had supported farmers with a guaranteed price for their milk, but it was closed in the 1990s and farmers needed to diversify. Some turned to cheese-making. Demand for local food was increasing; concerns about food miles were being voiced, and consumers wanted to support the local economy, including cheese-making. Traditional recipes were revived for old favourites such as Gloucester and Caerphilly, and new cheeses, like Stinking Bishop, some using goats' or ewes' milk, were invented. These unpasteurized cheeses sell well at a higher price than those made in factories because they taste better.

In 1986 Carlo Petrini founded the Slow Food movement in Italy as a response to the growth of fast food. Slow Food encourages people to enjoy food that is good for them as well as being good for farmers and the planet. The movement quickly attracted members around the world, including in the UK.

More people have turned to organic foods because they are better for the planet and usually taste better, even though they are likely to be more expensive. There is no evidence that fertilizers and pesticides used in conventional farming are unhealthy for human consumption, but they are certainly bad for the planet. They are not good for the ecosystem; they affect the soil, wildlife, rivers and streams, and the climate.

The anthropologist Kate Fox noted the English attention to food is 'ambivalent, highly discordant and often superficial'.[15] Food is not yet given the high priority it is accorded in many parts of the world. Until recently, if we were too interested in food, we could be regarded as food snobs. This has changed, and awareness and appreciation of good food, at least for the reasonably well off, is the norm. Fox also noted, as others have done, that many people watch a celebrity chef cooking a dish from fresh, good-quality ingredients on TV while eating a supermarket ready meal or snacks on their knees.

But some people are not able to cook. I was shocked to see in Belsize Park, London, that small flats built in new developments in the 1990s and later often do not have a kitchen. At best they have an alcove with a microwave, fridge and power point for a kettle. A slow cooker, an air fryer or electric steamer can be plugged into the power point, although such facilities for preparing a proper meal are not ideal.

Many food programmes on TV have concentrated on showing viewers how to improve their cooking skills. Delia Smith's TV shows in the late twentieth century were immensely popular; she paid great attention to detail and many women rushed out and bought her books along with the ingredients and gadgets she recommended. Some of those women may have had basic cookery lessons at school, but cooking was removed from the curriculum. Now, cooking and nutrition are taught again from primary school upwards and food technology has been replaced by food and nutrition in the GCSE course for fifteen- to sixteen-year-olds. However, many families still rely on processed foods. People who have been out all day at work have little energy and often too little money to buy good-quality food and make a meal.

Early in the twenty-first century Jamie Oliver's *Naked Chef* TV series had scores of people, especially young men, watching the show and cooking from his books. Oliver campaigned for good-quality food and started the campaign for better school meals. His programmes continue to be immensely popular and instructive. At about the same time, Nigella Lawson hosted the first of her highly successful television cookery series. They were followed by other writer-chefs who taught us how to cook and fed us well in their restaurants, among them Ruth Rogers, Simon Hopkinson, Shaun Hill, Rowley Leigh, Fergus Henderson, Raymond Blanc, Jeremy Lee, Tom Kerridge and Heston Blumenthal. Their food is nutritious and well presented: the best of Modern British. In addition, restaurants serving food from all parts of the world were spreading around the country, and more books were bought about how to cook dishes from Georgia to Peru as well as the now more familiar cuisines of India, China, Japan or Thailand.

In recent years there has been a proliferation of digital cooking channels worldwide as well as recipes posted on the Internet. They offer a variety of recipes (vegetarian, vegan, gluten-free and more). In spite of the rise of such websites, including chefs or cooking influencers on social media, and online cooking programmes, the number of cookery books increases.

There is certainly a significant and growing number of women and men in England who enjoy cooking and experimenting with foods from around the globe. Farm shops and farmers' markets draw increasingly large numbers of customers, and they all offer seasonal, local food, much of it organic. Waiting lists for allotments have increased as more people want to grow their own food. Around the country, the Incredible Edible network continues to spread. It began in 2008 when a group of women in Todmorden in Yorkshire decided, with the approval of the local authority, to plant vegetables in 'unloved places' around the town and encourage local people to take what they needed to cook. From small beginnings, this led to wide acceptance in their town; more people joined them, more gardens were planted, including at schools, and the movement has now caught on elsewhere. 'We believe in the lost arts. The art of growing and soil science, the art of cooking and preserving and the connection that is made to our planet when we learn about food. Incredible Edible believes reviving our hands-on knowledge of food is essential for all our futures.'[16] Look up your area online and you may well find a group near you, or start one with friends.

Over the centuries, English food has changed according to the socio-economic situation and it continues to do so today. Much of the food produced in Britain is not good, for the planet or for health; for many years the demand for cheap food has led to a race to the bottom and a lack of attention to preserving essential nutrients in food. Ultra-processed foods now make up a significant amount of the food eaten daily; they may be convenient, but they contain added sugar, salt, fat and more dubious ingredients. They lose many of their nutrients and are not healthy. Someone who lives primarily on a diet of ultra-processed food may feel well fed but is likely to be undernourished. Around the country many health professionals are working with patients to promote better diets and health.

New production methods are being trialled that will help to protect the planet. Organic farming is increasing but the produce is still not eaten widely enough, partly because, by necessity, it costs more. Awareness of food miles has been evident for some years; eating locally produced food is a solution, but it doesn't help the poor Kenyan or Peruvian farmer. Growing food in heated greenhouses and dispatching it long distances in lorries contributes to the damage to the planet just as air miles do. The impact of climate change is becoming increasingly evident across the globe. The role of the current agricultural systems in contributing to driving climate change has been well documented. Managing agricultural biodiversity has become urgent everywhere.

There is also a need to research more local crops and underutilized edible plants and to consider more seriously adopting a plant-based, or predominantly plant-based, diet. Vegetarian and vegan diets have become increasingly popular in recent years, and most restaurants now have vegetarian or vegan dishes on the menu.

Many edible plants are good sources of protein: oats, quinoa, spinach, broccoli, almonds and soybeans, and among fruits blackberries, apricots, cherries, avocados and guava. Nevertheless, many people think of meat, dairy and fish as the primary sources of protein. The search for alternative sources has led to some successful experiments with producing 'meat' in laboratories, which might in the future lead to a reduction in the number of animals kept. At present, laboratory 'meat' and 'chicken' are not licensed for sale in the UK, but plant-based milks and meats are on supermarket shelves.

Insect-based food is also being taken more seriously globally. For many years insects have been eaten in Asia and in parts of Central and South America; around 2 billion people worldwide eat insects as part of their normal diet, according to the UN Food and Agriculture Organization (FAO). More than a thousand species are eaten around the world, but thus far they have not been taken seriously in rich countries, though this is starting to change. Some entomologists agree; in *Silent Earth* (2022) Dave Goulson argues that we should eat farmed insects while moving to non-intensive farming and reducing the use of pesticides. A few companies in the UK are now investing in cricket and other insect foods. Crickets are nutritious, providing essential fats, proteins, minerals, vitamin B12 and amino acids. They consume little water and produce low greenhouse gas emissions. At present they are mostly made into snacks, but it is likely that insects will play a larger part in our diet in future. Farming insects requires less land and resources than farming livestock, which means more space for nature and potentially the ability to feed a growing population on a smaller footprint.

Food production should be considered as one of the solutions to climate change; people can change their eating patterns and learn to adapt to the new. After all, that is what we have done since earliest times.

Twentieth-century recipes

Potato salad

Lady Jekyll, *Kitchen Essays* (London, 1922)

Take the most waxy potatoes available, boil in their skins, peel while warm, cut into thickish slices, pour on 1 tablespoonful vinegar and about 2 tablespoonsfuls stock, but very gradually so that they may absorb it; add 2 tablespoonsful oil, salt and pepper to taste and 1 small finely chopped onion, and let it all stand for an hour before serving. A very, very thin mayonnaise sauce with a little French mustard and a drop or two of garlic vinegar, and a few capers with parsley and chives may be used as an alternative dressing.

Brussels sprouts with chestnuts

Elisabeth Ayrton, *The Cookery of England* (London, 1974)

2 lb (1 kg) brussels sprouts
½ lb (240 g) cooked and skinned chestnuts (good whole canned chestnuts may be used)
1½ oz (40 g) butter
salt and coarse black pepper

Prepare the brussels sprouts by removing all the outside leaves and hard stem ends, drop into about 2 inches (5 cm) boiling salted water, stir several times and boil gently till tender (about 20 minutes). Melt the butter in a pan and heat without allowing it to brown. Toss the chestnuts in it, breaking them up as they fry for 2 minutes. Add the sprouts and toss with the chestnuts 2 minutes more. Mix all lightly together, season highly with salt and coarse black pepper, and turn on to a hot dish and serve.

Serves 4–6

Mushrooms baked in cream

M. K. Samuelson, *Sussex Recipe Book* (London, 1937)

Arrange 8 large firm caps (gill side up) or 1 lb of small mushrooms in a shallow, buttered pan; sprinkle with salt and pepper and dot with butter. Add about ½ cupful of cream, and bake for 10 minutes in a hot oven. Place the caps on toast, and just before serving pour over them cream remaining in pan. An excellent simple method.

Staffordshire oatcakes

Elizabeth David, *English Bread and Yeast Cookery*
(Harmondsworth, 1977)

To make sixteen to eighteen 15–18 cm/6–7 in. oatcakes
or pancakes
250 g/½ lb each fine oatmeal and plain bread flour
(I use 85 per cent wheatmeal, but white will do)
2 tsp salt
15 g/½ oz baker's yeast
approximately 450 ml/¾ pint each warm milk and water
a little fat will be needed for the frying pan

Put the oatmeal and the wheatmeal into a bowl with the salt. Cream the yeast with a little of the warm milk and water mixture. Stir it into the flours, add the rest of the liquid and with a wooden spoon beat the mixture into a batter. If it is too thick add a little more warm water.

Make the oatcakes as for pancakes. I like them very thin and curling a little at the edges. Oatcakes can be kept warm and soft in a folded cloth; and if you want to make then in advance and reheat them in the pan or in a slow oven, dampen the cloth so that they remain moist.

Serves 8–9

Kippers with scrambled egg

Jane Grigson, *Good Things* (London, 1971)

A good dish for late Sunday breakfasts that merge into lunch. Try it too as an hors d'oeuvre, or in sandwiches. The kippers can be cooked or not, as you please. The main thing to notice is the use of garlic – Escoffier's idea – which enhances the flavour of the eggs without stridency.

The best garlic to use is the fat, white, juicy kind imported from France.

2 kippers
6 eggs
5 oz butter
large clove garlic
salt, pepper
buttered toast

Divide the cooked or uncooked kippers into large flakes, or strips. Beat the eggs for five minutes with a fork stuck firmly into the clove of garlic. Season with salt and pepper. Melt the butter in a thick pan over a low heat, pour in the eggs through a strainer and cook as slowly as possible, stirring from time to time. When the eggs are beginning to solidify, but are still fairly liquid, add the kipper pieces. Don't overcook. Serve on buttered toast.

If this dish is to be served as a cold hors d'oeuvre, it's best to scramble the eggs on their own, and lay strips of kipper across them just before serving.

Serves 4

Brill baked on green and white vegetables

Fergus Henderson, *Nose to Tail Eating* (London, 1999)

fennel, sliced across the grain
leeks, washed and sliced
onions, peeled and sliced
garlic, peeled and finely chopped
butter
1 large whole brill, gutted
sea salt and pepper
1–2 lemons

The size of your brill will dictate the number of mouths it will feed. A medium to large brill will satisfy four to six diners, a smallish one two. It should be reasonably large so that it will withstand a cooking time long enough for the vegetables to get to know the fish juices.

You want a whole fish for this, so see what your fishmonger has; also take into account your cooking receptacles and the size of your oven.

In a pan gently sweat your vegetables and garlic in butter, just to start the softening process, but not so that they give up all resistance. Season. Lay them as a bed for your fish in your oven tray. Place the fish on its vegetable bed, dot with knobs of butter and season, then pop it into a hot oven. Check the fish with a knife – when done the flesh should part easily from the bone. Keep a very close eye after 10 minutes. Serve with lemon.

Serves 3

Roast chicken

Simon Hopkinson with Lindsey Bareham, *Roast Chicken and other Stories*
(London, 1994)

110 g/4 oz good butter, at room temperature
1.8 kg/4 lb free-range chicken
salt and pepper
1 lemon
several sprigs of thyme or tarragon, or a mixture of the two
1 garlic clove, peeled and crushed

Preheat the oven to 450°F/230°C/gas mark 8. Smear the butter with your hands all over the bird. Put the chicken in a roasting tin that will accommodate it with room to spare. Season liberally with salt and pepper and squeeze over the juice of 1 lemon. Put the herbs and garlic inside the cavity, together with the squeezed lemon halves – this will add a fragrant lemony flavour to the finished dish.

Roast the chicken in the oven for 10–15 minutes, turn the oven down to 375°F/190°C/gas mark 5 and roast for a further 30–45 minutes with further occasional basting. The bird should be golden brown all over with a crisp skin and have buttery, lemony juices of a nut brown colour in the bottom of the tin.

Turn off the oven, leaving the door ajar, and leave the chicken to rest for at least 15 minutes before carving. This enables the flesh to relax gently, retaining the juices in the meat and ensuring easy, trouble-free carving and a moist bird.

Carve the bird to suit yourself, I like to do it *in* the roasting tin. I see no point in making a gravy in that old-fashioned English way with the roasting fat, flour and vegetable cooking water. With this roasting method, what you end up with in the tin is an amalgamation of butter, lemon juice and chicken juices. That's all. It is a perfect homogenisation of fats and liquids. All it needs is a light whisk or a stir, and you have the most wonderful 'gravy' imaginable. If you wish to add extra flavour, you can scoop the garlic and herbs out of the chicken cavity, stir them into the gravy and heat through; strain before serving.

Another idea, popular with the Italians, is something known as 'wet-roasting'. Pour some white wine or a little chicken stock, or both, or even just water around the bottom of the tin at the beginning of cooking. This will produce more of a sauce and can be enriched further to produce altogether different results. For example, you can add chopped tomatoes, diced bacon, cream, endless different herbs, mushrooms, spring vegetables, spices – particularly saffron and ginger – or anything else that you fancy.

For me, the simple roast bird is best, but it is useful to know how much further you can go when roasting a chicken.

Mishmishiya

Claudia Roden, *A Book of Middle Eastern Food* (London, 1968)

A splendid meat and apricot dish which derives its name from the Arabic name for the fruit, *mishmish*. Lamb seems to have a special affinity for apricots, and a similar dish was a great favourite in our family.

From al-Baghdadi's thirteenth-century cookery manual.

Cut fat meat small, put into the saucepan with a little salt and cover with water. Boil and remove the scum. Cut up onions, wash and throw in on top of the meat. Add seasonings, coriander, cumin, mastic, cinnamon, pepper and ginger, well ground. Take dry apricots, soak in hot water, then wash and put in a separate saucepan, and boil lightly: take out, wipe in the hands and strain through a sieve. Take the juice, and add it to the saucepan to form a broth. Take sweet almonds, grind fine, moisten with a little apricot juice and throw in. Some colour with a trifle of saffron. Spray the saucepan with a little rose water, wipe its sides with a clean rag, and leave to settle over the fire: then remove.

> 1 kg (2 lb) lean lamb, cubed, trimmed of excess fat
> salt
> 1–2 onions, finely chopped
> ½–1 tsp ground coriander
> ½–1 tsp ground cumin
> ¼ tsp pulverized mastic
> ¼–½ tsp ground cinnamon
> black pepper
> ¼ teaspoon ground ginger
> 250 g (8 oz) dried apricots, soaked and blended to a puree
> 60 g (2 oz) ground almonds
> ¼ tsp saffron (optional)
> 1 tsp rose water

This is one of the dishes in which the meat is not fried before stewing. It may seem dull at first, but the apricot sauce thickened with the ground almonds gives it a particular richness which makes frying superfluous. The apricots must be of a sharp (not sweet) variety.

The stew requires about 2 hours of gentle cooking, preferably on an asbestos mat. Leave out the mastic and saffron if you wish – I do not think they are at all necessary.

Beef olives

Arabella Boxer, *Arabella Boxer's Book of English Food* (London, 1991)

One of the best old dishes, rarely seen today. This would have been served for Saturday lunch in a country house.

6 thin slices buttock steak or topside
2 oz (55 g) shredded suet
1 oz (30 g) soft white breadcrumbs
2 rashers streaky bacon, chopped
½ tsp grated orange rind
1 tbsp chopped parsley
½ tsp chopped thyme, or ¼ tsp dried thyme
salt and black pepper
1 egg, beaten
1½ oz (45 g) butter
1 onion, thinly sliced
1 carrot, thinly sliced
1 leek, thinly sliced
1 stalk celery, thinly sliced
½ tbsp flour
½ pint (275 ml) beef or chicken stock

Lay the slices of beef on a sheet of cling film and cover with another sheet. Beat them out until very thin. Trim the edges to make a roughly rectangular shape; chop the trimmings and put them in basin with the suet and breadcrumbs. Add the bacon, orange rind, parsley, thyme, salt and pepper. Mix well, add the beaten egg, then divide the stuffing between the 6 slices of beef. Roll each one up and tie with string.

Melt the butter in a casserole and brown the sliced vegetables quickly, stirring constantly. When they have coloured, take them out and put in the beef olives. Brown them on all sides, then remove them also. Shake the flour into the casserole and blend with the butter. Cook for 1 minute, stirring, then add the heated stock and stir till blended, adding salt and pepper to taste. Put the vegetables back into the pan, and lay the olives on them. Cover and cook gently for 1½ hours, either on top of the stove or in a low oven, 325°F/170°C/gas 3.

To serve, remove the string and lay the olives on a bed of mashed potato. Spoon the vegetables over the top, moistening with the sauce.

Serves 6

An excellent Lancashire Hot-Pot

Florence White, *Good Things in England* (London, 1932)

This recipe hails from Bolton-le-Moors. The oysters may be omitted, but they are the correct thing in a real hot-pot. Another correct thing is to serve Lancashire Hot-Pot with a dish or glass of pickled red cabbage whatever recipe be used. This is traditional.

INGREDIENTS: 2 lb middle-neck mutton; dripping 1 oz; onion 1; flour 1 oz; hot stock ¾ pint; pepper; salt and sugar; mushrooms 4 or 5; kidneys 2; oysters 20; potatoes 2 lb. Time to stew in oven 2 hours.

METHOD: 1. Cut the meat into chops. 2., Make the dripping hot in a pan, brown the meat in it. 3. Lift out and put into a brown Staffordshire pot that can be sent to table, or, if you prefer it, a deep fire-proof baking dish with a lid. 4. Stew the onion and cook for a few minutes in the dripping. 5. Add the flour and cook till it is nicely brown. 6. Add the stock (hot) to the pan and stir in the brown flour, as you would when making gravy. 7. Season to taste with pepper, salt and a teaspoonful of castor sugar. 8. Slice the kidney thickly over the mutton. 9. Add the mushrooms, peeled, and if large, cut to small size. 10. Add the oysters (all of these are separate layers). 11. Peel the potatoes, cut them in thick slices and arrange them overlapping round the top of the meat, with the nobbly ends in the centre to cover the contents of the pot completely. 12. Strain the thickened stock over the potatoes,

put on the lid and stew in a moderate oven for 2 hours. Take off
the lid during the last 15 minutes to brown the potatoes nicely.

Peaches in white wine

Mrs C. F. Leyel and Miss Olga Hartley, *The Gentle Art of Cookery*
(London, 1925)

Peaches, sauterne, butter, sugar.

Take as many peaches as are required and cut them in half.
Put them into a dish and pour over them a claret glass of sauterne.
Leave them for an hour or more. Crack the stones.

Put two ounces of butter into a very clean pan; when it boils put
in the peaches and fry them lightly. Drain them carefully. Add sugar
and kernels to the wine in which the peaches have been soaked,
and make into a syrup. Pour it over the peaches and serve either
hot or cold.

Caramelled oranges

Mrs C. F. Leyel, *Puddings* (London, 1927)

6 oranges
¼ pint cream
4 oz sugar
¼ pint water
pistachio nuts

Carefully peel the oranges, removing all trace of white. Then cut
the oranges across into rounds, removing the pips and any white
in the centre.

Make a caramel of the sugar and water in a saucepan. Arrange
a layer of the sliced orange in a crystal bowl and sprinkle it with

castor sugar. Pour over it a thin layer of the golden brown caramel, then arrange another layer of oranges and repeat the process until the oranges and the caramel are exhausted.

Whip the cream and cover the oranges with it.

Chop the nuts and decorate with them.

Gooseberry Fool

Wartime 'Good Housekeeping' Cookery Book (Harmondsworth, 1942)

1 lb (450 g) gooseberries
water
sugar to taste
½ pint (280 ml) thick custard
little 'top of the milk'

Top-and-tail and wash the gooseberries and cook them in a very little water until reduced to a soft mash. Pass through a sieve, sweeten to taste, and allow to cool. Make ½ pint thick custard (with 3 teaspoonsful of custard powder to ½ pint milk or milk and water), whisk it well to give it a smooth and creamy texture. Mix with the gooseberry purée and put into a glass bowl or individual glass dishes. Just before serving pour a little milk 'tops' on the surface and stir round with the handle of a teaspoon to give a marbled effect.

NOTE – Other fruit fools, e.g. rhubarb, plum etc., are made in the same way. Soft fruits such as raspberries can be puréed without first stewing.

REFERENCES

1 First Settlements to the Earliest English Society

1 Claude Levi-Strauss, *The Raw and the Cooked* (Harmondsworth, 1992), p. 201.
2 Richard Wrangham, *Catching Fire, How Cooking Made Us Human* (London, 2009), p. 14.
3 Ibid., p. 12.
4 Strabo, *The Geography of Strabo*, Book IV, Chapter 5, [*c.* 24 CE], www.roman-britain.co.uk, accessed 7 August 2023.
5 The *Geoponica*, quoted in *Apicius: The Roman Cookery Book*, trans. Barbara Flower and Elisabeth Rosenbaum (London, 1958), p. 22.
6 Apicius, *The Roman Cookery Book*, trans. Flower and Rosenbaum, p. 167.
7 Ibid., p. 155.
8 See Thomas Miller, trans., *The Old English Version of Bede's Ecclesiastical History of the English People* (Cambridge and Ontario, 1999), p. 14.
9 H.P.R. Finberg, *The Early Charters of the West Midlands* (Leicester, 1972).
10 Elisabeth Ayrton, *The Cookery of England* (London, 1974), p. 78.
11 O. Cockayne, *Leechdoms, Starcraft and Wortcunning* [1864–6], quoted in A. Hagen, *A Handbook of Anglo-Saxon Food* (London, 1992), p. 55.
12 Ibid., p. 14.
13 A. J. Robertson, *Anglo-Saxon Charters* [1939], quoted in Hagen, *Anglo-Saxon Food*, p. 87.

2 From 1066 to Chaucer

1 John Burnett, *A History of the Cost of Living* (Harmondsworth, 1969), p. 29.
2 C. B. Hieatt and S. Butler, eds, *Curye on Inglysch* (Oxford, 1985), p. 3.
3 Urban T. Holmes Jr, *Daily Living in the Twelfth Century: Based on the Observations of Alexander Neckam in London and Paris* [1952], p. 93, www.archive.org.
4 Thomas Wright, *De utensilibus*, in *A Volume of Vocabularies* (London, 1857).
5 Elizabeth David, *English Bread and Yeast Cookery* (Harmondsworth, 1977), p. 227.
6 C. Anne Wilson, *Food and Drink in Britain* (London, 1974), p. 339. Chibols are spring onions; porray are leeks; 'lave' means rinse and wash.

7 At this time the weight of a sugar loaf was about 30 lb.
8 In 1345 the guild became The Worshipful Company of Grocers.
9 Wilson, *Food and Drink in Britain*, p. 287.
10 Geoffrey Chaucer, *The Canterbury Tales, The Nun's Priest's Tale* [1387–1400], trans. Nevill Coghill (Harmondsworth, 1951), p. 181.
11 Geoffrey Chaucer, *The Canterbury Tales, The Prologue*, trans. Nevill Coghill (Harmondsworth, 1951), p. 29.
12 Quoted in J. C. Drummond and A. Wilbraham, *The Englishman's Food* (London, 1939), p. 36. A francolin was probably a bird, now extinct.
13 Quoted from H. T. Riley, *Memorials of London Life*, in Sir Noel Curtis-Bennett, *The Food of the People* (London, 1949), p. 52.
14 Chaucer, *The Canterbury Tales, The Prologue*, p. 32.

3 Excess and Hardship in Tudor and Stuart Times

1 See Andrew Boorde, *A compendyous regyment or a dyetary of healthe made in Mountpyllyer, by Andrewe Boorde of physycke doctour, newly corrected and imprynted with dyuers addycyons dedycated to the armypotent Prynce and valyent Lorde Thomas Duke of Northfolke*, Chapter Fourteen, available at https://quod.lib.umich.edu, accessed 4 December 2023.
2 G. M. Trevelyan, *Illustrated English Social History*, vol. 1 (Harmondsworth, 1964), p. 195.
3 Paul Hentzner, *A Journey into England in the Year 1598* (London, 1757).
4 John Burnett, *A History of the Cost of Living* (Harmondsworth, 1969), p. 80.
5 F. G. Emmison, *Tudor Food and Pastimes* (London, 1964). Ingatestone Hall was built by Sir William Petre, soon after he had acquired the manor following the Dissolution of the Monasteries (1536–41).
6 Ibid. 6s 8d in 1550 would be the equivalent of £92 in 2017, or eleven days' wages for a skilled tradesman.
7 Ibid.
8 Thomas Moffett, *Health's Improvement* (London, 1655).
9 Maurice Ashley, *England in the Seventeenth Century* (Harmondsworth, 1952), p. 75.
10 Samuel Pepys, *The Diary of Samuel Pepys*, 1 January 1661.
11 Ibid., 13 January 1663.
12 Ibid., 25 September 1660.
13 Maximilien Misson, *Mémoires et observations faites par un voyageur en Angleterre* (Paris, 1691), quoted in J. C. Drummond and A. Wilbraham, *The Englishman's Food* (London, 1939), p. 116.

4 Prosperity and Conquest

1 Basil Willey, *The Seventeenth Century Background* (London, 1934).
2 Daniel Defoe, *A Tour thro' the Whole Island of Great Britain* [1724–6] (Harmondsworth, 1978), p. 83.
3 Arthur Young, *The Farmer's Letters to the People of England* (London, 1768), p. 84.
4 Quoted in Bee Wilson, *Swindled* (London, 2008), p. 82.
5 Tobias Smollett, *The Expedition of Humphry Clinker* (London, 1771), quoted ibid., p. 83.

6 Hannah Woolley, *The Queen-Like Closet* (London, 1670).
7 James Woodforde, *The Diary of a Country Parson* [1758–1802] (London, 1992).
8 R. Campbell, *The London Tradesman. Being a Compendious View of All the Trades, Professions, Arts, both Liberal and Mechanic, now practised . . .* (London, 1747).
9 John Nott, *The Cooks and Confectioners Dictionary* (London, 1726), entry 235.
10 Ibid., entry 51.
11 Defoe, *A Tour thro' the Whole Island of Great Britain*, p. 259.
12 James Boswell, *The Life of Samuel Johnson* (London, 1791).
13 François de la Rochefoucauld, *Melanges sur l'Angleterre* (Paris, 1784).
14 Boswell, *The Life of Samuel Johnson*.
15 See Friedrich Accum, *A Treatise on Adulterations of Food, and Culinary Poisons* (London, 1820).
16 Woodforde, *The Diary of a Country Parson*, p. 153. Hyson tea is a fine China green tea.
17 J. C. Drummond and A. Wilbraham, *The Englishman's Food* (London, 1939), p. 205.
18 David MacPherson, *The History of the European Commerce with India* [1812], quoted in Sidney W. Mintz, *Sweetness and Power* (New York, 1985), p. 114.
19 Sir Frederick Eden, *The State of the Poor* [1797], vol. 1 (London, 1966), p. 535.
20 Drummond and Wilbraham, *The Englishman's Food*, p. 197.
21 Ibid., p. 198.

5 The Birth of the Industrial Nation

1 Rowland E. Prothero, *The Pioneers and Progress of English Farming* [1888], quoted in John Burnett, *Plenty and Want: A Social History of Food in England from 1815 to the Present Day*, 3rd edn (London, 1989), p. 21.
2 Redcliffe Salaman, *The History and Social Influence of the Potato* [1949] (Cambridge, 1985), p. 131.
3 Prothero, *The Pioneers and Progress of English Farming*, quoted in Burnett, *Plenty and Want*, p. 30.
4 William Cobbett, *Rural Rides* (London, 1830), p. 372.
5 Friedrich Engels, *The Condition of the Working-Class in England in 1844* (London, 1892), quoted in Burnett, *Plenty and Want* (1979 edn), pp. 70–71.
6 Esther Copley, *The Complete Cottage Cookery* (London, 1859).
7 Dorothy Hartley, *Food in England* (London, 1954), p. 57.
8 E. P. Thompson, *The Making of the English Working Class* (London, 1963), p. 351.
9 Engels, *The Condition of the Working-Class in England in 1844*, quoted in Burnett, *Plenty and Want*, p. 70.
10 Charles Dickens, *Oliver Twist* [1838] (London, 2007), p. 382.
11 John Burnett, *A History of the Cost of Living* (Harmondsworth, 1969), p. 193.
12 George Dodd, *The Food of London* (London, 1856).
13 Charles Dickens, *The Pickwick Papers* [1836] (London, 2009), p. 254.
14 Friedrich Accum, *A Treatise on Adulterations of Food, and Culinary Poisons* (London, 1820), quoted in Bee Wilson, *Swindled* (London, 2008), pp. 2–3.
15 Mayhew's articles were collected into one volume: Henry Mayhew, *London Labour and the London Poor* (London, 1851).
16 Dudley Baxter's estimation of the distribution of incomes in 1867, quoted in Burnett, *Plenty and Want* (1979 edn), p. 293.

17 Eliza Acton, *Modern Cookery, for Private Families*, introduction to the 1855 edition.
18 Jane Austen, letter of Saturday, 17 November 1798, in *Jane Austen: Her Life and Letters*, ed. William Austen-Leigh (2017), ebook.
19 Major L…, *Breakfasts, Luncheons and Ball Suppers* (London, 1887).
20 Mrs Rundell, *A New System of Domestic Cookery* (London, 1843).
21 Mrs Beeton, *The Book of Household Management* (London, 1861), p. 959.
22 Ibid., pp. 956–9.
23 Dodd, *The Food of London*.
24 Stephen Mennell, *All Manners of Food* (Oxford, 1985), p. 155.
25 Dodd, *The Food of London*.
26 Ibid.
27 Dickens, *Oliver Twist*, p. 184.
28 Quoted in Gerald Priestland, *Frying Tonight* (London, 1972).
29 Acton, *Modern Cookery*, p. 313.
30 Priestland, *Frying Tonight*, p. 65.
31 Ralph Rylance, *The Epicure's Almanack* (1815).
32 See B. Seebohm Rowntree, *Poverty: A Study of Town Life* (London, 1901).
33 J. C. Drummond and A. Wilbraham, *The Englishman's Food* (London, 1939), p. 402.
34 Rowntree, *Poverty*, p. 211.

6 From Edwardian Picnics to the Microwave

1 George Orwell, *The Road to Wigan Pier* [1937] (Oxford, 2021), p. 66.
2 Sir Noel Curtis-Bennett, *The Food of the People* (London, 1949), p. 211.
3 *Report of the British Medical Association*, 1933, in J. C. Drummond and A. Wilbraham, *The Englishman's Food: A History of Five Centuries of English Diet* [1939], revd edn (London, 2012), Chapter Fourteen.
4 Arabella Boxer, *Arabella Boxer's Book of English Food* (London, 1991), p. 2.
5 Lady Jekyll, *Kitchen Essays* (London, 1922), p. 39.
6 Elizabeth David, 'Kitchens and Their Cooks', in *Is There a Nutmeg in the House?* (London, 2000), p. 1.
7 Mrs C. F. Leyel and Miss Olga Hartley, *The Gentle Art of Cookery* (London, 1925), p. vi.
8 Florence White, *Good Things in England* (London, 1932), p. 12.
9 *The Good Food Guide* had several editors over the years. The last edition was published in 2020 by Waitrose.
10 See Elizabeth David, *A Book of Mediterranean Food* (London, 1950), p. 9.
11 Jane Grigson, *English Food* (London, 1979), p. 14.
12 Claudia Roden, *A Book of Middle Eastern Food* (London, 1968), p. 14.
13 See Felicity Lawrence, *Not on the Label: What Really Goes into the Food on Your Plate* (London, 2004), Chapter Seven.
14 Eric Hobsbawm, *Age of Extremes: The Short Twentieth Century* (London, 1994).
15 Kate Fox, *Watching the English: The Hidden Rules of English Behaviour* (London, 2004), p. 29.
16 See the 'What We Do' page at the website for Incredible Edible, www.incredibleedible.org.uk, accessed 26 March 2024.

BIBLIOGRAPHY

Accum, Friedrich, *A Treatise on Adulterations of Food, and Culinary Poisons* (London, 1820)

Acton, Eliza, *Modern Cookery, for Private Families*, revd edn (London, 1855)

Ashley, Maurice, *England in the Seventeenth Century* (Harmondsworth, 1952)

Ayrton, Elisabeth, *The Cookery of England* (London, 1974)

Beeton, Isabella, *The Book of Household Management* (London, 1861)

Boxer, Arabella, *Arabella Boxer's Book of English Food* (London, 1991)

Brillat-Savarin, Jean-Anthelme, *The Physiology of Taste* (Harmondsworth, 1994)

Burnett, John, *A History of the Cost of Living* (Harmondsworth, 1969)

——, *Plenty and Want* (London, 1966)

Colas, Alejandro, et al., *Food, Politics and Society: Social Theory and the Modern Food System* (Oakland, CA, 2018)

Collingham, Lizzie, *The Biscuit: The History of a Very British Indulgence* (London, 2020)

——, *The Hungry Empire: How Britain's Quest for Food Shaped the Modern World* (London, 2018)

Copley, Esther, *The Complete Cottage Cookery* (London, 1859)

Curtis-Bennett, Noel, *The Food of the People* (London, 1949)

David, Elizabeth, *English Bread and Yeast Cookery* (Harmondsworth, 1977)

——, *Is There a Nutmeg in the House?* (London, 2000)

Dodd, George, *The Food of London* (London, 1856)

Drummond J. C., and Anne Wilbraham, *The Englishman's Food* (London, 1939)

Emmison, F. G., *Tudor Food and Pastimes* (London, 1964)

Engels, Friedrich, *The Condition of the Working-Class in England in 1844* (London, 1892)

Flower, B., and E. Rosenbaum, trans., *Apicius: The Roman Cookery Book* (London, 1958)

Fox, Kate, *Watching the English: The Hidden Rules of English Behaviour* (London, 2004)

Freedman, Paul, ed., *Food: The History of Taste* (London, 2019)

Grigson, Jane, *English Food* (London, 1979)

Hagen, Ann, *A Handbook of Anglo-Saxon Food* (London, 1992)

Hartley, Dorothy, *Food in England* (London, 1954)

Henisch, Bridget Ann, *Fast and Feast: Food in Medieval Society* (Philadelphia, PA, 1976)

Hennessy, Peter, *Having it So Good: Britain in the Fifties* (London, 2006)
——, *Never Again: Britain, 1945–1951* (London, 1992)
——, *Winds of Change: Britain in the Early Sixties* (London, 2019)
Hobsbawm, Eric, *Age of Extremes: The Short Twentieth Century* (London, 1994)
Hughes, Glyn, *The Lost Foods of England* (London, 2017)
Jekyll, Lady, *Kitchen Essays: With Recipes and Their Occasions* (London, 1922)
L . . ., Major, *Breakfasts, Luncheons and Ball Suppers* (London, 1887)
Lawrence, Felicity, *Not on the Label: What Really Goes into the Food on Your Plate* (London, 2004)
Leyel, Mrs C. F., and Olga Hartley, *The Gentle Art of Cookery* (London, 1925)
Mennell, Stephen, *All Manners of Food* (Oxford, 1985)
Mintz, Sidney W., *Sweetness and Power: The Place of Sugar in Modern History* (New York, 1985)
Nott, John, *The Cooks and Confectioners Dictionary* (London, 1726)
Priestland, Gerald, *Frying Tonight* (London, 1972)
Purkiss, Diane, *English Food: A People's History* (London, 2022)
Roden, Claudia, *A Book of Middle Eastern Food* (London, 1968)
Rowntree, B. Seebohm, *Poverty: A Study of Town Life* (London, 1901)
Rundell, Mrs, *A New System of Domestic Cookery* (London, 1843)
Smith, Eliza, *The Compleat Housewife* (London, 1727)
Stenton, D. M., *English Society in the Early Middle Ages* (Harmondsworth, 1971)
Thompson, E. P., *The Making of the English Working Class* (London, 1963)
Trevelyan, G. M., *Illustrated English Social History*, 4 vols (Harmondsworth, 1964)
Vogler, Pen, *Scoff: A History of Food and Class in Britain* (London, 2020)
White, Florence, *Good Things in England* (London, 1932)
Willey, Basil, *The Seventeenth Century Background* (London, 1934)
Wilson, Bee, *Swindled* (London, 2008)
Wilson, C. Anne, *Eating With the Victorians* (Stroud, 2004)
——, *Food and Drink in Britain* (Harmondsworth, 1974)
——, ed., *Banquetting Stuffe* (Edinburgh, 1991)
Woolley, Hannah, *The Queen-Like Closet* (London, *c.* 1670)
Wrangham, Richard, *Catching Fire: How Cooking Made Us Human* (New York, 2009)

ACKNOWLEDGEMENTS

Many thanks to my daughters Sasha Roth and Elinor Breman, who read and commented on the text at different stages. My husband, the late Paul Breman, and many of his antiquarian bookseller colleagues over the years brought me copies of old, and sometimes valuable, early English cookery books. I have cooked from many of these books and it is from these that I have drawn in writing *The English Table*. Colin Hamilton and Calum Paterson helped me track down an old icehouse in Scotland that had been used in the early days of shipping salmon to London under ice. I am grateful to Arabella Boxer, Claudia Roden, Fergus Henderson, Simon Hopkinson and the estates of Elizabeth David and Jane Grigson for giving me permission to quote their recipes. Alex Ciobanu did an excellent job of finding the illustrations, Amy Salter has been a careful, meticulous editor and Zoe Ross has provided a thorough index.

PHOTO
ACKNOWLEDGEMENTS

The author and publishers wish to express their thanks to the sources listed below for illustrative material and/or permission to reproduce it. Some locations of works are also given below, in the interest of brevity:

Alamy Stock Photo: pp. 80 (Robert Clayton), 86 (Susie Kearley), 87 (Christopher Jones), 162–3 (Heritage Image Partnership Ltd/London Metropolitan Archives); Balnagown Estate, photo Callum Peterson: p. 131; Bodleian Library, University of Oxford: p. 26 (MS Bodl. 764, fol. 44r); British Library, London: pp. 30 (Harley MS 1585, fol. 49v), pp. 44–5 (Add MS 42130, fols. 163r, 166v, 206v, 207r, 207v and 208r), 48 (Royal MS 14 E IV, fol. 265v), 64 (Add MS 5016, fol. 7r), 196 (*top*); Flickr: pp. 33 (photo LearningLark, CC BY 2.0), 77 (*bottom*; photo Michael Gaylard, CC BY 2.0), 227 (photo Jim Linwood, CC BY 2.0); from Charles Elmé Francatelli, *The Modern Cook, a Practical Guide to the Culinary Art in All Its Branches* (Philadelphia, PA, 1846), photo Library of Congress, Rare Book and Special Collections Division, Washington, DC: p. 165; from John Gerard, *The Herball; or, Generall Historie of Plantes* (London, 1636), photo Universitätsbibliothek Basel: p. 68; from Hannah Glasse, *The Art of Cookery Made Plain and Easy*, 3rd edn (London, 1748), photo Wellcome Library, London: p. 128; Imperial War Museum, London: p. 197; from G. A. Jarrin, *The Italian Confectioner; or, Complete Economy of Desserts* (London, 1820), photo Library of Congress, Rare Book and Special Collections Division, Washington, DC: p. 182; from G. A. Jarrin, *The Italian Confectioner; or, Complete Economy of Desserts* (London, 1829), photo Getty Research Institute, Los Angeles: p. 183; Lewis Walpole Library, Yale University, Farmington, CT: pp. 120, 133; Library of Congress, Prints and Photographs Division, Washington, DC: pp. 139, 201, 213; from A. B. Marshall, *Larger Cookery Book of Extra Recipes* (London, 1891), photo Getty Research Institute, Los Angeles: p. 184; The Metropolitan Museum of Art, New York: pp. 49, 135; Musée Escoffier de l'Art Culinaire, Villeneuve-Loubet: p. 196 (*bottom*); Musée de la Tapisserie de Bayeux: pp. 40–41; The New York Public Library: p. 199; from Denis Papin, *A New Digester or Engine for Softning Bones . . .* (London, 1681), photo Wellcome Collection, London: p. 98; Philadelphia Museum of Art, PA: pp. 159, 160, 161; private collection: pp. 185, 194; from Elizabeth Raffald, *The Experienced English Housekeeper*, 5th edn (London, 1776), photo Wellcome Collection, London: p. 121; The Sainsbury Archive, Museum of London Docklands: p. 204; Shutterstock: pp. 186 (*Daily Mail*), 221 (ANL), 222 (Edwin Sampson/ANL);

Tate Britain, London: p. 97; Tower Hamlets Local History Library and Archives, London: p. 220; Victoria and Albert Museum, London: p. 104; Wikimedia Commons: pp. 12 (photo Simon Burchell, CC BY-SA 4.0), 27 (photo Zephyris, CC BY-SA 3.0), 51 (photo NotFromUtrecht, CC BY-SA 3.0), 77 (*top*; photo Calstanhope, CC BY-SA 4.0); from Hannah Woolley, *The Queen-Like Closet; or, Rich Cabinet*, 3rd edn (London, 1675), photo Folger Shakespeare Library, Washington, DC (CC BY-SA 4.0): p. 122; Yale Center for British Art, New Haven, CT: p. 134.

INDEX

Page numbers in *italics* refer to illustrations